Trois Etoiles

Young Brown

The Law of Inheritance

Trois Etoiles

Young Brown
The Law of Inheritance

ISBN/EAN: 9783742807403

Manufactured in Europe, USA, Canada, Australia, Japa

Cover: Foto ©Andreas Hilbeck / pixelio.de

Manufactured and distributed by brebook publishing software (www.brebook.com)

Trois Etoiles

Young Brown

COLLECTION
OF
BRITISH AUTHORS

TAUCHNITZ EDITION.

VOL. 1445.

YOUNG BROWN BY TROIS-ETOILES.

IN TWO VOLUMES.
VOL. II.

YOUNG BROWN

OR THE

LAW OF INHERITANCE

BY

TROIS-ETOILES,
AUTHOR OF "THE MEMBER FOR PARIS," ETC.

COPYRIGHT EDITION.

IN TWO VOLUMES.
VOL. II.

LEIPZIG
BERNHARD TAUCHNITZ
1874.

CONTENTS
OF VOLUME II.

BOOK IV.
(CONTINUED.)

			Page
CHAPTER III.	"The George"		7
—	IV.	Good-bye, Sweetheart	12
—	V.	Mrs. Brown	20
—	VI.	Richmond	28
—	VII.	Noble and Ignoble	38
—	VIII.	Emigrants	45
—	IX.	A Marquis	51
—	X.	At Sea	60
—	XI.	Hereditary Rank	64
—	XII.	Auld Lang Syne	71
—	XIII.	The Sepoy Revolt	87
—	XIV.	British India	95
—	XV.	Rule Britannia	102
—	XVI.	After the Battle	111
—	XVII.	Raised from the Ranks	118
—	XVIII.	Race	126

BOOK V.

—	I.	A Last Love	135
—	II.	Lord Punjaub	144
—	III.	Peace	151
—	IV.	Coming Home with Despatches	159
—	V.	Sir Richard Porteous	168

CONTENTS OF VOLUME II.

		Page
CHAPTER VI.	Beaumanoir	181
— VII.	The Lost Letter	188
— VIII.	The Heir of Courthope	196
— IX.	Amabel Wyldwyl	205
— X.	The Anglo-Indian	217
— XI.	Wooing	228
— XII.	The Heir's Death	241
— XIII.	Humbled in the Dust	247
— XIV.	Requiescat	255
— XV.	In the Picture Gallery	261
— XVI.	The Soldier and the Lady	269
— XVII.	A Discovery	272
— XVIII.	Conclusion	280

YOUNG BROWN.

BOOK IV.
(CONTINUED.)

CHAPTER III.
"The George."

AT Southampton, and at every other town between Southampton and London, there is an inn called the "George." There is no particular reason why the Hampshire people should be so demonstratively loyal to the House of Hanover; but it is certain that they are so, and though the "George" inns are not such fine inns as the new monster hotels which we have imitated from the Germans and Americans, they are comfortable old English abiding places, with sound ideas of roast and boiled and beer.

While the grand party invited by the Duke of Courthope were breakfasting at Radley's there was a very different group of people assembled at the "George," a tavern of humbler pretensions, situated near the water side, at the bottom of the High Street. Mr. and Mrs. Brown and Mr. Mowledy had all found their way from Wakefield-in-the-Marsh, to take leave of the soldier boy who was about to drift for ever away from them in search of fortune.

Young Brown met his mother with rather a shameface at first, and felt by no means so proud of his uniform in her presence as he was out of it. But by-and-by, perceiving, rather by some mysterious instinct than from anything she said, that his mother was not really displeased with the career he had chosen, he began to take heart, and patronised her, as boys will, and showed her about the town.

As for Thomas Brown, the events which had lately succeeded each other in his family had been altogether too much for him. First, there had been that queer start in London, of which he could neither make head nor tail, except that Madge had been ill-used by somebody he would have liked to punch till he was tired. Then there was that surprising seven-months' child of his first "'listing for a sojer, an naew gwine to Injy," why, he could not make out, seeing that the boy had a good home and plenty of victuals.

Moreover, Tom Brown was utterly lost in his Sunday clothes, and almost disappeared in a portentous blue coat with brass buttons, twenty years old, and much too large for him, except at the waist, where it was too short, and displayed a pair of pocket flaps half the way up his back. Upon the whole an uncomfortable coat, and Mr. Brown passed the day chiefly by the taproom fire of the "George" inn wondering whether he might take it off. Not so his wife. She quite bloomed back into youth and beauty under the excitement which oppressed and fatigued her husband. Her step was as light and elastic as that of a girl while she walked arm-in-arm with her tall son through the streets of the merry seaport. A line from Mr. Mowledy to Colonel Oakes had obtained the young recruit a day's leave to accompany his family, and it is doubtful whether mother and son had ever before been so happy as during the last hours they ever spent together.

Madge had brought her ten pounds with her, carefully wrapped up in paper, and had given her son injunctions not to open the packet till he got to India, fearing with motherly foresight that the precious hoard she had kept for him so long might waste away before he really wanted it if he touched it now. She had brought him, too, a very respectable kit of linen, and much flannel, which rather embarrassed him when he got to his destination. Whatever she had of value, or that she thought might be turned to some account— an old silver pencil-case, a turquoise ring perhaps worth half-a-crown, and a broken garnet brooch which she had found among her things and had mended, were brightened up and scoured till they shone, and put aside for him. The Curate had added a Bible and two sovereigns to these treasures as his gift, and Tom Brown had bought a serviceable clasp knife at Dronington, that being the instrument he had personally found of most use in life; and his son had often occasion to rejoice, on many a toilsome march, and at many a night bivouac, that it had not been forgotten. He said afterwards that this clasp knife was the best friend he had during the campaign which followed, and it now hangs up in his library, a well-worn relic of the wars.

They dined together at one o'clock, father, mother, and son, Mr. Mowledy being discreetly absent: too perfect a gentleman to intrude his presence where it could only be a source of embarrassment. Tom Brown took almost a solemn leave of his son, bidding him be an honest man let what would come of it, and as he had turned to soldiering to set about it with a will. Then he drew out his big silver watch, as large as a turnip, and thrust it awkwardly into his son's hand.

"She had better go wi' yow, lad," said the rough fellow. "I' wunt much matter to Oi wats o'clok till you be back wi' us agin."

His wife gave him a sounding kiss in exchange for his watch, and called him her "old man" with rustic fondness, after which they all took a deep draught of beer from the same pot in silence, Mrs. Brown joining for the first time in the family potations.

" 'T yale be sweeter, Madge, since thee hast put thy beak into 't, wench," said her husband, and, lighting his pipe, he sat behind it, blinking like an owl, watching wife and first-born with a tenderness perhaps none the less deep and eloquent for being inarticulate. They sat at a little distance from him near the window, while he smoked by the fire. The mother and son were wonderfully alike; and to-day, looking as she did so young and spirited and handsome, they might have been taken for brother and sister.

They did not speak. William Brown had exhausted all the gallant babble with which he had tried to hide his feelings in the morning, when he patronised and protected his mother, stopped her to gape at the Indian jugglers who tumbled for pence in the streets, or to listen to the German bands, who performed before every hotel where there was a new arrival of importance. All his boyish bravado was gone now, and his heart sank with a sad foreboding that mayhap he should see that sweet matronly face, and those dear, loving, motherly eyes no more. Possibly she may have answered his unuttered thoughts unconsciously and without speech. She took the boy's shapely hand in her own, and patted and caressed it as she sat beside him, cheering and comforting him with unspoken hopes and silent blessings, and an inward assurance of his future welfare. She was very proud of him; she loved him above everything on earth; she would have died for him; he was the one link betwixt her and happiness. When he was gone, her life would be very dull; but she had no wish to detain him. She would not have stopped him on his way now if she could have done so. Something told her that her boy had found the occupation fitted to him, and that all was for the best.

"Mrs. Brown—William," said the mild voice of the Curate, interrupting her at length in these day-dreams, "the *Tanjore* will be ready for sea in two hours, and whatever you have left to do must be done at once. If you will come with me, William, I will present you to your new colonel."

So the kit of linen and flannel, with stout pairs of boots, and a large home-made cake, and some bottles of currant wine, with two hams and a flitch of bacon for contingencies, were hoisted into a donkey-cart, which Tom Brown had hired for the purpose that morning, and the soldier, with his kinsfolk and the parson of his parish, walked soberly to the wharf where the great ship lay.

CHAPTER IV.

Good-bye, Sweetheart.

THE *Tanjore* got slowly under weigh, and as the Curate found out that she would anchor again in Southampton Roads to wait for the latest news and despatches from land, an hour after the advertised time of her departure, the little company from Wakefield-in-the-Marsh remained on board till she got into deep water; being permitted to do so by the special intercession of Colonel Oakes, whom the Curate had already interested in his old pupil and fellow-fisherman.

Mr. Mowledy almost felt himself young again, as he talked with the Colonel about their school days at Winchester, and walked up and down the deck conversing with the smart officer who bore such a perfume of life, enjoyment, and adventure about him.

"You don't remember Courthope at Oxford, do you? Kinsgear he was then."

"No," answered the Curate, "he was after my time; but I have often heard of him."

It somehow happens that poor clergymen generally *do* hear of the noblemen who go to their college, and Mr. Mowledy had often derived a quiet satisfaction from the thought that he was educated fully up to the standard of the highest class of Englishmen.

"Ah, I am sorry for that," continued Colonel Oakes, "but it doesn't much matter, I can introduce you: and it is worth your while to know the Duke, as you take an interest in young Brown—because his Grace's son,

Lord Kinsgear, has just got a troop in my regiment, and, as all his letters and parcels are sure to come out in the Government despatch bags post free and carriage free, you can send anything you have for young Brown under cover to Kinsgear, if you are on terms with the Duke."

The Curate was quite worldly wise enough to acknowledge the advantage of a friend at court under every possible circumstance, and he said so.

"Well," continued the Colonel, straddling all about the deck with his bold cavalry swagger, "there's the Duke's yacht *Osprey* in the offing yonder. He has taken refuge there, I suppose, with the General and a large party to be out of the din going on here, but he is sure to come on board with Kinsgear, so look sharp and stick near me that you may not be out of the way at the right moment, for time is almost up I fancy. The captain came on board with the latest mails five minutes ago."

As the Colonel spoke a signal flew up to the masthead of the *Tanjore*, and was immediately answered by the yacht, whose boats were already manned and lowered. The boatswain's whistle piped all hands on deck, for there was man-of-war's discipline on board the *Osprey*, and presently the Duke of Courthope, Lord Kinsgear, and his guests, were seen descending the companion ladder, while the boat crews held their oars aloft in the attitude of saluting. His Grace, the Marquis, General Violet, and the Right Hon. Hermann Schnapsgelt, stepped one after the other into the long boat. The Marquis's valet and stud groom got into the other, and several cases of champagne were put after them.

"Give way, boys," cried the captain of the Duke's yacht, who had taken the helm of the long boat. He was an ex-lieutenant in the navy, who had lost an arm at Navarino, and he had been glad to accept domestic service, because he had no interest at the Admiralty. "Give way, boys!" cried this veteran, jollily. The crew bent to their oars, and the long boat of the *Osprey*, with its illustrious freight, flew over the sea towards the *Tanjore*, where the captain of the steamer, Colonel Oakes, and the chief officers of the Queen's and merchant's services stood waiting to receive them. They were all in high spirits, and a brisk breeze which was blowing set the very ends of their neck-handkerchiefs dancing and fluttering. It had, however, prevented Lady Overlaw from accompanying them, lest she should not appear to advantage wet through and raked by the wind.

"I feel twenty years younger, Violet," said the Duke, as the spray from a wave struck the boat's prow and dashed over him. "I have not had such a ducking since we ran for the coast of Norway together to look after ptarmigan."

"Why don't you make the voyage with us, Duke, at all events to Aden? The *Osprey* would go out as fast as we shall, and you might be home for the grouse on your Scotch moors," observed General Violet.

"What do you say, Benbow?" asked the Duke laughingly of his captain. "Would the *Osprey* weather a white squall?"

"Aye, aye, sir," answered Lieutenant Benbow, R.N. "She would stand up to anything that the Mediterranean could show her, and more too."

"Will you join us if we run out with the first wind

and give Dullington the go-by?" said the Duke to the Right Hon. Hermann Schnapsgelt. "Or are the cares of State too much for you?"

"I am afraid I am not a free man, Duke," answered the junior Lord, who did not take a joke very quickly.

"Egad, I have a great mind to go myself," continued the Duke. "Is the ship well found with provisions, Benbow?"

"Plenty of junk, your Grace!" replied the old sailor, slyly, "if that will do."

"Rough it. Nothing like roughing it," said the Duke, showing those handsome white ivory teeth of his, glistening and even as ever. His Grace had not the smallest intention of setting out on a broiling voyage to Egypt; there were at least a hundred and fifty reasons why he could not have done so if he would. He was involved in perfect mazes of correspondence which nobody but he himself could conduct, and which could not be left for a week to take care of themselves without an explosion, which would have been a windfall to all the cheap newspapers in the world. There were half-a-dozen people he was obliged to call on or to meet on particular days and at appointed hours. There was a whole family somewhere in Pimlico who knew him as Mr. Johnson, and who had for ten years believed that he was an old gentleman's steward, who could only get leave to come out on Saturdays. He had bills and notes of hand at short date to be renewed, annuities constantly falling due to pay, or he had to pacify and negotiate with the annuitants. He had children's schooling to pay, Chancery suits to answer by interrogatories, arbitrations which had been going on for a dozen years, and might be suddenly brought to a close if not attended to. He was trustee under marriage settlements; he was guardian of noble young wards who were travelling in Syria, and out-running their credit. He frequently received a score of letters by a single post, and could no more have absented himself from England than a horse harnessed to a mill wheel can go for a pleasant roll in the meadows. Noblemen have their troubles like other people, only the Duke of Courthope just now had forgotten his, for he had lunched delightfully; and besides he was naturally courteous and kind, so that he delighted to give pleasure to those about him. It was a very ingenious compliment to assure them that they were bound upon a voyage which he, the Duke of Courthope, would not disdain to make himself.

The Minister of State fell back and made way, the general commanding in chief of an army in war time stood aside, the naval veteran of a dozen sea fights got up and held his arm in the form of a banister, the boat's crew lifted their oars aloft again in salute, and then the Duke of Courthope rose from his place of honour at the long boat's stern, a smile and kind word on his lips, and stepped on board the East Indiaman, followed at a respectful distance by his gallant company. The shrill whistle of the boatswain of the *Tanjore* piped out its honours to the great nobleman, in correct man-of-war's notes, as his foot touched the vessel's plank, for there, too, the captain had notions of discipline, and was also a naval officer, who had been pushed out of his country's service to make way for the son of a distinguished, yarn contractor, aforetime in office.

"Mowledy!" Colonel Oakes called hastily out to the Curate, "bring up young Brown's mother. She seems a decent looking body, and the Duke is very good-natured, perhaps he'll take notice of her. He's always doing kind things, and the General is with him, which is better still."

The Curate turned to look for Madge, and found her leaning against the bulwarks of the ship, deadly pale, and cowering as if she had been struck down. Her large blue eyes, almost starting out of her head, were fixed upon the handsome figure of the Duke of Courthope, who stood with his head thrown back and a winning smile upon his lips, paying lofty compliments to the captain of the Indiaman on the state of the *Tanjore*.

"Mrs. Brown!" said the Curate, gently taking her arm and trying to rouse her; "that tall gentleman just come on board is the Duke of Courthope, and standing near him is his son, the Marquis of Kinsgear, William's captain. Colonel Oakes has promised to say a good word for your son; and you had better stand near me in case they should wish to ask you any questions about him."

But Madge was far beyond questions and answers for a while; the fixed and rigid look upon her poor startled face had gradually relaxed, her eyes closed as if to shut out the sight of some evil thing that had haunted them, and she fainted, so that the good-natured intentions of Colonel Oakes and the Curate were frustrated.

"What's the matter, Oakes?" inquired the Duke, seeing the two gentlemen look a little vexed.

"Only a woman fainted. She is the mother of one of my raw recruits in Lord Kinsgear's troop, and my old friend the parson here wanted to present her to him," answered the Colonel.

"Bless my soul! Woman fainted! Benbow, do you happen to have your medicine chest in the boat?" exclaimed the Duke, speaking rather thickly, for the reaction of the wine and sea air was overtaking him. "Where is she?" and his Grace strode to the place where Madge lay deprived of consciousness by some sudden emotion stronger than her powers of resistance. Her husband was seated on an officer's bullock trunk behind her, and supported her head on his coarse knees, gnarled and knotted by a lifetime of labour. He looked up with blinking puzzled eyes at the stately noble, so straight and tall, so condescending and impatient of grief or sickness.

"Is there any danger?" inquired the Curate of the ship's doctor, and the surgeon of the 1st, who had both hurried benevolently to offer their services at the first call for them.

"Oh dear, no!" said the Duke, overriding disease and pain with his high-pitched strident voice, which brooked no contradiction. "It is only the heat of the weather and excitement, and that kind of thing." His Grace never would admit that anybody was in danger till they were dead. His mind had no place for pity in it, it was so full of grandeur.

"She is very weak, poor thing," remarked the surgeon of the 1st, compassionately, "and that hectic flush, which looked so pretty half-an-hour ago upon her cheeks, does not promise her a long life." As he spoke, and administered some simple cordial to her, Madge slowly opened her eyes, and the colour which had attracted the army surgeon's attention came back to her wan cheeks and lit them up again. The Duke of Courthope passed his hand across his forehead, as if he were trying to remember something he had forgotten, but without success, and it was not until Madge had been lifted into the last boat for shore, and the Duke was speeding back again to his yacht, that he recollected the country girl he had admired on the night which he passed at the "Chequers" inn, when he had been thrown out of the Cloudesdale hunt by the lameness of a favourite horse. Then he turned very pale; an anxious expression came into his countenance, and it was succeeded by that determined wicked Wyldwyl look, which appeared in old busts and portraits at Beaumanoir, and which had evidently been seen upon the features of many generations of his ancestors when troubled or angry.

As the boat which carried Madge and her husband with their friend the Curate back to Southampton parted from that which bore the Duke of Courthope ever farther and farther in an opposite direction, the band of the 1st struck up the old soldier tune of "The Girl I left behind me," to which generation after generation of our troops have said good-bye to home and country when they went away to the wars. Then from boat and from terrace and balcony in the town —on the pier, and along the pleasant shores of the Hampshire coast, there went up prayers to God from fervent lips and over-burthened hearts. White kerchiefs fluttered out their kisses and blessings that the winds might bear them ever farther—farther than speech, farther than sound.

The crew of the *Osprey's* long boat, and the clumsy fleet of barges from the town, having got clear of the troop ship's mighty draught, rested on their oars to see the last of her. The Duke of Courthope stood erect and proud, waving his hat to Lord Kinsgear, who might be plainly seen a prominent figure on the quarter-deck between General Violet and the colonel of his regiment. Madge also stood up, supported on the one side by her husband, and the other by the curate of her village, straining her fond eyes towards the spot where only a mother's vision could discern her boy among the crowd of soldiers who leant cheering or weeping tearlessly over the ship's side, about the forecastle. At last the huge paddles of the East Indiaman turned heavily round with a mighty thud, the sails of the *Tanjore* swelled, flapped and swelled again steadily, bellying to their work; and as women wailed with sharp cries, and strong men hid their faces from each other, the Union Jack was hoisted, and the crowded transport stood out to sea.

CHAPTER V.
Mrs. Brown.

THAT was the last time Madge ever saw the Duke of Courthope; and she died soon afterwards. She had met him once at the commencement of her life, and she now met him again at its close. Nothing had ever effaced the image of the handsome nobleman from the poor ignorant woman's memory. She had been married; she was a faithful wife and a contented mother, but he had taken the bloom and joy from her existence, nevertheless. What could he have said to her during that brief time, upon a stormy autumn evening which they passed together when she was but a girl, and he little more than a boy? What do fine gentlemen generally say to village girls who captivate their fancy? The young Duke had been fascinated by the rustic beauty. He had given her ten pounds, and, perhaps, intended to come again and again, when at leisure. It was a notable project, and such a one as hath been often formed and executed by wealth and idleness at a loss for a day's amusement. But it so chanced that his Grace had been caught up and whirled away by a vortex of pleasure. He had lost a fortune at a horse race, and won another, then hurried away to Paris to spend it before it melted in his purse. There he had met Mademoiselle Zephirine and Madame Désirée with that queenlike Pantaleoni of the Italian stage, in whose fetters he had been led captive about Europe for a whole month. Then he had had adventures, had gambled, fought duels, had married and been separated by chance or inclination, and had then fallen into a sea full of sharks and difficulties; having had ever since to swim for his life with the sharks after him as we have seen. So that he had forgotten poor Madge till Mr. Sharpe had all at once recalled her existence to him by the strange tidings that she was heiress of those great estates which had been brought into the Courthope family by the good Duchess, wife of a deceased Duke, now long since dead and buried. Then he had sometimes thought of her with a sort of terror, and had dreaded lest she should some day start up with a dreadful solicitor behind her, and put him in grave peril or to grievous charges. Once or twice he had seriously considered if there were any prudent means of getting rid of her; and it might have been a bad thing for Madge if his Grace had known of her arrest by the police. It would have been quite possible that she would next have been heard of some distance from England. Only a few days ago he had sent for Mr. Sharpe, and inquired in that light, easy way of his whether "those Browns of Wakefield could not be vexed a little by Dick Porteous's trustees, and induced to emigrate." Mr. Sharpe had promised to think of it, had thought of it, and, being a well-meaning man, had come to the conclusion that it would be better to leave them alone, "unless they showed their teeth at any time."

"By Jove," replied the Duke, biting his lips, "if they begin to show their teeth it will be too late to collar them; I would rather you got them off at once!" His Grace was a wiser and more resolute man than the Yorkshire attorney. Fully aware of his own strength, and never having been thwarted—never having been opposed to any one who could resist him, he was very brave. If left to his own devices, he would have ridden down to Wakefield, laid hands upon the Browns without more ado, shipped them to South Australia, and left them to their remedy, with a hint to an under secretary at the Colonial Office to help them. Mr. Sharpe, however, being a man who had risen from humble beginnings, always liked to have the letter of the law upon his side. The bold stroke of kidnapping and transporting a country innkeeper and his family because they might some day be troublesome, and doing it entirely on his own hook, would never have entered Mr. Sharpe's head, and it made him stand aghast with astonishment when it was coolly proposed by the Duke as he lit a cigarette with his hunting-whip under his arm, and rode off to the cover side, Mr. Sharpe and amazement following him at a proper distance.

The Yorkshire solicitor would have done the same thing if he had as clearly seen the necessity for it, but he would have gone about his business in a different manner. Thomas Brown would have become involved somehow in difficulties with the quarter sessions. He would have been had up before the magistrates again and again, on one pretext or another, till even Mr. Mowledy and his old neighbours had been brought to look shyly on him. Constables would have gone to the inn with search warrants. Actions for trover would have been commenced against him by the Lord of the Manor. His children would have been had up for trespass, and shut up in reformatories and penitentiaries as incorrigible vagabonds. If his wife had picked up a stick or an acorn in a lane, she would have been sent to pick oakum; and a something darker—more stealthy than ruin would have brooded over the "Chequers," till Mr. Mowledy, probably, or Mr. Sharpe himself, who would always have been friendly with them, had suggested emigration in their own interests, and would have generously given them a few pounds to pay their passage out; perhaps even he would have been so good as to recommend to them an emigrant ship rather overloaded and undermanned, never likely to reach its destination. Such things have been done, and we English defend our monetary concerns by grim and secret methods now and then.

Madge, however, had no notion that her appearance or disappearance was of importance to anybody—so little, that about fifteen years before, when an advertisement had appeared in the *Times*, offering a reward for Margaret Brown, otherwise Wyldwyl, and a heavy local lawyer had ridden over from Dronington to see if any costs were to be made out of it, old John Giles had sent him away without his errand, saying he knew "nowt, und wuddn't know nowt;" and now, if inquiries were to be made again, the panic which naturally seizes on the poor at the bare mention of a lawsuit, and Madge's own experience when taken before a magistrate, would have certainly prompted her to deny her own identity rather than have anything further to do with legal persons or proceedings.

But the visit of the stranger huntsman had been the day dream and night thought of her existence for eighteen years, and now she had found out that the man whom she had supposed to be some country squire of a rank and degree comprehensible to her, or perhaps some Sir John or Sir Harry at most, was one of the demigods of the earth, a Duke, at whose name even Mr. Mowledy bowed his head, and in whose august presence her son's colonel and the very Queen's general held their breath. A spell had been cast from the first over her, and now it grew stronger when all besides was fading away.

No wonder. It so frequently happens that a human existence is thus sicklied and blighted. There is no mercy for women. Untold millions of young girls who know nothing, have seen nothing, who have neither learning, wisdom, strength, nor experience, find themselves exposed in the dawn of womanhood to strong Temptation with his wily ways and subtle tongue. It is half touching and half ludicrous to see a skilful statesman, an orator whose fame fills many mouths, or a consummate soldier, bring all the force and subtlety of a master mind to deceive a child of seventeen. They would be ashamed to hoax a boy with falsehoods; but from the moment their victim is a frail foolish girl she becomes fair game to hunt and harry. Thus a gentleman will flush his quarry in a farm yard or an inn kitchen, striking it in the breast and leaving it fluttering to die or recover. It very seldom recovers. Its daily life is made insipid to it after that sweet pain.

A bumpkin, however honest a fellow he may be, does not speak like a gentleman, or look like a gentleman, or act like one. Then come comparisons, and heartaches, and pinings for that which can never be, and which therefore had better not have been known. The familiar voices of old times, the homely pleasures, and simple vanities which sweeten life, have been made distasteful, and their best enjoyment is mingled with a sort of shame because of the corroding idea of something better and finer which is fixed for ever in the victim's mind.

Whether it was that Madge caught cold on her visit to the sea side, or whether the many conflicting emotions of the few weeks preceding had exhausted her strength, or whether the loss of blood had been too much for her, and in her eagerness to return home and see her son once more before his departure she had left the hospital too soon, certain it is that she arrived at Wakefield in a very weak state and was observed to sink rapidly. All through the summer she still managed to do such household work as could be got through without much exertion. She cut the loaf for her children at their morning, midday, and evening meals, thus fulfilling to the last the functions of the lady, or breadgiver of her household; but when the leaves began to fall she changed visibly from day to day. At first her busy footfall was missed soon after dawn, and she rose a little later, only coming down stairs when her eldest daughter had already set out the breakfast, and moving about very pale and quiet, but with the old gentle, protecting, motherly expression in her soft eyes. Then she was confined to her chair, and looked placidly on when her family gathered round her, taking nothing but a cup of tea or a little milk herself. So she grew weaker and weaker, and her husband, honest Tom Brown, became haggard as he watched her wearing away like snow in the thaw. For some time longer she was busy with her needle, and there was not a rent in a stocking or a pinafore but she mended it with patient, uncomplaining toil.

It was upon a day in October when the end came. Her children were all at work or at play in the garden and in the fields, and her husband only was with her, for he never left her now night or day. She sat very upright, as she was wont, in her large wooden armchair, by the ample hearth of the inn kitchen, where she had passed her life. Some thin shawls and wraps were round her, and an old hound (she had all the noble likings and instincts of the Wyldwyls) lay dozing in a pale autumn sunbeam full of motes which fell athwart the few and smouldering ashes of the neglected fire, which had never burned so low upon an autumn day before since she kept house. Surely the rich and learned have a great advantage over untaught poverty. If Madge or Thomas Brown had ever been well schooled, she might have read, or he might have read aloud to her long after she could work no more, and so have charmed her life to linger here; or the sacred messages which Faith received from Heaven might have revealed to her the glad tidings of a world beyond the grave, and cheered the last steps of her pilgrimage thither. But she had nothing to relieve the awful tedium and solitude of a mortal sickness. No mental food from without, no conversation, no news, no comfortable words. She was alone, quite alone with God and her own thoughts, while that great uncouth silent love of her peasant husband brooded sorrowfully over her. So the last afternoon of her life's journey stole on hour after hour uneventful, without sign or token that the Betrothed of the World* was about to claim another bride ere the night came on. The smell of the earth refreshed by recent rains, the merry chirp of birds, the far glad voices of children at play, the clash of a spade as it struck against a stone, and the wild shriek of a steam engine speeding to the haunts of trade and pleasure —all were borne from time to time into the dull room where Thomas Brown sat watching his wife with an aching heart, and that stolid, miserable foreboding of the boor who can find no voice, and looks pitifully

* The Betrothed of the World is an expression used for Death in old legends.

like a dumb thing in his helpless anguish. He could do nothing, poor fellow. He was afraid even to smooth the pillow at the back of her chair with his rough, clumsy hands. He could only wait; wait without moving, almost without breathing, as time rushed onwards tearing his hopes away with it. It must have been at the turn of the day, when the light had just begun to grow fainter and the air more chill, that she called him nearer to her and leant back in his arms and bade him kiss her, smiling calmly as she did so. Then she took both his rude hands in hers, thanked him sweetly for having been so good a husband to her, and asked him gently to be kind to "her Willie;" and when the poor clown fell on his knees, sobbing, a strange light passed for an instant over her face. It was but her answer to the Bridegroom's smile; or perhaps a ray of light which fell in a parting gleam from him of the Amaranthine wings, as he spread his angel plumage and bore her Home.

CHAPTER VI.
Richmond.

THE Duke of Courthope learned the news of Madge's death as he was giving a breakfast to a festive party at a villa which he had upon the banks of the Thames near Richmond. He was very fond of giving breakfasts; they kept his friends together, and what was better, at hand, and in sight if needed. They kept his creditors in a good humour with him. It is astonishing to see what things people who are neither hungry nor thirsty, nor poverty stricken, will do for a breakfast or a dinner. They will inconvenience themselves extremely, incur great expense for dress and equipage, offend their benefactors, clients, or customers, throw away time, health, and temper, to eat an uncomfortable meal with a stranger, when they might feast with infinite ease and appetite at home. But to breakfast or to dine with a man of influence is quite another pair of shoes. There are people in London, and, for the matter of that, many more in the country, who would go down on all fours to be served with a scrap of cold fish and egg sauce, and a bit of boar's head, in fine company; yet there are few people in the United Kingdom who have really intelligent cooks, and some of them never give parties.

It is a great mistake for a man of rank not to give parties—almost as great a mistake as it is for a vulgar man to attempt to entertain his superiors, because the vulgar man's pretension to eat his way into society is resented, and he is certain to incur some contempt, as well as to meet with open affronts. But a man of position may really do what he likes if he will only give enough dinners or breakfasts, and invite the right people. Lord Palmerston used to say that "dining is the life and soul of diplomacy," and it is indeed the life and soul of our social system altogether. It costs very little to entertain discreetly. When once a man has a well mounted establishment, he must pay his servants whether they do something or nothing. His game, fruit, mutton, poultry, cost him nothing, or rather they will cost him just as much whether he eats the shattered birds and pecked fruit —which are unfit for market—or not. His gamekeepers must be maintained, and so must his gardeners; not a shot less will be fired in his preserves, not a block of wood less will be burnt away in his conservatories, whether he has guests to enjoy his hothouse grapes and fat pheasants or not; and the serious influence which a politician may wield with his knives and forks is very valuable and may be very useful.

Let any shrewd observer only consider with attention the composition of an intelligent party like that which the Duke of Courthope had assembled round him, at his ornamental cottage by the water side, upon one of the latest fine days of an English autumn. His Grace, and every one else worth knowing, had been with the grouse among highland heather in August, and when the birds got wild they had been yachting at Cowes, and then busy in the stubble after partridges. The hunting had not fairly begun, for the scent will not lie while the sun is still powerful, and some of the late crops were still in the ground. Parliament and the law courts were closed, and it was too soon for stumping: so there was just a week's breathing time, during which agreeable people could run up to London before the winter campaign commenced. They did not reopen their town houses; they stopped about at snug hotels in Berkeley Square and Bond Street, or took furnished houses by the week. When they met they tried to amuse themselves and sometimes succeeded, though not always.

It was certainly with some object of profit, or advantage, that his Grace had invited Sir Joseph Demurrer, whom he had met a few days before in consultation with Mr. Mortmain, touching the amendment

of an amendment of a Bill in Chancery, which was
going up in a year or two before the Rolls Court.
That great Equity lawyer had been hastily summoned
to London in consequence of a closely-kept Cabinet
secret which had unfortunately oozed out through
somebody's indiscretion. It had been long known that
the Lord Chancellor had lost the faculty of hearing,
and had tried his cases by sight; but it had been
carefully concealed that his Lordship had for some
time past lost the faculty of speech also, and the
Government had hoped to tide over the session without being obliged to introduce a new man into their
confidence. The indiscreet somebody had frustrated
their expectations in after-dinner oratory. Of course,
however, the Chancellor would continue to hold office
till arrangements could be made to appoint his successor, and might even fill his office with his usual
dignity and wisdom for a term or two longer. Still,
it had become advisable to entertain proposals for his
retirement, and the large place-holding family which
then happened to be in power were looking about to
ascertain which of the distinguished lawyers below the
bench were most eager for advancement—who would
bid highest for the vacant Chancellorship, accept it
with the least share of influence and patronage, and
give the most trustworthy guarantees not to make
himself troublesome to the family. It seemed probable
that Sir Joseph Demurrer would do this, and it was
known that both Sir Coke Littleton and Sir Gascoyne
Bacon would not; because they had ideas and purposes of their own, unconnected with the family.
Besides, neither of them were so popular as Sir Joseph,
so that the family could well afford to snub them in

his favour for their own benefit and peace of mind. A runaway Chancellor would have been an awful infliction on the family, and Sir Joseph was an amiable, obliging person of whom everyone spoke handsomely; he was such a worthy and excellent specimen of mediocrity. The Duke of Courthope, who had many Chancery suits, cordially approved the Government choice, and had intimated his satisfaction to Lord Dullington when they had discussed the subject just after the great St. Leger race was run at Doncaster that year. Sir Joseph Demurrer was aware that the vote and influence of the Duke of Courthope with his party had been exerted for his elevation, and against his rival Sir Gascoyne Bacon. He therefore naturally resolved that he would not be ungrateful to a magnate whose friendship conferred so much honour upon him, and who was never likely to stand in his way. He had been delighted to receive an invitation to breakfast, and the Duke was delighted to see him.

Philip Poynings, the shrewd Parliamentary agent and wire puller of the Dullington party, was there too. The Duke of Courthope did not himself care for place, and as he expressed it his Grace was "out of the running altogether." But he liked to know what was going on and to watch the moves upon the political chess board with an interest half amused, half cynical. Now Poynings always knew what was going to happen next week, and the true story of the latest job or scandal, if he chose to tell it; which was indeed not often. But he could not be expected to keep a secret from a Dullington Duke. It would not be honourable, and the Duke's headkeeper sent him a haunch of venison every Christmas from Beaumanoir. If his

Grace had ordered a jack snipe to be sent to him from the uttermost parts of the earth, he would have felt personally flattered by the attention, and the Duke used his vanity without scruple. His Grace was always wanting some piece of patronage for a dependent, and had asked for everything, from the primacy to a tide waitership, since his party had been in power. But he could not well ask himself, for none of his own private friends in the Cabinet dared wag a tongue in their own departments. When he wanted a place for somebody who could not be coaxed or silenced without one, and whom it was not expedient to defy, he spoke to P. Poynings, and P. Poynings spoke to the Secretary of the Treasury, or to a clerk at the Admiralty, or an agent at the Foreign Office, or to the real man who had the place to give away, and made terms with him. Sometimes the Secretary of the Treasury stipulated for the Duke's influence in a borough which belonged to him, the Reform Bill notwithstanding, because every house in it was upon his property, and his tenants had leases drawn up by a Parliamentary solicitor, which leases were afterwards copied by an Irish peer, with perceptible results. Sometimes the Admiralty clerk or Foreign Office agent bargained for an invitation to Beaumanoir once a year, with a fixed annual commission or per centage upon the salary of the place. His Grace had also given his proxy to Earl Placard, after the custom of the period, so that whether he was absent or present, his vote in the House of Lords was steadily recorded in favour of Ministers. He had therefore in a manner taken out his license to deal in commissions and appointments while his party were in office.

The other guests were a pair of able editors who praised and printed their way into big houses, where they were used and hated; a raffish Irish baron, who had succeeded to the till of a country banker, which banker had bought his coronet from an impecunious Minister. He was welcome, for he submitted to be a dupe because he was a snob. He was trying to buy his way into good company, and played high and betted high while doing so. There was a spare, keen-eyed man from Australia, with a black satin waistcoat and a beard growing out of the top of his chin. He was giving immense prices for brood mares and salmon roe, and dreamed of squatters and Crown lands. Then there were, for pleasure's sake, a few guardsmen, Parliamentary colonels, and stray dandies who make the padding of agreeable society; with charming Lady Overlaw, the Hon. Mrs. Manning, the Countess of Trimmington, and other beautiful women who lived on the frontiers of propriety, but had never passed over the border. The party had both salt and savour in it. The Parliamentary colonels and ladies were pleased to meet the future Chancellor, and he, De-murrer, and the vulgar baron were glad to meet them.

"When you get on to the woolsack you must abolish wigs, Sir John," said Lady Overlaw to the lawyer.

"Abolish wigs!" echoed Sir John, smiling incredulously over his partridge.

"He thinks you mean Wigs with an *h*," said Lady Trimmington.

"Oh no, I meant nothing personal—only the horse-hair wigs, Sir John."

"Wigs lend much to the dignity of the human

face," put in the Duke with his pompous falsetto, not suspecting as usual that there was a joke afoot.

"They were great social equalizers," observed P. Poynings. "When everybody wore a wig, men past fifty were not handicapped as they are now with respect to ladies."

"Do you think our grandmothers couldn't tell a man's age through his horse-hair?" asked Lady Overlaw, halving a peach with a young guardsman.

"I doubt it," replied P. Poynings. "The Duke of Richelieu married for the third time when he was past eighty. His bride was sixty years younger than himself. He would never have ventured upon such an exhibition if he had been obliged to figure at the altar in one of our modern black coats and with a bald head."

The breakfast was over. Some of the guests were preparing to row back to London, some to drive back in drags and barouches, some to return by rail or to ride over and visit the Orleans Princes at Twickenham while they were in the neighbourhood. The Duke of Courthope meant to have a quiet club dinner, because Lady Overlaw had offered him a place in her box at the Haymarket, and he had just ordered his phaeton when a telegram was put into his hand. Her ladyship was taking leave of him before she stepped into her britzka, and therefore his Grace, who had a delicate sense of the becoming, laid the telegram aside unopened.

"Were you pleased with your breakfast?" asked the Duke of his cousin, in a business-like sort of way.

"Were *they* pleased, you mean?" answered her

Ladyship, shrugging her fair shoulders. "I am always pleased: you know that. Why should they not be pleased, I should like to know? They had plenty to eat and drink."

"Two pounds six shillings and fourpence," observed the Duke, sententiously. "Everything but the cold roast beef came from Beaumanoir yesterday; and I have included the carriage of the things and the porterage in the price of the breakfast. It is under three shillings a head."

"Quite enough too," laughed Lady Overlaw, decidedly. "It is no use spending money on people. They never pay it back again, and they are glad enough to come and be looked at. Good-bye, and mind you are not late to-night. I dislike sitting in my box with nobody but my sister Jane. Bring the Australian Savage with you. Jane wants to weed her husband's stables, and anything with a good name in the stud book will do for Australia."

"I will obey orders," replied the Duke; "I can send a note from you by the club messenger to the man from Australia at his hotel. I had better not ask him myself, or he would expect dinner: those aborigines have wild notions of hospitality, and we don't dine strangers at the Carlton."

"I will send my footman to you with a note from the Clarendon, where Jane is staying with the Strogonoffs," answered Lady Overlaw. "I have no coroneted paper with me at Thomas's, but she always has some, and it is better to write to savages in state." So saying, her Ladyship tripped into her carriage and rolled away with the best flowers in bloom in the villa gardens and hothouses that day made up into nosegays, so that the Duke's gardener had nothing to sell for twenty-four hours, and he wished that her Ladyship had been in Palestine, for she did not give him a sixpence.

"You will take care to have the unbruised peaches that were left at breakfast, with the Windsor pears, and all the pheasants that are not knocked about, packed in separate baskets and addressed as I told you, Giovanni," observed the Duke, who sold the finest of his fruit and game like other noblemen now-a-days. Then he sauntered to the table where he had laid the telegram and carelessly opened it. He opened it carelessly because nothing that could possibly happen in the world would much disturb him, and he read:—

"The dark horse is dead. Interview requested.— SHARPE."

He knew that the "dark horse" meant Madge, and mounting his phaeton in high good humour he took the well-rounded brown reins in his hands and drove to London, sending up an answer to the Yorkshire attorney's telegram by the way—so numerous are the conveniences of modern life—and when he pulled up an hour afterwards in Pall Mall, there was Mr. Sharpe waiting for him hat in hand in the doorway of the Carlton.

CHAPTER VII.

Noble and Ignoble.

"WELL, we shall hear no more nonsense about those people at Wakefield—is not that the name of the place?" said the Duke of Courthope, apparently much refreshed, as he entered one of the underground rooms of the Tory club with Mr. Sharpe behind him.

"I should not go quite so far as that, your Grace," replied the lawyer, "but we have got rid of the worst part of our botheration, broken the neck of the difficulty without laying a finger on it, which is always a convenient mode of settlement because there are no afterclaps."

"It does not much matter how you get the right side of a fence if you don't tumble down as you clear it," said the Duke.

"I'm not so sure we are quite clear of the brambles yet, Duke," observed Mr. Sharpe, putting his hand to his hat deferentially in a horse-dealing way he had. "There's an okkerd old fellow named Brown, who still prints an advertisement in the papers now and then, and he might make himself troublesome if he happened to live in London instead of Calcutta, and had a wicked chap behind him."

"What d'ye mean, Sharpe?" asked the Duke. "If the dark horse is dead, what have we to do with any one else? Lord George Wyldwyl is the next heir in tail, and you know from Mortmain that we are on the best of terms. Nobody else would have any interest in disturbing my possession of the estates even if they had the power to do so, which I utterly deny."

"Steady she goes, your Grace, if *you* please," objected Mr. Sharpe. "There are quite a litter of young Browns, and the lad who has gone out soldiering to India would be Earl of Winguid if his mother's claim were established; only fortunately he does not know it. Besides, the claim is now three generations old; and although the sixty years of undisturbed possession necessary to establish a valid title in law has not elapsed, it would be very uphill work to attack us. Nevertheless, it might be done, your Grace; it really might be done now by a resolute man with money; and this Brown of Calcutta has money, there is no doubt of that."

"What do you advise?" inquired the Duke, briefly. He was fond of hearing what other people had to say before he spoke himself, for he was by no means an original minded man.

"Let me see," replied Mr. Sharpe, reflectively. "Brown of Calcutta is, as I have said, an okkerd customer, your Grace; but Brown of Wakefield isn't: we had better get rid of him. He might, I don't say he will, but he might fall into queer street some day now his wife is dead, and if his name were to get into the cussed noosepapers, that Brown out in Calcutta would see it, and might turn up in a troublesome shape."

"I told you my opinion long since," said his Grace. "Why didn't you send the whole lot of them off to some out-of-the-way place by hook or by crook?"

"It wasn't quite so easy while the woman lived," mused Mr. Sharpe. "I often used to drop in at the

'Chequers' for a glass of ale, just to see if I could make anything of her; but you'll hardly believe it, your Grace, she turned me round her finger she did, and was a good deal harder to draw than a badger. I used to tell her that I knew of a good offer for the tumble-down old house they lived in; and she told me I must speak to her Master about that; when I did speak to him, he said I must go to 'his Missus.' Once I tried to tell them a fine story of the gold fields, and brought them a coloured picture from an illustrated paper about the wonders of California; but Mrs. Brown knew in a minute I was up to something, and I could never get her into talk after that. She distrusted herself, and she distrusted me still more, so that there was nothing to be made of her. Her husband, too, is a north-countryman, and much shrewder than he looks. He contrived in a roundabout way of his own to put it into my head that he had taken my measure, and I gave him up as a bad job."

"It is a very strange thing," remarked the Duke in his grand, haughty way, "that the moment any insignificant person is opposed to me he becomes possessed of unsuspected qualities of resistance, and starts up into a separate power. Once I drove over an old apple-woman when I was coming home sprung from the Derby, and she roused three Whig Secretaries of State and twelve judges before I got the better of her."

"Very likely, your Grace. It costs a good deal to have your own way if you are stubborn about it and the wind is contrary; but I think I can manage this move for you, if I have time. Slow and softly wins the game, your Grace," remarked Mr. Sharpe.

"I do not see why I should possibly be pestered some day by people who live at Wakefield-in-the-Marsh," said the Duke. And, to do his Grace no more than justice, he really did not see why he should be inconvenienced at any time, or by anybody.

"I suppose your Grace will pay something for their outfit, if we have them gammoned off to the other side of the water?" inquired Mr. Sharpe.

"Certainly *not*," replied the Duke, decidedly. His Grace, in common with most great spendthrifts, had the profoundest disinclination to part with money upon some occasions. "There are the Emigration Commissioners, Sharpe. You can bleed them, can't you? All you will have to do is to give these Browns a good character." The Duke, after all, was ten times cleverer than the Yorkshire attorney; or perhaps it would be truer to say that the patrician was accustomed to do everything by influence, and the plebeian had always been obliged to have recourse to money.

"To be sure," said Mr. Sharpe, "I never thought of that, now; and I can get them a bit of land out there, I dessay, through your Grace's good word. Live and let live." The money-lender was not an unkind man. He would have wrung an elephant's neck, of course, for one of his tusks; but he would not willingly have harmed a fly unless something was to be got by it, and all his instincts, like those of most men who deal in horses, were merciful.

The Duke of Courthope smiled inwardly. He had been all his life so habituated to be considered by others, and to see their interests and feelings give way to his, that his heart was as hard as adamant. He felt, also, that the crafty and successful usurer was a mere child to him in knowledge of the world and diplomatic astuteness. If the Duke of Courthope meant to crush a man, he had no regard for small delicacies. He put his ducal heel resolutely on the man's neck and stamped him out, without exultation and without pity. The thing had to be done, and he did it—thoroughly. He did not half do it.

"Tread upon a worm and it turns," said a baffled and smarting antagonist to his Grace once upon a time.

"Ah," answered the Duke with easy scorn, "I have heard your proverb, but you have only repeated half of it: 'tread upon it *again*, and it turns no more.'"

The Duke of Courthope in his youth had ruined that baffled antagonist in more ways than one, so his Grace knocked the fellow down when he was impudent enough to remonstrate. Animated by a similar spirit upon the present occasion, he replied to the benevolent suggestion of Mr. Sharpe in the very dryest manner, and with a peculiar metallic ring in his voice:

"Take my word for it, your wise course is to leave those Browns to shift for themselves, and get them no grants of lands or anything else. Never raise up an opponent; if he is in the mud, so much the better. Were the Browns ever to see themselves in a snug farm, they would be asking how they got there, and perhaps find out. There is no such thing as a secret."

"I can't say I fancy the job altogether, your Grace," remarked Mr. Sharpe, "but I would go a long way to oblige you; and, besides, it would hardly soot my own book to see them there Browns git their eds above water—that it wouldn't." The Yorkshireman often dropped his h's and spoke in a strong provincial dialect when perplexed.

"*I* should say," suggested the Duke, good-humouredly, as if he was conferring a favour on his visitor, "do not move at all in the business yourself; keep out of sight. Isn't there a parson down there who belongs to old Porteous?—a washed-out man, with his head in the clouds. Lady Dowdeswell-Mowledy spoke to me about him the other day only, and said he was some connection of hers. She wanted me to give him one of my livings; to be sure women are impudent enough for anything." The Duke tossed his head, and smiled at the recollection of Lady Dowdeswell-Mowledy's impertinence in supposing that he, the Duke of Courthope, could or would give away a good Church benefice to a good churchman.

"I declare your Grace knows everything," cried Mr. Sharpe in some astonishment. "There is a parson—the Reverend Something Mowledy—who lives down there, and he has always taken an interest in the Browns."

"I know he has," assented the Duke. "Old Porteous told me he was sweet upon the girl—Madge was her name—I remember now—before she married, and he moved heaven and earth to get her out of the police row, breaking his way even into your friend Johnny Bodger about it, and wanted to have Krorl, the magistrate, dismissed for something he said or did. A regular tartar of a parson!" added the Duke with a sneer. "By the way, you didn't make the most of the police business, Sharpe. You should have squeezed Mrs. Brown when she was caught in that trap, and left the reverend gentleman to his remedy afterwards. He would not have made much of his grievance at the Mundane Office if Alfred Wyldwyl had stood in his way."

"I see my way a bit clearer now than I did then," said Mr. Sharpe, rather abashed. He had never quite taken the measure of the Duke's mind before, and now he felt for the first time that if the business between them should ever come to a wrangle, he would not be so certain to get the best end of it as he had supposed.

"Ah, you see it now," observed his Grace. "I have often noticed that my best thoughts are only a month or two ahead of those of my solicitors, and they generally come round to them after they have had time enough to reflect. I'll tell you what it is now, Sharpe; your plan should be to work the oracle through the parson. Don't do it yourself; set old Porteous on him. This is the way to do it. The Doctor always catches fire at the touch of print, and I have told the Clerk of the House of Lords to send him my Parliamentary papers. He is a mellow old boy, and they amuse him. He fancies they give him importance in the eyes of that termagant housekeeper of his; and he has done several things for me lately —showing a proper feeling. I will take care he receives the latest report of the Emigration Commissioners this evening; and if you get a letter written to him by some one at Dronington, asking his assistance for the Brown family, there is no fear but he will put this and that together, and never rest till he and his Curate have shipped them comfortably off, without either you or I having had so much as a little finger in the pie."

Mr. Sharpe took leave of the Duke of Courthope after this conversation with a much higher opinion of his Grace's intelligence, and a wholesome fear of provoking him beyond a certain point, which simplified their future intercourse. Nothing is so common a sentiment in the breast of a vulgar man as a secret contempt for the intelligence of his superiors, and if ever circumstances combine to assure him that he is under some misapprehension on this subject, he is as unaffectedly astonished as if a statue reputed inanimate had abruptly cuffed his ears.

CHAPTER VIII.
Emigrants.

It may be frequently observed that the death or removal of one member of a family brings ruin upon all the rest. Some quiet, unobtrusive influence kept them together, and working in harmony; when it is gone the connecting link between them is destroyed. The "Chequers" was never the same after Madge was taken from it. Until the very day of her decease it had seemed a respectable road-side inn, as it had done any time since its ancient sign-board was first put up. But from that time an air of desolation and decay fell upon it. Tom Brown slouched about with his hands in his pockets, or sat upon stiles and leaned against posts with his clodhopper's boots half unlaced, and his beard unshorn. He had nothing to do, and had no heart to seek for work. If he went to dig a bit in his garden, his strength failed him, and he might be seen soon afterwards brooding upon his wheelbarrow, with a pipe in his mouth at noon-day. His children, uncombed and unwashed, went whooping and straggling all over the village, and out into the fields, and got flogged for scaring colts, and milking cows, and stealing apples. Their mother's death had converted them into little vagabonds. Their dinner, which had been such a decent and orderly meal, was turned into a saturnalia. The children crowded round the saucepan, where a heap of unwashed potatoes boiled, and picked them out with their fingers before they were done, and they fought and yelled among each other as they did so. They climbed up to the rafters where the side of bacon hung, and helped themselves, spoiling more than they ate, and making themselves half sick. Then they set off, shouting, for the mill-stream, to catch sticklebacks, emptying the hen-roost of its eggs by the way, and did not turn up again till nightfall. There was nobody to put them to bed, so they laid down to sleep as they were, undressed, and got up again, unwashed, and became shocking dirty little children. Mrs. Jinks came in to them once or twice and scolded them, and slapped the youngest; but they were too strong for her now, and laughed at the old grandame who had seen most of them born.

It was almost touching to see Tom Brown upon his knees in the chill autumn mornings, trying to blow up a bit of fire to boil the kettle and make himself a cup of tea. It was not long before he ceased to do so, and went over the way for a mug of warm ale and a hunk of bread and cheese, which well-nigh choked him; for his old chum and rival, Harry Jinks, had set up a Tom and Jerry shop since Madge's death, and all the village saw that the "Chequers" had gone wrong.

One night as Mr. Mowledy returned through the glebe meadows from visiting a sick parishioner, he stumbled over something in his path, being more near-sighted than ever now, and stooping down he was grieved to perceive that the lifeless log was well-behaved Thomas Brown, apparently drunk and insensible. It was not that he had drank much; but the beer at the Tom and Jerry shop was not so good as his own had been; some said it was adulterated, and often made the villagers ill; moreover, he was weak from living on bad food and sorrowing.

So ultimately things happened at Wakefield-in-the-Marsh very much as the Duke of Courthope had anticipated that they would happen.

Mr. Mowledy, the best friend and staunchest protector of the Brown family, fearing they would come to no good in that state of life to which they had fallen, was made the unconscious instrument of getting them out of the country, lest by any accident they should be discovered by a relative who was seeking for them, and have fortune thrust upon them. He did them no harm, for riches and titles have nothing to do with human happiness, and to have called a dozen loutish country lads and wenches who were too old to be sent to school the Honourable John and the Honourable Giles, the Lady Susan and the Lady Jemima, would have profited them nothing in the end, and have been very offensive to rational people. Still, Mr. Mowledy would not have stood in their way and perhaps deprived them of lands and a peerage, if he had known what he was doing and had had a free choice submitted to him. On the contrary, he would have felt it his duty to do them a great injury by helping them into a position for which no one knew better than himself that they were totally unfit. Providence, which always acts for the best, and shames all human wisdom, decreed otherwise. When Tom Brown moped about day after day and let his business go to the dogs, so that Harry Jinks opened an opposition beer-shop over the way, the Curate spoke to him seriously, and mentioned the benefits of emigration; which had opportunely been brought to his notice by his Rector, Dr. Porteous. At first honest Thomas hearkened without understanding what was said to him.

But his brewers, finding their account unpaid, and their old customer doing no butts a week, sent a broker over from Dronington, and sold off his goods. They were only a few poor sticks when they came to be put up for auction; but Thomas Brown had been proud of them in his silent way, and could never face his neighbours with his head up after this disgrace had come upon him. So he listened with more attention to the Curate's talk about another country, where land was cheap and victuals plentiful, and spoke to his eldest daughter, who was growing up a bold, slatternly, motherless girl, and to his slouching, lazy sons, about it. It chanced too that an emigration agent happened to pass through Wakefield-in-the-Marsh at this time, and got likewise talking to his boys and girls till they were all agog to be off. He was a smart, glib-tongued fellow, and he promised to go with them.

So within three months after Madge's death Mr.

Mowledy accompanied her husband and children one day to Gravesend, and saw them on board the good ship *Royal Oak*. The Curate had contrived to fit them out with all things needful. Their copyhold property had realised nearly a hundred pounds after both brewer and distiller had been paid; and as hope revived in them their self-respect seemed to revive also. They looked clean and decent again in their country-made clothes; and some scraps of mourning which they still wore for the departed wife and mother gave a pathetic interest to their appearance as the emigrants trudged through the streets of London on their way from one railway station to another, with the parson of their parish guiding them.

They were received on board the emigrant ship at Gravesend by a trim, clean-shaven man, who looked like a horse-dealer, but who was a dealer in men. He numbered them carefully with a neat gold pencil-case in his hand, for he received a commission of so much a head on them from the government of the colony whither they were about to proceed. He was a smooth-tongued gentleman, very pleasant; and the emigration agent who had been to Wakefield and had used so many persuasive arts to lure them from their home was merely one of his young men, who was persuasive in the way of business for two pounds a week. His master, however, being better paid, was, if possible, a still more persuasive person. He assured Thomas Brown and his family that Australia was the true Tommy Tiddler's ground, and that lands and cattle were to be had for the asking. Then he told them how fine a ship was the *Royal Oak*, in which they were to sail and steam by turns across the world—

how it was the latest experiment in ship-building, approved by the Post-Office, and especially built for speedy and prosperous voyages, because it would not need to stop for coaling purposes, being a screw clipper, which was rated A 1 upon the books of Lloyd's. The emigration agent said briskly that the one hope and desire of his life was to make a voyage to the Antipodes in the *Royal Oak;* and then, having carefully noted their names and ages, to prevent mistakes, he went to dine at the London Tavern with the Honourable Company of Fishcatchers.

Thomas Brown and his family scratched their heads when he was gone, and felt a little strange in the overladen vessel, as she crawled down the Thames in the wake of a tug. But there were so many hopes on board, so much life and energy, such big projects, and great expectations, that soon they fell to cheering whenever they passed a ship going up stream, sending noisy good-byes behind them. And sometimes a young collier or bargeman bringing up coals from the northern ports, or the captain of a smack in the coasting trade, would answer their cheer and look wistfully after them, as he bade them God speed through all the dangers of the seas to the other side of the world. Hundreds and thousands of coast-folk, as they saw the ship stand out farther and farther from the shore, longed to go with her, away from hard landlords, stern tax-gatherers, and meagre food; and the emigrants felt proud and satisfied with themselves for that they had made so bold and wise a venture.

How they might have fared in their new home, what strong men and fair women might have sprung from their loins, what new nobilities and empires they might have founded, is a secret which will never be revealed. For yet a few days later, and a thrill of horror went through the very heart of England, as the news flew from mouth to ear that the famous screw clipper *Royal Oak*, the most successful experiment in modern shipbuilding, and which carried in it so fair a dream of fortune, had gone down off the Anglesea coast, with all hands on board.

So perished the family of the Browns of Wakefield, all save one—there being, as far as mortal judgment could discern, no reason why they should have been born, or why they should have died. The very house where they had lived their uneventful lives, and which had been known for two centuries upon one of the ancient high roads of the kingdom as the "Chequers" inn, was pulled down to make way for some saw-mills, which the blacksmith's son erected to cut sleepers by contract for the Dronington Railway. After a year or two more all recollection of Madge and her immediate kindred, and the very name of the house wherein they dwelt, passed away from their birth-place, and it knew them no more.

CHAPTER IX.

A Marquis.

"WHAT is a marquis?" asked William Brown of a comrade as they leaned over the ship's side, fishing, off Malta, where the *Tanjore* had stopped to take in more coal and deliver her mail bags.

"How should I know?" answered William Brown's

comrade, a Kentish hop picker; and then he added, "a marquis is a lord, isn't he?"

"Hoot, man! a marquis is a title of dignity in England, France, and Italy, next in rank to that of a duke," replied a decided voice with a strong Scotch accent. It belonged to a passenger bound for Calcutta, and who seemed to be upon very good terms with the deputy sub-assistant Commissary-General of her Majesty's troops, also on board the *Tanjore*.

William Brown was a well-mannered lad, and had been taught by Mr. Mowledy to show habitual deference towards his seniors; so he made way for the Scottish gentleman, who seemed disposed to continue the conversation. Therefore, after eyeing the two soldiers with a benevolent glance, he allowed himself to be carried away by the national longing of his countrymen to impart knowledge in its dryest details.

"If ye would wish to have the requisite information about marquises, ye'll not have far to seek it," said he. "The title of marquis is a ridiculous thing we got from the Germans, and might as well have left it to them. The military chieftains in the Teutonic kingdoms and empires which arose on the fall of the Western Empire of Rome, and were entrusted with the defence of the frontiers, were called Mark-grafen, or in the Latin tongue Marchiones. Carolus Magnus, who is improperly named Charlemagne, appointed some of the first of them, though they had already got a footing upon other people's grounds before him. They were intended to be military governors, but they took their places into their own hands and made themselves hereditary under weak bodies of kings. The first English marquis was created by that poor creature Richard II. in 1387. He was named Marquis of Dublin. The next creation was John de Beaufort, Earl of Somerset, but he refused to bear the dignity because it was a strange and novel one. The first marquises had the power o' life an' death. They were just petty princes: the latest marquises are commonly little better than tailors' touts."

The two soldiers gaped at the Scotsman who thus expounded much to his own satisfaction the historical origin and present value of the second hereditary honour of the British peerage; but they did not derive much advantage from his discourse. Their captain, Lord Kinsgear (for they were both in the same troop), certainly did not answer either of the descriptions of a marquis which had been given them. He was very good-natured, but he could not have put either of them to death if he would, and as for tailors—General Violet certainly had more to do with them than this marquis.

The Scotsman perceived their dilemma, and having nothing better to do, he sat down upon a coil of rope, and taught them; rather to relieve his own mind of its abundance than from any thought of whether his teaching might be of use to them.

"Hereditary titles," said he with a strength and breadth of accent to which no vowels or consonants can do perfect justice, "have died out everywhere but in England. In France they are not used at all, and a Duke is called Monsieur, which is merely the French for Mister. The terms your Grace and your Lordship are only heard of in the mouths of the English; and we have taken all meaning from them, so that they will soon come to be laughed at. By-and-by we shall only use those titular distinctions which have still a meaning, such as Doctor, Colonel, Captain, or Bishop. If the time ever comes when we make captains out of bankers, call a man a doctor because his grandfather turned his money in physic, and so on, we shall omit these titles too. Already, I'm told, 'tis offensive to use sham titles between friends, and peers are only my lorded by their servants."

"Men!" said the Marquis of Kinsgear, coming down from the quarter-deck and kindly addressing the two soldiers, "have you had any sport?"

"Yes, my Lord, we are pulling them up almost as fast as we can bait our hooks," replied Young Brown, answering his Captain's question, and giving him his hereditary designation as a matter of course. He even paused respectfully in his occupation till the nobleman had passed on.

"Aw!" observed the Scotch gentleman, shaking his head at the trooper when he returned to his fishing again, "it is a pity any man should be born with the right to make other men tell falsehoods to him every time they open their mouths. There is no Lord but One."

Whether it was that this full private soldier had the nameless power of attracting the good will of all who were brought in contact with him, or whether people on board ship are often at a loss for something to do, it is certain that the Scotch gentleman appeared to take an unusual fancy to William Brown. He was a hale, strong man, long past middle life, with a bold, open countenance, and shaggy hair. The expression of his face conveyed the idea of mingled shrewdness and honesty, with something of the pedant and more of the humourist. Perhaps he liked William Brown because he was a good listener, decorous, attentive, intelligent. Perhaps he was insensibly drawn to him because they were namesakes, he by a curious coincidence—such strange things will happen—having been also christened William, and his patronymic being Brown.

The trooper, too, had plenty of time at his disposal. He had learned his drill, and got a good character at the depôt in England. So Colonel Oakes had relieved him from regimental duty, and he had been selected as servant by Lord Kinsgear, who never wanted to be served.

The Marquis had also a great liking to him; and sometimes when they were together they might have been taken for two brothers, only that Young Brown was the stronger, the more stoutly built, and the more upright of the two. Lord Kinsgear himself had been struck by his servant's resemblance to a family picture at Beaumanoir, and even the tone of William Brown's voice often sounded to him strangely familiar. They seemed drawn towards each other by some subtle sympathy. The Marquis, who was himself a draughtsman of no mean skill, soon found out that his servant could draw, and asked him to make certain plans and sketches for him. His Lordship liked to talk with his servant over the details of these drawings better than to listen while Lieutenant Highlowes explained to him that his real name was Wyldwyl, his (Highlowes') grandmother (by his *father's* side, which made the strength of his case) having married Sir Lovelace Wyvil, a descendant of the Ducal House of Wyldwyl, who had apparently determined to spell his name upon phonetic principles, or had been unacquainted with its true orthography. The rest of the officers had mostly some similar craze. One was fifteenth cousin to Lord Hanaper, another claimed the Barony of Trecorne, and loved to converse upon peerages, which had little interest for the acknowledged heir to half a score of them.

Once or twice Colonel Oakes, however, rallied the Marquis on his unusual kindness towards a trooper and a servant. The English theory has always been that privates in the army and domestics belong to a different order of creation from officers and gentlemen. But William Brown conciliated even the Colonel. He never took a liberty or presumed in any way upon the favours shown to him. He was civil, and prompt to obey orders. On the other hand, having been used to the companionship of Mr. Mowledy, his manners were free from all loutishness or embarrassment. He spoke excellent English, and his address to his superiors was marked by that candid, inoffensive freedom, that frankness and perfect absence of undercurrent in the mind which infallibly pleases brave men. He could not understand that he was a different species of being to his officers; and at length even they themselves began to entertain doubts upon the subject. Not but what they tried his temper, and tried it very sharply, before they gave him their confidence. Lieutenant Highlowes ordered him under arrest; Cornet Peebody damned him; and even Colonel Oakes blew him up sky high, owing to a mistake which that gallant and kind-hearted officer had himself made. But Young Brown never complained. He took his punishment like a gentleman and did not sulk after it. So Lieutenant Highlowes told him afterwards that his arrest was a fluke, and Cornet Peebody looked sheepish when General Violet, who seldom spoke louder than a whisper, heard he had used bad language. While as for Colonel Oakes, he told Lord Kinsgear he was very sorry he had jawed Young Brown, who had not been in fault, instead of breaking the head of private Sloper, who was. "But," added the Colonel, heartily, "the young beggar is a trump, and did not turn rusty, so I shall make him a lance corporal as soon as can be."

The young fellow, too, was equally popular with his comrades because he did not stand aloof from them, took rough jokes without snarling, and shared any good thing he got with them. If the Colonel or Lord Kinsgear gave him a bottle of wine, or the remains of a ham, or a preserved pie, he was off at once to the forecastle with it, and cut it up with his clasp knife, giving a hunk and a drink to whomsoever was nearest, till it was gone. He was always ready to fight any of them, or to write or read a letter for them, or to play leap-frog, and "tuck in his twopenny" on deck of an evening with the rest.

They were a queer lot; many of them among the most consummate scoundrels in the world. Owing to our valiant prejudices against conscription and against general compulsory service, and owing also to the decay of everything like patriotism or a thirst for military glory consequent upon the dissemination of cheap literature among the lower classes, the difficulty of recruiting the army had already begun to be felt. In no calling did men earn so little at the cost of so much humiliation, and therefore no youngster of energy and character ever dreamed of joining the ranks except under the influence of drink or despair. Our regiments had become, what they were for many years, and still perhaps are, the habitual refuge of the worst kind of criminals. While newspapers were filled with the advertisements of the police offering rewards for the apprehension of forgers, thieves, swindlers, murderers and others, these persons had discovered that the Queen's uniform was the safest hiding-place in the world for a fugitive who had offended the laws. When tracked by the police he had only to run for the nearest recruiting office to baffle his pursuers. No questions were asked of him. He needed only to crop his hair in military style, put on a red coat to disguise himself effectively, and then to lead an exemplary life in barracks or on board a transport till the hue and cry after him had gone by. Then he might safely slip out of his uniform and go in again for any course of misbehaviour he liked best. The military authorities folded their hands and twiddled their thumbs. They called the deserters "runners," and thought no more of them. The Government stores were merely minus a uniform; and whatever the deserter thought proper to steal from his comrades in order to give himself a fresh start in life after he had deserted. The military authorities did not think him worth looking after. His name was simply inserted in the police sheet, and if he was unluckily caught they dealt with him as leniently as possible. He very seldom was caught: neither the Horse Guards nor the War Office wished to catch him; for they did not know what to do with him. If brought back to the regiment, he only stayed long enough to corrupt better men, and then took himself off with more spoil. So any fine enterprising fellow with a taste for other people's lives or property, who fancied the criminal business in preference to any laborious undertaking, might drive a pleasant trade if he would only take the reasonable precaution of enlisting now and then in a new regiment, and passing a little of his spare time in heroic society, whenever he might be in danger of being molested by a magistrate. In short, the military profession was adopted by a large class of ingenious and dangerous persons, simply in order to defeat the ends of justice.

Among William Brown's comrades were roguish bank clerks, and defaulters of all kinds; expert swindlers, passers of sham cheques, hotel sneaks, and other good-for-nothing fellows. There were also a few country lads like himself, who had wandered away into the army with a sore heart for a sweet face.

The lad might not have got on so well with his companions but that he had an uncommonly hard fist, a ready wit, a sharp tongue, and an excellent temper. Besides, he had not leisure or inclination to get very thick with any of them. He joined none of their boozing parties with rum and dice between decks of nights; he had no cronies. What with his master's plans and drawings, old Mr. Brown's long-winded discourses upon things in general, and his own concerns, he began to feel tired long before the tipsy time began with his fellow-troopers, and rolling himself up in his hammock while they cursed or swore by turns, he usually slept soundly between supper and breakfast.

There was only one thing which surprised him in

the early part of the voyage, and that was the marked antipathy shown by Mr. Brown to Lord Kinsgear. Once the old gentleman snapped his fingers indignantly as the Marquis passed, and said, "He's just one o' the wicked Wyldwyls."

CHAPTER X.
At Sea.

IT came out in various ways during the voyage of the *Tanjore*, that Mr. Brown was a rich and enterprising merchant, who had been for many years established in Calcutta. At the first outbreak of the Indian Mutiny he had, with characteristic caution, determined to place his property in security; and, having made enough money for his own needs, he resolved to settle in Scotland. His adventures in search of a dignified retirement, however, were of a sort unhappily too common. He had purchased a rude old granite house and some wild moorlands near Dumfries, which had once belonged, so Tradition said, to the Red Comyn, from whom he was, Tradition also said, descended. The name of this territorial acquisition was "Scrappiecraggs," and Mr. Brown, being like most Anglo-Indians a great stickler for ancient customs, had fondly hoped to be personally known as "Scrappiecraggs" for the rest of his days, and to be recognised as one of the ancient hereditary lairds of the soil by his neighbours and dependents. But somehow it happened that all his neighbours who had comfortable homes were attorneys, or, as attorneys are named in Scotland, "writers to the Signet." When they spoke to him they addressed him as "Mister Broon;" and when they wrote to him they directed their letters to "——Brown, Esq." Moreover, he very soon discovered that all the happiness and comfort of provincial life in Scotland depends upon the favour and protection of the resident old lady. No sooner had he bought property and settled in the country than a bitter-tongued spinster called upon him in an antediluvian carriage, and put him through a regular genealogical examination. He passed it well, for he was a Scotchman; but having been long abroad, he got thrown out in the history of a county family, and as soon as she perceived that he was not aware of the stupendous fact that she was Miss Blinkie of Blinkie, she refused to acknowledge him as Scrappiecraggs. "Who is the canting auld wife who drove over from Dumfries in a boat upon wheels?" Mr. Brown had innocently asked of one of the elders of the Kirk over a dish of toddy: and the elder had told his wife, who had told her sister, who had told Miss Blinkie, who had flown to arms in wrathful indignation. Miss Blinkie was the more angry because a peerage, which she kept in abeyance, could only be revived by her speedy wedding. Thus, for a reason which should have been known and admired by all Scottish patriots, she was not disinclined to matrimony, and upon the appearance of a marriageable man of good family in her vicinity, she had considered it her most sacred duty to take possession of him without further loss of time.

"An auld wife is it?" therefore shrieked Miss Blinkie of Blinkie, greatly incensed. "When a' Scotland kens I have the barrenee o' Blinkie to my tocher, for the heirs of my body lawfully begotten, an' me a maiden woman! I'll teach the gowk manners!"

So ever afterwards Miss Blinkie of Blinkie, whose opinions had great weight at Dumfries, asserted with persistent animosity that the last laird of Scrappiecraggs had fallen beside her own great-grandfather in the final charge which had sent "Cope's pockpuddings fleein'" before Charles Edward's hielandmen at Preston Pons." Then, as for dependents, there were no longer any such persons. The farmers who held leases on the Scrappiecraggs estate talked politics, and their daughters played the piano. They were in favour of reform in the land laws, and considered that the obligation was very much on Mr. Brown's side whenever they paid their rent without deductions for short crops. Nobody called Mr. Brown "Scrappiecraggs" indeed but a medical man who paid him an unexpected visit. Even he, moreover, had been sent to carry out a grim practical joke devised by the vindictive Miss Blinkie, who had suggested that "the rich pedlar Broon might be suffering from the effects of a sunstroke he got in India, for he was obviously labouring under mental hallucinations about his own identity."

Now all this made things extremely unpleasant; and, moreover, it always rained at Scrappiecraggs when it did not snow. Mr. Brown, who was accustomed to a more genial climate and to a considerable amount of domestic attendance, did not like to be scolded when he got up in the cold by an hereditary old encumbrance whom he had invited to keep house for him, and who insisted upon his breakfasting invariably off an oatmeal poultice and a bare sheep's head. He was not pleased by any of those dry and humorous remarks respecting his "eegnorance" of local affairs, with which his acquaintances delighted to beguile their leisure. Therefore one day it occurred to him that the best thing he could possibly do for his own comfort would be to run away from Scrappiecraggs, as the earth was not likely to open and swallow it up. His spirits revived at the first commercial town he reached on his way southward; and by the time he got to London he had a fine appetite for the latest Indian news in any evening paper, as he sipped an excellent glass of Madeira at a snug Anglo-Indian hotel on the borderland between the West End and the City. The result of Mr. Brown's cogitations over his wine sent him on the following day to Leadenhall Street; and for a week or two afterwards he was seen in the neighbourhood of the House of Commons and the public offices about Whitehall. Then somehow or other it happened that Mr. Brown (of the eminent firm of W. Brown, M'Canny & Co.) returned to Calcutta with several large contracts for clothing, provisioning, and arming Her Majesty's forces.

That is how he came to be on board the *Tanjore*. He could not rest and do nothing. The man was a trader at the heart. He had none of the resources in himself which make the opportunity of leisure delightful to the poet, the philosopher, and the noble. He had no world within himself to make him indifferent to the world beyond, or scornful of it, or compassionate to it. The small echoes of gossip, little hatreds, petty envies, and pestilent moral squibs had murdered his peace in retirement. He did not care to read, he had never written anything but business letters, and he did not know how or where to seek enjoyment. It had been revealed to him that his business was the only pleasure which he was capable of appreciating, and he sensibly returned to it; not for the sake of gain, for he was childless, and had already more than he wanted, but for an occupation. He desired something to convince him that he was of some use in the world, and had his place in it.

Half amused and half angry at the old gentleman's contempt for Lord Kinsgear, a contempt which he did not care to conceal, Young Brown looked laughingly up at him one day and said, as the spray from a stiff nor'-wester dashed over the bows of the ship.

"You do not seem to like the nobility, sir."

CHAPTER XI.
Hereditary Rank.

THE acquaintance between the frank, sympathetic young soldier and the merchant had ripened as it only could have done at sea, where people are shut up together in a small space, and see more of each other in an afternoon than they would under ordinary circumstances in twenty years. There is nothing like a sea voyage for contracting friendships or marriages.

"Wait now till I tell you, young man," answered Mr. Brown, making himself up to deliver a homily. "There is a notable difference between nobility and hereditary nobility. Nobility when it has any true foundation is to be aye revered. But we must not omit mention of the cunning device made use of by the usurper Hugh Capet for establishing his unlawful power when he had taken the French crown from Charles of Lorraine. Here in a mere bastard's trick you see the first origin of hereditary nobility."

"Hugh Capet lived in 987; was Count of Paris and son of Hugh the Abbot, wasn't he, sir?" replied Young Brown, briskly, for he was pretty well up in his dates.

"Ye speak like a book, my laddie," answered the elder man; "and when this war is over there in India I shall be glad to converse with you as to how far it may suit your purpose to remain a private soldier, when you may do better." Then resuming the thread of his discourse he continued, "formerly all magistracies and honours, such as Dukedoms and Earldoms, were conferred upon select and deserving persons in the general conventions of the people, and were held only during good behaviour; whereof, as the lawyers express it, they were but beneficiaries. Hugh Capet, however, says Francis Hotoman the civilian, in order to secure to himself the affections of the great men, was the first who made these honours perpetual, which were formerly but temporary, and ordained that such as obtained them should have an hereditary right to them, and might leave them to their children. It was well enough as long as titles and estates went together, for at all events the title meant something, but"——

Here the Scotch merchant's lecture was interrupted by one of the mules which had been shipped for the transport service at Aden, a place which has been for two thousand years the emporium of trade between Europe and the East. Suddenly the beast fell into convulsions, then turned upon its back and died.

"That makes the seventy-ninth of them dead since yesterday. The Barbary horses are dying too, yet Lord Kinsgear's horse is right and tight enough," observed William Brown, taking the warm, comfortable nose of the English charger in his two hands and stroking it.

The Scotchman took snuff. "Aw," he remarked presently, shaking the dust from his fingers—"they are like Hugh Capet's nobles, they were bought dead. My friend the deputy-sub-assistant Commissary and some of his patrons are not sorry to get rid of them, to buy more. They do not spend their own goods or money any more than the French king did."

Young Brown could not quite understand what the merchant, meant at that time, but when some years afterwards he heard of the deputy-sub-assistant Commissary-General as a very rich man, and a member of Parliament, the Scotchman's words were invested with a clearer signification.

"The Law of Inheritance which is now in force," resumed Mr. Brown in a plain, business-like way, "by which I mean to say the transmission of hereditary rank and entailed properties, has long made a family a curse instead of a blessing to the nobility. It produces shocking and unnatural results. Whereas children should be a source of strength and prosperity, according to all Gospel law, they have been degraded into the signs of poverty, and too often of shame. Many noble gentlemen pass a considerable portion of their lives in leaving their children about in all parts of the world like so many cuckoos. The poor young things are abandoned to chance because their noble forbears cannot or will not afford to educate and bring them up at a cost of ten thousand pounds each; and they will not own a labouring man or a servant girl for a relation. If the children do well when they come out of foundling hospitals and charitable institutions, and ever show their heads in society, they are unable to recognise their own fathers and mothers or any of their nearest kindred; and this, while we have so many fine colonies where a dozen tall sons and daughters could earn fortunes for themselves and all connected with them; and where children would mean wealth, happiness, and honour. Now there is many a nobleman in Britain who won't own his offspring; and such of them may be compared to those droll birds of passage, the Zygodactyli, who have two sets of limbs, some turned before and some behind."

"But, sir," said Young Brown, gravely, and remembering the Curate's lessons—"the son of the bondwoman, you know?"

"Ye do not inquire properly concerning that matter!" replied the Scotchman, sternly, "we are expressly told in the fourth chapter of Galatians and the twenty-fourth verse that these 'things are an allegory?' Now, listen to me, and I'll tell ye, my lad, what is an allegory.

"An allegory is just a figurative sentence or discourse, in which the principal subject is described by another subject resembling it in its properties and circumstances. The principal subject is thus kept out of view altogether. We are left to collect the intentions of the writer by the resemblance only of the secondary to the primary subject. "Claudite jam rivos, pueri;

sat prata biberunt," is an example of an allegory. It does not mean that music is water and that men's ears are fields.

"I would be loath to meddle irreverently with Scripture texts," pursued the Scotchman with some solemnity, "but surely the sons of Bilhah and Zilpah inherited the blessing of Israel equally with those of Rachel and Leah, and there were princes of Dan and princes of Naphtali. It was foretold that Gad should be a conqueror, and that Asher should feast upon royal dainties. Besides," added the Scotchman in a practical manner, as if he puffed dispute disdainfully away from him, "the world is wide enough for all of us; there is bread always to be won by honest working hands. Wealth comes to those who look after it. If any man is poor at forty it is his own fault; and if you know him you will see the reason of his indigence. It is not far to seek—he is either a fool or a rogue. A fool if he could not make such a trumpery thing as money, a rogue if he lost, having once got it together, because that would imply dishonesty followed by retribution." It will be generally seen that successful men make small allowance for mishap or evil fortune, and Mr. Brown of Calcutta was no exception to persons of his own class. He thought that everybody with two ideas might be as successful as he had been himself, and had a very poor opinion of them if they failed.

"It is curious enough," observed Mr. Brown on the following day, as he took his place again on deck beside the young soldier, "that there is no collection of bastardy laws in English law literature." It was just after lunch, and most of the passengers on board the

Tanjore, except such as drank no wine, slept away the noonday heats; among the latter, however, were the Scotch merchant and the youthful trooper, towards whom he felt so strong and irresistible attraction.

"The subject," continued Mr. Brown, "interested me so much that when I was last in England I consulted the librarian at Lincoln's Inn, who was introduced to me by Mr. Bodger, of the Mundane Office. All that the librarian could show me, and all that I could find, were two 'sections' on the subject, one in Burn's *Justice* and another in Oke's *Magisterial Report*. The English law, which is the common law and not the statute law, is so distinct on the subject that it requires no extra definition. Born a minute after the solemnization of marriage in church or before a magistrate, and the child is legitimate; born a minute before, illegitimate, which would be alone sufficient to prove the absurdity of the rule. The Civil and Canon Law, which is the Scotch law, makes the child legitimate if the parents ever marry, though it may be years after the birth of the child. The only questions even raised in 'Burn' and 'Oke' are in relation to proofs of bastardy, namely: 'How many days after the father's death is a child illegitimate?' About three hundred days is the extreme limit fixed, but there have been nasty lawsuits on this point. Such is the brief and explicit, the cruel and nonsensical code which daily and hourly consigns unborn millions of human beings to a life of disgrace and infamy. It is a scoundrelly thing, invented by a devilish pride, and sanctioned and maintained by a not less devilish greed. It seems to close the very gates of heaven against repentance, and to make a hell upon earth for the innocent."

"You speak strongly, sir," said the young soldier.

"I have cause to speak strongly," answered the merchant. "I am a Scotchman. Now, by the law of Scotland, marriages merely contracted by declaration, acknowledgment, or before witnesses, are held valid. But the question of the validity in one country of marriages good according to the laws of another, is one of the most complicated, and it may be added, one of the most unsettled which remains in international jurisprudence. Marriages are void if solemnized in a wrong name, and if a poor deceived lassie gives out that she is legally married, and cannot furnish the requisite proof, she may be condemned to silence and heavy costs. It is not always easy to prove a Scotch marriage after the lapse of a few years; and if it cannot be proved," added the merchant, dejectedly, "it might as well have never happened."

"Save for conscience' sake, sir," interposed the younger man.

"Ay, lad, it is a braw thing to have that with us. If conscience will not cure a heartache, it will ever help us to support it—not without wincing, may be, but still with the courage which sustains us under all forms of suffering but remorse. Listen, my lad. It will be full two hours before those sluggards will awake after having slept off the fumes of the wine, ale, and stout in which they have drowned and burned their livers; so if you will fetch me my large white cotton umbrella to ward off the sun, I will tell you a story of a Scotch marriage."

It was thus that William Brown became acquainted with a series of events which concerned him very nearly, though he heard them at the time with little interest. It was not for years afterwards that he remembered them clearly, and every word in which they were narrated was engraved in his memory. He did not learn them all at once; but the tale once begun, it pleased the merchant to complete it, and indulge the garrulity of age with a patient listener. They were still many days at sea, and after lunch there were always some quiet hours on deck. So bit by bit, fact by fact, often seemingly confused and contradictory till he had unravelled their mystery, the young soldier learned unconsciously, as many a man has done before him, the history of his own family.

CHAPTER XII.
Auld Lang Syne.

"My father," said Mr. Brown, "was one of 'John Company's' servants, employed at Fort William, and he got his place through the influence of Lord Pigot, who was under some obligations to his uncle, a saddler. Though the East India Company was then a trading community, everything that was worth having in it fell into the hands of some lord, and what the lords did not want themselves they gave away. It has always been so, and always will be, in all times and in all countries, whether they called their lords peers or citizens. Now the first establishments of the English in India arose out of the alleged necessity of providing factories or warehouses where British traders might store their goods in safety and carry on intercourse with the natives. In my father's time those factories had already become armed strongholds and fortifications. They were not tenanted by peaceful clerks and supercargoes, but garrisoned by armies of cyphering soldiers. So when Hyder Ali began to overrun the Carnatic, my father, like the other young commercial men of his standing, chucked away the pen from behind his ear, and joined the raw levies of Sir Eyre Coote. He might have done well, for he was a brave man, and a personal friend of Popham, the hero of Gwalior. But unfortunately he got wounded in his first skirmish with the French under Bussy, and was invalided home upon a small pension.

"He settled on the banks of the Nith, near Dumfries, and was treated with a good deal of respect by his neighbours, not only because he had seen far and strange things, such as were only revealed to a few in those days; but also because he claimed kindred through his mother with Sir Brown-Comyn, and was known to all the country round as a personage of good birth and character. He married a Miss Hope, of the famous Hopes of Ayr, and had two children; firstly, my sister Meggie, and then my mother died in giving birth to me.

"We lived in a very poor way, but the respectability of people in Scotland was not then measured by their money, and we were always considered as among the most honourable folk within a day's ride of Dumfries. We owed nothing to any one. Our homespun clothes lasted a long while, and my father's pension from John Company, small as it was, sufficed to buy us kail and oatmeal. We wanted little else; and if we had, my father, who was of the old blood of the Browns, or 'as it might be more precisely and accurately stated, the Brown-Comyns, of Scrappiecraggs,'" insisted the merchant, "was too proud to follow any trade or calling in sight of his own kith and kindred. He spent his leisure chiefly in catching salmon, and was renowned for a particularly killing fly which he had himself devised, and which attained such a reputation that it was sold in fishing tackle shops as far as Glasgow and even in Edinburgh as the 'Brown-Fly.' It was he who hooked the big salmon of eighty-three pounds weight, which is the largest ever taken in British waters, where they seldom exceed thirty-five pounds full grown. So as soon as the fishing season commenced, my father would receive letters from anglers in every part of England and Scotland, soliciting his advice; and upon more than one occasion the Government consulted him, asking his guidance especially with respect to an Act of Parliament for the regulation and encouragement of British fishers, which nearly destroyed the produce of our rivers entirely, as may be seen on reference to 25 Geo. III. c. 65, 1785. It was on account of the unfortunate results of a legislative enactment in which he had so large a share, that my father conceived some disgust for politics; and he was also, I think, displeased because an elaborate report which he had drawn up with all the care which distinguished the writings of the East India Company's servants had been merged in the general report of a select Parliamentary committee, without any complimentary mention of his own name. He had built, I suppose, some hopes of employment under the Crown upon his report, and when they were disappointed, he was no better satisfied than people usually are when they fail to obtain what they want.

"It must have been somewhere about this period of his life, and now nearly fifty years ago, that a young Englishman, apparently travelling about upon a pedestrian tour, arrived at Dumfries and put up at the Rose, which was the principal inn there. I was nearly seventeen at the time, and you may be sure I soon found him out, for a stranger in those parts was a rarity. It was he, however, who first called upon us. He came with a letter from Mr. Majoribanks, of Majoribanks, a mighty fisherman, who bespoke my father's countenance and 'Brown flies' for Mr. Odo Wyvil, a young gentleman who wished to rent fishing on the Nith for that season; and in some manner or other it seemed, although the fact was not mentioned in express terms, that he desired to keep out of the way of pursuit or discovery, a circumstance which invested him with a romantic interest both for my sister and me. It was Meggie, I remember, who opened the door to him on the morning he first came to our house. She had bare feet, and her frock tucked up nearly to her knees, for it was washing day. But as soon as she had seen who it was, she morriced off to her room, put on her Sabbath stockings of grey ribbed worsted, and twisted a bit of blue ribbon in her hair; but was ashamed to show herself, and hid giggling and blushing behind the door till he went away. He was a very handsome young fellow, tall and well grown, with black hair and large eyes. I think I never saw so handsome a man. He came very often after he had once made our acquaintance, and I had a vast admiration for him; but it was a long while before Meggie would open the door for him again. She always seemed to avoid him, and whenever he came she used to hide herself away with her foster-sister, a clanswoman of ours, though only a weaver's daughter. I have heard since that she married an English gentleman's servant, and drifted far enough away from Dumfries.

"But I think the person who took most interest in the Englishman's society was my father. It was so long since he had enjoyed familiar intercourse with any one who could talk to him about those things which he had seen or done in his youth. Even Burns, our neighbour, of whom he had seen something in the sad decline of his life, was but an inspired peasant; whereas the affairs of India seemed as familiar to Mr. Wyvil as the affairs of our parish were to the minister. He would talk for hours with my father about the capture of Tanjore, the alliance of the Nizam and the Mahrattas against Tippo Sahib, the administrative acts of Sir John Shore, the acquisition of Rohilcund, and the cession of Cuttack by the Rajah of Berar, all events which are now forgotten, but which were then quickening the pulses of all true-born Britons. I never noticed but one bad point in him, and that was his utter and mocking indifference for the feelings of others whom he did not know or like. He appeared to entertain an unaffected belief that all things were created either with a direct or an indirect reference to himself, and that they were bound to minister to him. He was gallant and graceful, however, even in his selfishness; and though he claimed an extravagant degree of personal attention as his due, and had the whole of our small household running about for him upon wild goose chases, he said kind things, which we all thought more than enough payment for our trouble; and he looked most pleased when he was most unreasonable.

"He was very clever, very impassioned and eloquent where his own interests were concerned. He was brave even to rashness, generous, headlong in pursuit of what he then called Truth and Justice because he suffered himself from ill-treatment. I remember that 'Truth and Justice' were his favourite words. They were the words which occurred most frequently in his conversation, and which coloured all the rest. He was what is called in these days a philosophic radical, and I am even now convinced that had he not been connected with a titled family, and had he been obliged to rely on his own wits for distinction, he was so athirst for fame that he would have ripened into a great and good man, as soon as years and experience had mellowed his intellect into something softer and sweeter. But he was, in a manner which I did not clearly understand, connected with the Duke of Courthope, a rank old Tory, who had brought about the Emmett rebellion in Ireland by his high-handed ways. And now I come to think of it, you are as like to him yourself as two peas in one pod," observed the merchant, pausing and looking wistfully at his young companion. "I can find no explanation of such things, save that I sometimes fancy when I look at you that his face haunts me, and that I must imagine a likeness where none exists.

"We had only his own account of himself, but we had no reason to distrust it. He was poor, poorer even than we were, and he made no pretence to be rich, though there were many signs about him of those relics of wealth which are the waifs and strays, the jetsam which wrecked Fortune strews upon the sands of ruined lives. He wore a valuable repeating watch which struck the minutes and was a great rarity in those days. Upon the case of it was one of those Petitôt enamels of a young tambourine player dancing upon a bed of violets, which I have since been told must have been worth the fee-simple of all we possessed, and his sleeve-links, his very shirt-buttons, were of massive gold.

"My father, who had no great reason to be pleased with the Government, and who thought he had been ill-used because he had been disappointed, listened eagerly as the hot-headed young man poured forth his passionate love of liberty in words of flame. It was possibly because my father was himself a cool-headed man, slow of thought and tongue, that he delighted in the intellectual flights and the fiery torrents of speech which poured from the lips of his daring guest. They would sit together talking harmless treason round the pine-wood fire upon a Saturday night when sport was over, while the spoil of the stream hung to kipper in the chimney, as my father looked over his tackle and trimmed his flies for the coming week.

"By-and-by Meggie would steal in on pretence of mending my father's landing-nets, which he kept very white and strong, or she would bring him some cuttings of silks and wool for his famous fly. So the evenings sped on month after month; my father and Mr. Wyvil debating the affairs of the nation, and Meg and I listening till nine or perhaps ten o'clock, when my father opened his great family Bible, and read the lessons for the evening; after which not another word could be got out of him, and Mr. Wyvil was fain to take his departure till next day. But we could hear his musical whistle and elastic step, with his gay goodnight to the watchman, long after he had disappeared in the mists of evening. My sister soon began to listen for those sounds, and after a little while, I remember he always whistled the same tune, that of an old Jacobite song, the first she had ever sung to him, and which embalmed one of the most exquisite myths of the Stuart—'King of the Hieland Hearts, Bonnie Prince Charlie.'

"We soon learned his history, or as much as he chose to tell us, and I do not think that he concealed anything, except the spelling of his name, which we found out by accident on the back of a letter was Wyldwyl, and not Wyvil, as he pronounced it. He was the son of a lord by courtesy, one of the numerous family of the 'Wicked Wyldwyls,' as he himself described them, with a mixture of pride and contempt that used to make me laugh and my sister sigh. He had no title himself, and was accustomed to say in his careless way—half bitter, half bantering—that he was born with the tastes of a duke and the income of a groom. I can only tell you for certain what I know of him, and that is very little, but I am under the impression that he must have been very much in debt, and that he was staying at Dumfries partly to hide away from his creditors. I do not think he was dishonest in money matters, but he was thoughtless, and what few shillings he still had he flung away. I remember he gave his last half-guinea for a bunch of violets he might have had for a bawbee upon my sister's birthday; and when he offered them to her with one of his courtly speeches, she turned pale

enough, poor lassie, for violets are thought unlucky
to girls in their teens by our old northern superstitions.
He always seemed to me happier without money than
with it. He would come and eat his oatmeal porridge
with a little buttermilk at our house in the highest
spirits, all fun and good humour; but whenever a
letter reached him containing a remittance, he would
always insist on having me with him at his inn, and
making us both stupid with claret. A day or two—
at most a week—after he had gotten a new supply of
money it was all gone again, though he was kept very
short, and I doubt if he ever knew when he should
see any more. Yet I do not think he had ruined
himself by the ordinary extravagances of young men.
He was not fond of drinking or games of chance,
and when he played at games of skill he won. My
father, who had learned whist and piquet, then a
favourite game in India, said that Mr. Wyvil was the
best player he had ever seen. His memory was re-
markably retentive, and he never made a revoke. As
far as I could ascertain the cause of his embarrassments, from those scraps of his graver conversation
with my father, which I picked up, as boys will, when
I was not supposed to be listening, I believe he had
contrived to affront the people in power, and particularly that rancorous old Duke of Courthope, who
had made such a noise in Ireland. He must have
held at some time or other one of those sham commissions in the Household troops, which are an excuse for idleness; and falling into a state of discontent with the authorities, he had printed a pamphlet
upon army reform, and had been betrayed by his printer
to some of the influential underlings of the Horse

Guards, and the War Office, who had determined to punish him, and had carried out their threat. Adjutant-General Sir Ajax Bodger, K.C.B., had instituted a private inquiry, which had resulted in his being placed upon half-pay. Lord Hanaper, who had married a daughter of Sir Ajax, and was at that time commander-in-chief, had refused him a court-martial, naturally fearing that the Adjutant-General might have made some mistake, which would be thus brought to light. Lord Trecorne at the War Office, who was Lord Hanaper's brother-in-law, and whose wife was first cousin to Sir Ajax Bodger, had been unable to see any reason for interfering with the decision of Lord Hanaper, and there had been a paper war, and a Parliamentary riot, and a newspaper scandal about his case in the usual way, till it had been rendered quite unintelligible. So we looked at Mr. Wyvil with a sincere sort of hero worship, and considered him as much of a martyr as Clive or Hastings, with whose names the very air was then resounding.

"I recollect that upon one evening when he was with us a question unexpectedly came up as to what was to be done with me. It seemed to take us all by surprise. I was a big-boned, gawky lad, with red hair and a fine appetite, recurring regularly four times a day. I had received a solid sort of education, partly from my father, who was himself no contemptible scholar, and partly from a dominie at Dumfries, who had taught me my humanities for an occasional supply of kippered salmon. But nobody had thought what I should do for myself and Meggie when in the course of nature it must happen that our father should be taken away from us, and he had of late shown certain signs that his constitution, impaired by wounds and unnourished by any gleams of hope or prosperity, was now fast breaking up. When he died we should be left without any resource, unable to dig and ashamed to beg. Whether it was that something which Mr. Wyvil had said suggested this doleful train of thought, or whether I had arrived at that age when the desire of adventure, the longing to go forth and do or suffer, makes itself invariably felt in all healthy youngsters, sure it is that the uncertainty of my prospects in life impressed us all very seriously, and my father's withered hand (it was the one which had been struck through by an Indian spear at Arcot) rested with a mournful pathos on my sister's head, as he owned he had been unable to set aside any provision for her. Within a week from that day I received a cadetship in the Honourable East India Company's service, and as my father had no influence with the directors, who disposed of such things, we knew such a piece of luck could only have come to us through Mr. Wyvil, though he had had the good taste not to excite our expectations till he could fulfil them. Indeed he acknowledged, after some hesitation, that he had represented my father's unrequited services to Lord Overlaw, who was at the head of the Board of Control; "and his Lordship, who is a connection of mine, and one of the few friends I have left, has been pleased to pay attention to my request," added the young man, with a comical assumption of importance, which we were too grateful to ridicule, or even to perceive, though I thought of it with a sort of pained and shamefaced feeling afterwards; and I was, I think, honest enough to regret that I should owe my first start in life not to any merit or fitness of my own, but to the recommendation of a stranger who had seen but little of me and knew less, to another stranger who had never seen me, and did not know me at all.

"It was a long voyage then to India, and I could not afford to shorten any of it by taking the overland route through Marseilles and Egypt. The mails, therefore, which left England some time after my departure reached Calcutta before me, and the first news which I received on my arrival was contained in a black bordered sheet of paper. It was written by poor Meggie, and announced our father's death. She was, she added, staying with her foster sister, and would remain with her till I was promoted in the usual course, and she could join me, as we had arranged together before I went away. I forwarded her some money from my first pay. It was not much, but it was all I could spare; though I was proof to every temptation and inducement to spend a groat upon myself till she was provided for, and all the allowances of the Company at that time were liberal. Therefore, while most of my fellow cadets had three or four servants and a couple of horses about them, and pawned their future to the Parsee money-lenders as soon as they arrived at the Presidency, I managed to do with half a servant. He was an old clansman, and had followed the chief of the M'Gillies, who was in reduced circumstances. We paid him together more than either of us could have paid him alone, and we were all three satisfied: though some of the wilder youngsters cut their jokes at us, till the M'Gillie fingered his dirk and looked ugly at their jests. I cannot say myself, however, that I ever cared for them.

Jokes break no bones," observed the merchant, sententiously.

"It was a long while after that before I heard from my pretty sister Meggie. She wrote to me from Naples, and her letter was signed 'Margaret Wyldwyl.' She said she was in great distress and alone in Italy, and that her husband had left her. She told me a wild tale of her having been shut up in a convent, and of her having escaped and given birth to a daughter. Her letter was the outpouring of a broken heart and a head almost distraught with prolonged and hopeless misery. Her husband seemed to have got rid of her, and to have suddenly disappeared; so there she was in a foreign country, without friends or money, with an infant child.

"I am glad at this hour to say," continued the Scotch merchant, wiping his forehead, "that I did not hesitate as to what I should do. I tossed up the commission which had been begged for me by the scoundrel who had betrayed my sister, and hurried back to England. The first person I sought there was Lord Overlaw. I had some trouble to gain speech of him, because all men of title, especially those in place, become invisible to any one who wants to punish them for a misdeed. But I felt I had been duped and got out of the way for a purpose: so I waited near Lord Overlaw's office till I saw him come forth, and I could recognise him by the arms on his carriage. His Lordship looked at me out of the corners of his eyes, and was evidently averse to be inspected, still less interrogated; but he must have seen I was in grim earnest, and he was not a man to screen a friend at any risk to himself. So after the first double or two he no longer attempted to shuffle with me, as I had been warned it was his habit to do, and from him I found out that Mr. Odo Wyvil was neither more nor less than the fine Duke of Courthope and Revel. The hard-hearted old peer who had harried the Irish was 'deceased without issue,' as the heralds say, and a collateral heir had also died to make way for him. I suppose such grand fortunes coming suddenly upon him had turned his head and made him dishonest. Few heads are strong enough to bear being lifted up very high.

"I went in hot haste down to a big house which he had at Whitehall, and bluntly charged the base Duke with having married and abandoned my poor sister, and also with concealing his new name and rank from her and me. He tried to pacify me, and when I insisted in stern, strong words that he should at once acknowledge her as his wife, he told me he had married a woman of title a week before, and that he would do anything I pleased for my sister if I would be quiet, but that he had never wedded her. Then I told him that he lied in his throat, and I beat him—beat him till there was well-nigh murder done between us, and his servants rushed into the room where I had forced my way in to him, and parted us. I was taken up by one of the police who kept guard before his palace doors, for it was night; but no charge was ever made against me.

"As soon as I was set at liberty I went to Italy. I could find no traces of her who was in Heaven's sight and mine an English duchess, and who I was determined to see righted if justice could be won upon earth. I wrote to her foster sister at Dumfries, and my letter was returned through the post-office. I went there and found that she had married and settled in England, no one knew whither. All I could ascertain was that her husband had been a gentleman's servant, who had become a tavern-keeper, as most of them do who thrive well. I found out the 'gentleman' too: he was an insolvent debtor living at Boulogne; but I traced him, and he sent me, as I now believe, upon a false scent to Ireland! I wandered about trying to find my sister, till every shilling I had was exhausted. I went to lawyers and they asked me for proofs of my statements and belief: I could give none. I composed advertisements which the newspapers refused to insert, handbills which the printers would not print. I walked on foot through half England in search of her, till in passing through a country village on the borders of Oxfordshire, I was waylaid and very roughly handled; though, strange to say, neither my watch nor anything I had about me was stolen.

"When I came to myself I was in the county hospital, where the doctors seem to have thought me crazy, for they had shaved my head, and were not at all disposed to let me go. Chance, however, if there be chance in human affairs, came to my rescue. It happened that one of the hospital directors had made acquaintance with me on my voyage out to India, and had taken some such fancy to me as may be I have to you. He was in a large way of business in the City, and had a branch house at Calcutta. He asked me if I would go out as clerk, and he said if I did well I might perhaps become his managing man. I was glad enough to close with his offer, for I saw no chance of finding my poor sister, and I half hoped, half believed, that she was dead and her child also. I was advised to put all further search for her into the hands of a lawyer named Sharpe; but I have never had any tidings of her, though I saw him only the day before I left London.

"I prospered greatly in India. Before I was thirty-five years old I had made enough money to come home and leave others to do my work. I must have had nearly 40,000*l.* well secured. I had been first managing man and then partner in the old established firm of M'Canny. The hospital director who had started me had gone the way of all flesh, and I trust I had not shown myself unmindful of the benefits I had received from him in the day of my poverty and sorrow. Well, the first thing I did when I got back to England was to find out how I could thwart or anger the Duke of Courthope, and as I learned that he was very anxious about the representation of a rotten borough of his, I determined to contest it against his Grace's nominee. It was just after the first Reform Bill, and his power was almost absolute; but I broke it, and humbled the pride of the Wyldwyls in their own birthplace to the dust, as they had done mine. I could not win the election, though I spent every sixpence I had made upon it. But I ruined the Duke, and so held him up to execration, so terrified and cowed him, that he never more ventured to go abroad beyond his own park gates; and he died, frightened to death. Since then I have spent my life in India, doing what I could for others and myself."

CHAPTER XIII.
The Sepoy Revolt.

WHILE the good ship *Tanjore* is making her swift course to the Indies it may be worth while to consider the cause which sent an English marquis and an English peasant to fight against a people they had never seen, with the full consent and approbation of those who loved them dearest; and which had likewise induced a shrewd Scotch merchant to accompany them as long as he could do so without danger. It was indeed a cause which had placed in sudden peril the dignity and revenues of the noble, the peasant's home, the merchant's moneys, with much that Britannia still retains of her dominion over the seas.

The rebellion which burst out in British India in 1857 created as much astonishment in the House of Commons as if it had been something altogether unprecedented and wonderful. But in fact it was neither a new nor a strange thing, and there must have been at least several peers who had seen or heard of a similar occurrence more than once before. As far back as the year 1806 there was a revolt of the Sepoys in which the family of the late Tippoo took an active part. It flamed suddenly into mischief on July 10, at a place called Vellore, which has long since slipped out of Parliamentary memory, but which was, nevertheless, a real place, situated in the south-east of India. It was strongly garrisoned by British troops, because it had been made the residence of the heirs of the dethroned Sultan of Mysore, whom we had caged up during the warm weather, worried at ease, and then gone to sleep as usual, nothing doubting. Indeed, we had not taken the trouble to garrison Vellore ourselves. We had put Sepoys to do our work for us. The word Sepoy is a corruption of Sepáhi, which is merely the Hindustanee for soldier; and very queer soldiers they were—cunning, obsequious, treacherous and venal. Moreover, they liked the family of the Sultan of Mysore, whom they were set to watch, and did not like us. We had adopted the rash practice of arming and disciplining them from the French, and they had profited by our own lessons to upset us as soon as they felt they were strong enough to do so. One Colonel Gillespie, another forgotten name, was obliged to kill eight hundred of them at Vellore before they were convinced they had acted prematurely, and were quite ready to cringe before us and to cheat us again. The next Sepoy mutiny made itself felt at Madras in 1809; and Lord Minto was sent out in a hurry to publish a general amnesty that the Sepoys might mutiny henceforth without fear of consequences. Lord Minto was selected to govern India at a critical period because he had been to Vienna. There was no other reason, there seldom has been a better reason, for the selection of any ruler of British India.

The next time the Sepoys showed their teeth was in 1841 at Cabool, when Sir Alexander Burnes, Sir William M'Naghten, and about twenty-six thousand other persons were massacred, with the sanction of the Foreign Office and the Board of Control. In 1850, again, the 66th Regiment of Bengal Native Infantry were disbanded for mutiny; and signs of discontent might have been seen smouldering everywhere within our dominion.

The natives had long been disaffected, for they smarted under the most amazing and contemptible tyranny which has ever ground the bodies and souls of men for greed. We never sent out one single man of real note and importance, who had a character and fortune at home, to govern the largest dependency ever possessed by any nation. We handed it over to our small-minded middle class, and gave it wholly up to a grasping mercantile Company, who neither knew nor cared anything for Hindostan and its 176,000,000 souls save for their marketable value.

It was quite true, as Mr. Brown had observed with plebeian envy, that noblemen were allowed to fill the higher offices of state, and had some scanty scraps of patronage at their disposal; but they were only dummies or lay figures; and no viceroy of India, with the exception of Clive and Hastings, who were both Company's men, ever wielded any real authority. Lord Pigot was imprisoned by his own council, and died of the shame and anger of his confinement; and from the time when a Captain Keigwin invested himself with the government of Bombay till that when the Company dismissed a peer from their service for not having publicly saluted them as "Honourable Sirs," the British rule in India had been confided almost exclusively to tradespeople, with the thoughts, desires, and education of tradespeople, determined to make money, no matter how, no matter where, no matter when. They appointed their sons and brothers and nephews to wield absolute sway over vast kingdoms and principalities; stipulating only that they should remit a sufficient amount of taxes to Leadenhall Street. They did not call their relatives by the names of monarchs; on the contrary, the immense and uncontrolled authority bestowed upon them was hidden under the modest appellation of resident, collector, agent, or secretary. They never went beyond some of these discreet titles, and were fond of adding the qualifying adjective "sub," "sub-assistant," "under," "officiating under," and even "deputy-sub-assistant-officiating-under-agent," of an occult power not named, in order to conceal themselves still more effectually. One officer of considerable importance even went so far as to call himself "deputy-assistant acting resident in the Persian Gulf," where it would have seemed impossible to go and look for him; but he was above ground, and a troublesome person in his way too for those who thwarted him — indeed a colonel in the twenties who had risen rapidly because his mother was a director's cook and housekeeper; and the director had poisoned many of the far Chinese with opium. It is now known, though it was long and impudently denied, that torture was systematically employed to wrench from a peasantry poorer than that of Greece or Portugal, taxes which could not have been paid by the graziers of Lincolnshire or the vinegrowers of the Gironde. Madras and Rangoon were fired by despairing hands worked to the bone by ruthless taskmasters, and crowds of bankrupt wretches weary of life voluntarily perished in the flames. Famine smote whole provinces again and again, as their miserable populations writhed under cruel extortioners. Those active and remorseless taxgatherers seized not only shawls and jewels, hoards and horses, fruit and cattle, but the very seed corn which was the life of their slaves; till the smug traders in one district alone (Orissa) caused the death by hunger of fifteen hundred thousand persons.

But the British pedlars made money—much of it, and purchased many coronets and fine estates with it in England and elsewhere. The sturdy hucksters were very proud too of their power and achievements. They had quite a picturesque language of their own. They described themselves as griffins, and vultures, and lions. They included all the descendants of the Khilgis and of Toghlak, of Genghis Khan and of Timurlenk, under the generic name of "niggers." They had a good deal of dry humour about them; and many of them were sharp and resolute gentlemen who wrote admirable despatches, not unlike special pleaders' speeches, whenever they were called upon for explanations. The student of history, however, looks in vain among the Woods, Roes, Hartlands, Hobarts, Hislops, Shores, Bayleys, Elliots, Birds, Greys, and Cheapes for a single statesman whose sayings or doings posterity has deigned to preserve. From the establishment of the first British factory at Surat in 1612, to the partial termination of the Commercial Government of British India on September 1, 1858, all is a blank.

So there is upon the whole nothing astonishing in the fact that the "Bombay Gazette," a newspaper published under Commercial Government inspiration, should have announced on May 1, 1857, "India is quiet throughout," and that just nine days afterwards another mutiny should have begun at Meerut. Upon the same day, as a pungent practical commentary upon the foresight of Commercial Government occupied in collecting taxes by torture, the mutineers seized Delhi, and proclaimed a nigger emperor as the lawful successor of Arungzebe.

Of course the revolt originated in an official blunder. Upon the death of Bajee Rao, ex-Peishwa of the Mahrattas, some mole-eyed mercantile man at the India Office refused the claim of his nephew Nana Sahib for the continuance of the pension assigned to him. Now it is quite possible for an irresponsible person to commit any high-handed act with impunity, as far as he himself is concerned; but somebody is sure to suffer for it, whenever such a man as Nana Sahib is mishandled. Scorning all discussion with the clerk, he placed himself silently at the head of the malcontents of his own people, and soon found a war cry.

It had happened that somebody, wanting a contract, had introduced a new sort of musket from England into India, and it was necessary to load this gun with greased cartridges, which were an abomination to the native soldiers. All the money, however, which could be made out of the contract for muskets and cartridges having been made, nobody objected to a new contract for other guns and other cartridges, and those in use were immediately ordered to be discontinued. But this did not pacify Nana Sahib. Then, as the Commercial Government of India had created a very astute and powerful enemy, it disbanded thirty thousand of its troops, who immediately joined him; it also hung one Sepoy private and one Sepoy officer, as a terrible example; and immediately afterwards thirty-four regiments were lost to the British flag.

Moreover, having fully resolved, in January 1857, to change the greasy cartridges, upon the 9th of May following, or more than three months afterwards, Commercial Government committed eighty-five troopers of the 3rd Bengal Native Cavalry to prison for not using them. The next day these eighty-five troopers killed their commanding officer, Colonel Finnis, fired their barracks, and rode away to Nana Sahib on Commercial Government's horses. At the end of June, no less than twenty-one cities were in rebellion against the unknown clerk, who had refused Nana Sahib's claim for the money which he claimed; and at nine of those places the very European women and children were massacred, so fierce was the wrath of Bajee Rao's nephew at the high-handed dealings of the clerk. That irresponsible official likewise caused the proclamation of a public fast, and 280,749*l*. were subscribed for the widows and orphans which the clerk had made. The command in chief of the Queen's troops in India had been given to a well-known London man, who dressed exceedingly well. He knew little of soldiering beyond mounting guard at St. James's Palace; he marched at once to Delhi, and got killed. He could do no more, honest gentleman.

The Punjaub was saved by an obscure person, bearing the ancient name of Montgomery, who somehow or other came at once to the front; and the old warrior line of the Irish Neills was notably represented. Then it occurred to somebody that the newspapers, which had been rejoicing, in their best leaded types, over the quietude of India, were rather too free, and the liberty of the press was restricted, in the firm belief that Nana Sahib would be put down that way. The plan did not answer, however; and Messrs. Mangles and Co., East India Directors, who had insisted that the only way to stifle a rebellion was not to tell the truth about it were astounded. Another general soon followed the man of fashion to an untimely finish before Delhi; and he was succeeded by a third general, who bore the ill-omened name of Reed, and was promptly beaten by the "niggers," being the first British officer who had come to signal grief since General Whish. Wilson had not much better luck, and we got horribly beaten by niggers at Arrah; but that Irish Prince, O'Neill, turned up again when our affairs were at worst, and won a sort of victory for us. A hard-fisted Baptist, too, with nothing of the mercantile man in him, and who had been very ill-treated by Commercial Government in consequence, stepped suddenly forward, and showed some of the old, patient, heroic stuff which was seen in Cromwell's Ironsides. His name was Havelock, and he had been called "Old Phlos" at that famous Charterhouse School which has bred some of the best of the Anglo-Indians. He had just relieved Lucknow, where Irish Neill was killed, when General Violet arrived with reinforcements from England, some apprehension of the true state of the case having at last reached Leadenhall Street, and stirred up everybody there but the clerk who had first done the mischief. His name even has never been published to this day, though it is tolerably well known.

CHAPTER XIV.
British India.

It was rather a serious business for English residents in India when the *Tanjore* arrived out with reinforcements of raw recruits, and many incomprehensible instructions from the home country. Unseasoned lads marched about in the heat, drank, and died very fast. Middle-aged military dandies from Pall Mall were laid up in scores. The contradictory orders of official personages who knew much of the Parliamentary game of question and answer, but little of our Eastern Empire, confused the heads of local authorities already sore perplexed. Moreover, many alarmed personages in high place now began to understand for the first time that they were not beloved by the natives; and they were conscious of an uneasy presentiment that if the British arms received another check they would be all massacred. Not only India proper, but Afghanistan, Cabool, Candahar, Turkistan, Persia, and Koordistan, were watching events, and ripe for revenge against the hated infidels. The Mohammedan revival, of which so much has since been said, had commenced; and had another successful blow at our power been struck after that at Dinapore, it is probable that not a living Frank would have been left to tell the story between Calcutta and Trebizond. When the well-appointed British cavalry therefore rode through the streets on their way to war, with music playing and colours flying, they were greeted by deafening cheers from their fellow countrymen;

and as Colonel Oakes reined in his charger, and made him curvet beneath the balconies where groups of ladies waved them welcome and strewed flowers on their way, he nodded to Lord Kinsgear, and said:

"This looks as if we were going into action pretty soon. The General won't play with his command: we may be sure of that."

Their hopes or expectations were not disappointed. They were marched and counter-marched wherever cavalry could do service. Moreover, Lord Kinsgear was almost immediately attached to the staff of General Violet, and Young Brown accompanied him. They were present at the capture of Secunderabagh— at the taking of Cawnpore and the brilliant affair of Jhansi. The two young men, though so different in rank, were drawn still closer together during the campaign, because they were often obliged of necessity to occupy the same tent, and to take their meals in sight of each other, if not together. They rode often within earshot of each other for hours, and with no one else to talk to. They were together in many dangers and successes; they were friends and comrades in all but name.

It was not that William Brown, who had been bred a peasant, and was now a soldier in the best sense of the word, presumed in the slightest degree upon the kindness which was shown to him by a nobleman who was his captain. Not all the sad things he had heard of the Wyldwyls in any way influenced or diminished his respect to his superior officer; and indeed he had not imbibed many of the merchant's democratic theories, or, if the truth must be told, had he very clearly understood or cared to understand them. He was by nature docile, obedient, simple. He knew his duty and he did it; and that is the stuff of which veterans and heroes are made. He never intruded his presence upon Lord Kinsgear unless summoned, or entered into conversation with him without saluting; but he was removed from the rank and file of his regiment by his duties as an orderly; and so the young men were seldom separated for more than an hour or two at a time.

Also Colonel Oakes had kept his word, and Young Brown had advanced as rapidly in the regiment as possible for one not born to military honour. He was made a lance corporal, and soon after a full corporal; then, after the Jhansi affair, where several non-commissioned officers of the 1st were slain, and where Young Brown twenty times looked death in the face, he was promoted to a sergeantship. As a sergeant, having more leisure and ease on his hands, he generally spent much of his time in reading when alone, having no taste for rum and skittles; and he probably owed his life and health to the interest he found in a few books among the Marquis of Kinsgear's kit. Thanks to the rough life of campaigning, the Marquis could without impropriety converse more freely with Young Brown than would have been possible or seemly at home. He lent him all his books, so that Young Brown eagerly devoured works upon history and tactics, and often got absorbed in the study of a good map. He loved to go minutely over the positions of the decisive battles of which he read, with a few pins and corks and a sheet of cardboard. He was a silent and reserved young man, never tired of his own company, and never impatient of solitude. He neither drank nor smoked, and was a very moderate eater, living chiefly upon rice, which seemed to him cleaner and more wholesome than the greasy messes prepared by the Indian cooks. Therefore, as he kept his blood cool, the heat of the climate did not affect him as it did Lord Kinsgear and most of his brother officers. Abstinence was not, perhaps, any great credit to him. It was of course easy enough for Young Brown to do as he liked about eating and drinking. No one pressed him to indulge in iced Clicquot and old Madeira, of which there was no great supply but at General Violet's own table; where the Marquis dined whenever there was a halt long enough for the tents to be pitched and the commissariat waggons to come up, the case was very different. Thirsty young aides-de-camp, who had been galloping about under an Indian sun with field-glasses held to their eyes in a blinding dust, were glad to slake their parched throats and revive their spirits with as much wine, pawnee, pale ale, and cigars as they could get. Tiffin and sherry cobblers, and cheroots and punch were going on under the tent, or in the quarters of one or other of them, all day long; and the Marquis of Kinsgear, who was not of a very strong constitution, would sometimes lie down in the small hours under his own canvas with throbbing temples, and a head which felt like a lump of lead upon his shoulders.

One evening after a very late sitting with the General's staff, where Windham, Seaton, Grant, and Rowcroft had been all present to fight their battles over again, the Marquis of Kinsgear returned to his tent with a heavy footstep, made somewhat unsteady by the length of an Oriental dinner where the hookah and the narghilly had succeeded the wine, and the younger men had gone off to eat anchovy toast and drink again afresh afterwards. Young Brown, who had come into his captain's tent with a troop roster which needed inspecting, was so immersed in a book he had found on the table that he did not hear the young officer, and Lord Kinsgear went silently up to him and looked for a minute over his shoulder and down at the book without speaking.

They would have made a fine picture of Work and Play: the one so calm and placid, so tranquil and happy; the other hot, fevered, dissatisfied, and sorrowful.

The Marquis seemed to feel the contrast, and to stand rebuked before himself. He was not naturally given to excess, but he had been of late beguiled into intemperance by the contagion of example, the influence of companionship, and the fear of ridicule. He almost envied the studious sergeant, who had passed so quiet and profitable an evening with a good author, for he saw that Young Brown had been reading Macaulay's bright description of the gallant death at Killiecrankie of Bonny Dundee.

"How goes the day?" asked the Marquis, repeating the latest words of Claverhouse, as he remembered that deathless and beautiful story.

"Well for King James, my Lord," answered the young man, smiling and saluting his officer.

"Then it matters the less for me," added the Marquis; and there was a sad tone in his voice, as if the words were an augury of evil.

The nephew of Bajee Rao, ex-Peishwa of the Mahrattas, though he had been easily overcome and snubbed by an unknown clerk in the India Office, was nevertheless the most remarkable chief who had appeared in Asia since Jeswunt-Rao-Holkar. He was recognised by his countrymen as Rajah of Bittoor, and was a smooth-tongued, sleek creature, with a face like as human face can be to that of a tiger. It was of the tawny colour of that wild beast's skin. His forehead was low, his cheek bones high, his mouth wide, his teeth sharp, narrow-pointed, shining, his chin extremely short, almost deformed. His round eyes glittered like burnished steel, and were of the same uncertain colour, changing in the light. All his movements resembled those of a panther. He was rather long than tall, and looked longer than he was, for, like most of the fanatics among his people, he adhered strictly to the Eastern dress, and the least costly of the shawls he wore entwined about him would have been a fitting gift to a queen. The impression he produced on one who knew him well was that of an animal more than of a man. He seldom stood up, and was fond of reclining upon cushions, with his lithe limbs curled under him. He always looked ready for a spring, and though his words were so soft and low, his back so supple, there was a certain scorn, an evident intention to insult, under his flowery talk to Europeans. He was probably an Eastern philosopher at heart, inclined to rest and pleasure and lotus-eating. He might have lived and died scoffing securely at the conquerors of his country, and keeping out of the way of reprisals, if it had not been for that irrepressible clerk at the India Office.

Indeed, when he first felt the clerk's pen in him,

he entertained a sublime Asiatic disdain for such a wound, and set off for London, thinking reasonably enough that he should get justice and a hearing. But the clerk was no other than Anonymos, Despot of Great Britain and India, whose friends and business connections blocked up the grand staircase of the Queen's palace and all the private entries.

Nana Sahib soon ascertained, to his surprise, that he could only appear at court by the clerk's permission, and Alee-Zwingh, a personal friend of his residing in London, assured him over a pipe of opium that if he presented a petition, comparing Her Majesty to the Sun and himself to her most devoted worshipper, it would be so much waste adulation, for it would only be read and answered by the clerk, who was the beginning and end of all things Anglo-Indian. So the Rajah grew angry. His wrath was of a white heat, almost imperceptible, but very fierce and deadly. Not even the clerk who treated him with haughty condescension when they met at London dinners that season, ever heard the footfall of his vengeance as it drew nearer. He had his share of condescension too, and scattered cheques about with astute discrimination. He saw a good deal of London Society, and if he had employed his money more prudently might have got what he wanted from it. "There is," says a French proverb, "a way of negotiating with Heaven," and Indian jewels and Indian rupees have worked wonders with the clerkly mind, when transmuted by a discreet alchemy. If only Nana Sahib had not been so ferocious and bloodthirsty in his displeasure—if, instead of cursing by his gods in secret, and cringing in public to premiers and peers, he had got at Johnny

Bodger, or Lady Overlaw, or any one of some dozen people who could pull the wires he wanted pulled, and who would have pulled them for the usual consideration, he might have possibly got what he wanted; but perhaps he was ill advised.

Then he went to the Crimea, and watched, with all the keen-eyed malice of an intense resentment, our blunders at the commencement of the Russian war, especially our helpless transport and commissariat arrangements. He took peculiar care to make the personal acquaintance of our leading generals, and to find out what was in them. He spent about six weeks at Misseri's Hotel in Constantinople for that purpose; and having satisfied his shallow understanding, blinded by rage and mortification, that we were not a very wise or terrible people, he returned through Egypt into India, rousing the faithful in many a secret midnight meeting upon his road home. Big with his project of vengeance on the clerk who had impoverished and despised him, he headed the mutiny at Cawnpore, besieged that city with the forces upon which his foes had counted to defend it and obtained possession of it, with such direful results as history has recorded in its most mournful pages.

CHAPTER XV.
Rule Britannia.

It was not until after the victories of Kooneh and Calpee, the surrender of the Rajah of Jeypore, and the rout of Tantia Topee—that is to say, after much blood had been spilt and much treasure had been expended—that it seemed as if the high-handed proceedings of the unknown clerk at the India Office might yet once more be remedied without the loss of British India.

Nevertheless, and notwithstanding the heroic stand which our armies had made, as usual, for this functionary, without was fighting and within were fears. Tantia Topee, though beaten at Guzerat, still kept the field. A guerilla warfare continued in Rohilcund, and Nana Sahib, with the Begum of Oude, hovered with a countless horde of horsemen upon the frontiers of Nepaul. So General Violet, with a few British troops, moved steadily down to give them battle.

It was a fearful march through a country devastated by fire and sword and famine. Often as far as the eye could reach from a high hill top not a tree, nor a living thing, nor a human habitation could be seen. Sometimes they passed by heaps of rubbish, which a few months ago had been smiling villages; and the bones of men, horses, and elephants, dried by the sun, bleached by the wind, and half-gnawed by jackals, strewed the way at irregular intervals.

Every now and then, as the slender column of Europeans toiled through the dust and heat of an Indian summer, Lord Kinsgear, Mr. Highlowes, or another of General Violet's aides-de-camp would gallop up to the front and salute, with the awful announcement that some scores or hundreds of the rebels had been captured.

"Taken with arms in their possession?" would drawl the General, in that affected voice of his; and if the reply was "Yes, sir," as usually happened, he waved his white, womanly hand gracefully, as one who would have done quickly with a tiresome subject, and added, "To the rear; Oh yes, to the rear;" which meant that they were to be shot—and they were shot there and then, just as if the unknown clerk at the Indian Office had signed their death warrant for execution at the Old Bailey.

Indeed, there was no help for it. Prisoners were brought into the British camp and line of march in such numbers from the flying hosts of Beni Mahdo and Ferozeshah, after the successes of Lugard, Mitchell and Lord Clyde, that it was impossible to detain or to feed them. There was not a crumb of bread, or an ounce of meat, but what the English wanted for themselves, nor a draught of water; and to drag forward a rabble rout of prisoners, more numerous than themselves, would have been an experiment too dangerous for any general to risk. So thousands of these dusky-skinned Indians were sent daily and hourly into eternity, without any fuss or outcry beyond the whistling of balls through the air, and the dull thud with which they sank buried in living flesh. Fortunately there were no newspapers to look on, and scream "murder!" Our own correspondent kept enterprisingly out of the way. If he had not done so, General Violet had privately determined to hang him, because it was no time for trifling, and writing sensation articles about what could not be helped. When a clerk has once loosed and unchained the dogs of war, we all know how they moisten their fangs, whether ink is shed for the fate of those they tear or not."

General Violet overtook Nana Sahib and the Begum of Oude rather suddenly at last. It was during the hottest part of an Indian day when the pickets came galloping in with news of the enemy, and the pale face of England's bravest general became tinged with a pink as delicate as the colour upon a piece of Sèvres porcelain.

"We have got them now, gentlemen," said he, turning with a languid smile to his staff; and in the same calm, polite language he would have used on parade, he made the necessary arrangements for the coming battle before a standard was unfurled. Ten minutes afterwards the opening thunder of the Begum's guns cast a death shade over the ranks of the little army.

"We must hit hard, and hit quickly," said the General, affably; and as the trumpets sounded the advance, regiment after regiment, or what remained of them, moved down into action, with music playing, and colours flying—the bagpipes of the Highlanders answering the fifes and drums of the English, and some Irish shouts of "Erin-go-Bragh."

The battle began with infantry, as usual, and General Violet watched it with his staff from a commanding position. The Indians fought like wild cats: but their nervous excitement, terrible as it was, and frantic as the clerk had made them, was no match for the dogged pertinacity and the burly beef-fed strength of the mighty Western islanders by whom they were opposed. They came on again and again, furiously, drunk with excitement, drunk with bhang; but they were always beaten back, and they seemed to break themselves when they met the British troops, as waves break upon a rock. By-and-by their fire began to slacken, and there were signs of wavering in the Asiatic ranks when the smoke cleared away.

From the height which General Violet had occupied during the battle, with the officers of his staff around him, he could now see through his field-glasses that the enemy was bringing forward some teams of artillery horses, and was evidently preparing to retreat over the Nepaulese frontier, carrying his guns and treasure with him.

The General looked round to his officers, his eyes agleam with the fire of battle, and their was a mute appeal in them, as if he were about to call upon brave men for desperate service.

The Marquis of Kinsgear rose in his stirrups, and bent forward with eager response in his face, while the boldest held their breath for a time.

The English commander turned to the Quartermaster-General who was close at his side, and dictated an order, which that officer quickly embodied in a few pencil lines, written on a slip of paper resting upon his sabretache. It was very short:—

"General Violet wishes the 1st Lancers to advance rapidly to the front, and try to prevent the enemy carrying away the guns. Immediate.
    (Signed)   "A. BRACEBRIDGE,"

which was the name of the Quartermaster-General. Nothing more—few words to brave men.

General Violet gazed for an instant upon the clouds of Indian horsemen scouring the plain beneath him, and the fierce hail of hot iron which ploughed it up, so that nothing could pass through it save by miracle, and with a natural movement not wanting in chivalrous grace, he involuntarily raised his plumed hat and saluted the Marquis of Kinsgear. Then laying his hand upon the young lord's bridle rein, he said: "You see your regiment posted at the skirt of the wood yonder. All depends on the speed with which our squadrons advance. Now or never is the time when cavalry may be used with effect."

Lord Kinsgear brought down the point of his sword in salute, and the next moment he was gone. Old grey-beards still remember how the brave noble rode away. The hill on which the General's staff was posted was a thousand feet above the level of the plain beneath, and its sides were steep and rugged. Yet neither horse nor horseman faltered, but went down it straight as the crow flies, swift as an arrow.

Settling himself firmly in his seat, and taking a strong grasp of the rein with his bridle arm, he seemed to lift his horse off the ground, and he descended with a swoop as true as a falcon's to the wood side where his regiment was posted, impatient of the delays which had hitherto kept them idle, and longing to take part in the honours of the fight. He had no consciousness of his danger. In that supreme moment his thoughts turned only to some minute improvement in his horse's bit, about which he had talked the day before with William Brown; and he congratulated himself upon it, as it enabled him to dodge and distance every attempt at capture, so well it kept his striding thoroughbred in hand.

Colonel Oakes was sitting in the saddle in front of his troops, and longing to take active part in the battle, when Lord Kinsgear arrived with the General's order, and never was command more welcome to a soldier.

"Now, men," he called out, in a deep, sober voice, "remember what I have told you, and keep together." So he put spurs to old Sampson, his favourite charger, and cantered once down the ranks to see that all was well. Having thus done all things in order, he turned quietly to his people, and said: "The regiment will advance."

So in serried ranks the small group of European horsemen moved along the plain, apparently enveloped in clouds of dusky enemies, and unable to see before them from the smoke around, although it was every moment riven by a lurid glare, which showed that another messenger of death had been sent among them. The crash of lancers overthrown only alternated with the dry word of command—"Back, right flank!" "Keep back, Sergeant Brown!" "Close in to your centre!" "Look to your dressing; right squadron keep back!"

But as they drew nearer the enemy, the regiment gradually became more impatient of restraint. The troopers, whose numbers were thinning so fast, longed fiercely to close with the foe whose guns were galling them; and a feeling of contempt for the enemy added to their fury. William Brown was one of the last who retained some command over his horse, but a flesh-wound in the neck from a rifle-ball made the brute lose temper. He was then within sight of the Indian battery, and a torrent of flame burst forth in front of him. The next moment his horse made a mighty jump, a plunge, a scramble, and he was in the midst of the enemy. Far divided from his comrades, he had driven full into the Indian ranks, and being instantly confronted by a gigantic Nepaulese, he soon came to grief, because he incautiously gave point to his adversary.

Meantime, Lord Kinsgear, who had no regimental duties, had ridden home in the charge as a volunteer; with his orderly, William Brown, who, owing to the risk, had been charged with a duplicate order to Colonel Oakes, following behind him. Lord Kinsgear was not a good swordsman, and conscious of his deficiency, considered for a moment how he should best act when his troops broke away from him. He determined to rely on the main strength of his horse, hurled at full speed against the enemy; and singling out an Indian chief whom he perceived to be a leader of the opposing force, he resolved to overthrow him by the shock of a heavy concussion. So his Lordship clenched a rein in each hand; and, as though he were forcing a cantankerous horse at a nasty jump, drove full at the Indian. The man fell as if struck by a catapult, and the next moment Lord Kinsgear had broken into the centre of the enemy, and blinded by smoke, scorched by fire, hacked at by a dozen scimitars, he turned to bay, and defended himself by twirling his sword like a millwheel. He was hurled from his saddle, however, speedily, and beaten to his knees with an Indian lance thrust deep into his breast, when there was a mighty clash above him of contending horsemen, and then there came all at once a mist before his eyes.

On recovering his senses he found his head supported on Sergeant Brown's knees, and around them was an open space covered with the remains of the wounded and the dying. The Indians had gone down before the English swords like corn before the sickle; still the day was not won; and unless William Brown could assist his captain to remount and take him to a place of safety, they might both be shot dead at any moment. The sergeant did not hesitate. Hoisting Lord Kinsgear into his own saddle, he supported him to the rear, walking slowly through the ghastly scene around him, where dying men to whom no help could come shrieked madly for water, and broken-backed horses, raising themselves on their forelegs, looked piteously for help, in their horrible anguish.

But he bore the Marquis with unflinching pluck to the ambulance-waggons, supporting him in the saddle with hand and arms as he walked beside him. Having there given his captain over to the surgeon of the regiment, he rode back to the front and took part in the final charge which completed the victory of the day. The Indians, beaten at all points, threw themselves off their horses and crept under them to find shelter. They whined and entreated for quarter, grovelling in the dust in their abasement, after their guns, to which they attributed an almost miraculous power, were silenced. But then occurred that fearful sight which shows how grim a thing is war. Some of our men, and even of our officers, performed ghastly wonders in the way of slaughter. They were seized with the blood phrenzy, and did what they could to confirm the belief of the maddening effects of that wholesale killing which is said not to be murder. Some raged wildly against the miserable wretches who cringed and cried for mercy, slashing them down with reeking hands already besmeared by gore; and others made ceaseless use of their revolvers. Among the few who tried to check this ghastly butchery of the unresisting was Sergeant Brown; and again he heard the manly voice of Colonel Oakes above the crash and roar of the fight, speaking words of approval to him.

It was a great success for the English arms, the most decisive victory of the war. It definitively dispersed the insurgents in Nepaul. It enabled us to hang Rao Sahib and Bahadoor Khan, the ex-king of Bareilly; and it entirely broke the power of Nana Sahib at last, sending him away into Chaos, or the wilds of Tibet, where he has ever since remained. It also occasioned the foundation of a new order of knighthood. General Violet, who won it, was raised from the rank of Major-General to that of Lieutenant-General. The largest amount of loot and prize-money gained by any British force since the peace with the Burmese fell into the hands of the conquerors. Thus what was called the Indian difficulty was disposed of for nearly eleven months.

CHAPTER XVI.
After the Battle.

IF it were the purpose of this tale to deal further with a curious episode of Anglo-Indian history, it might be easy, and perhaps instructive to relate how General Violet's great victory was won, notwithstanding *another* Sepoy revolt broke out within the year at Sikkim. Nana Sahib and his fanatical adherents, oddly enough, refused to be satisfied, even although the clerk at the India Office, apparently impressed with the consequences of what he had done in running off with the Rajah of Bittoor's property, very handsomely gave away five hundred and twenty thousand pounds to the alleged descendants of a Rajah of Mysore, who had no claim at all upon us. Indeed, one of these alleged descendants, a certain Kootoobood-deen, was so astonished at the clerk's liberality, and flourished the proceeds of it so offensively, that he was killed by his own servants, who promptly made off with our money, and were never more seen. It has all ended happily. We put things to rights for the clerk at Sikkim, as we had done at Delhi, Cawnpore, and Nepaul. There has been another famine, and we have subscribed again for the sufferers. We have also more recently fined and imprisoned an Oriental scholar, who incautiously warned us of danger by translating a popular Hindu drama which explained the "niggers'" view of quite a new sort of extortion now practised on them. The other day one of our Envoys was seized at Bhootan, and compelled to sign a treaty. He, and we, got quit for the fright. We have long ceased to care much for treaties in practice, no matter how they are made. We have a war, a famine, and a scandal generally about once a year or more, and the Great Unknown still reigns supreme over us. Upon the whole, therefore, it cannot be denied that we have done, are doing, and shall do well by our splendid national inheritance of the Eastern Indies.

The manner in which we have dealt with this vast bequest from our ancestors, and how it has been passed from hand to hand by methods legal and illegal, might naturally enough fall within the scope of a story which professes to treat of the laws of succession. Many marvellously interesting things might be related upon the subject, but at present the reader of these pages is only concerned about the transfer of a trumpery dukedom, and one or two nicknames, with estates not much larger than those of a single indigo planter, though lettable at a somewhat higher rental.

Upon the fortunes of William Brown, moreover, the Sepoy Mutiny had a most favourable effect, however inconvenient its results may have been to several other persons. It raised him, for one thing, from the ranks of the army, and obtained for him a commission in Her Majesty's service. The advancement of the young soldier was not brought about very easily. Lord George Wyldwyl, who had just been named Commander-in-Chief, took the nobleman's side of the case, and declared that promotions from the ranks lowered the "tone" of the army; whatever that might mean. When his Lordship, however, had conversed with General Violet and Colonel Oakes, he promised to offer no active opposition to the commission being made out, but he added, significantly, that "it must be done in the usual way." Now, among the precious legacies which have been bequeathed to us as a people, is the inestimable blessing of "Routine;" and therefore, when Lord George Wyldwyl remarked that Young Brown's commission would have to be made out in the usual way, he meant in the routine way, which was saying a great deal more than he expressed. Accordingly, six weeks after the recommendation of Sergeant Brown's superior officers, that his conduct in the field should be rewarded by a commission, a very formal document was received from head-quarters. It was marked "confidential," but its contents of course transpired; and they were to the effect, that "Lord George Wyldwyl was unable to give his support to a request which was so little in accordance with the good of the service, and might interfere with the proper discipline which it was necessary to preserve between officers and men, by confounding the distinction of ranks. Lord George also considered it right to add that the wife of an officer raised from the ranks often felt herself in a false position among the ladies of her husband's regiment, and that the apparent honour conferred upon him by a commission was really nothing but a source of vexation and expense to himself, as well as of dissatisfaction to those gentlemen who had obtained their military rank in the customary manner by purchase, and who had sufficient means not only to maintain their position, but to join in the expenses and hospitalities of the mess without inconvenience." This document, which resumed in a windy and rigmarole manner all the platitudes which were current in garrison towns, to show that money made all the difference between a commander and a private, was signed by the august and puissant name of Dodger; Sir Ajax Bodger, K.C.B., K.S.I., &c., &c., &c., being at that time Adjutant-General of Her Majesty's forces in India. Moreover, what was more to the purpose in the present instance, one of his connections was Adjutant-General, and another private secretary to the Commander-in-Chief at the Horse Guards at home; and the telegraph was perpetually at work between them.

"George knows nothing about it—I dined with him yesterday," said General Violet: referring to the Commander-in-Chief.

"We must try again," observed Colonel Oakes; "the beggars never give in the first time. Young Brown has fairly won his commission, and by Jove he shall have it. The mess has sent in a round robin about it to Lord George."

"Won his commission!" drawled the General, shaking some eau-de-Cologne languidly over his handkerchief; "he deserves to be made a captain instead of a cornet. I never saw a cooler fellow of his age under fire—a salamander, I declare. Let us go and talk to the Commander-in-Chief; perhaps he will give us a wrinkle."

The two officers ordered round their horses, and it being towards the cool of the day they rode off to catch Lord George Wyldwyl before he went out for his ride. He could give them no help about Young Brown, however.

"Things must take their course, Ned," said the Commander-in-Chief of the Indian Army to the most famous general under him. "I can do nothing, you know."

"I suppose there's a way of managing it if we could only find out how to pull the wires," answered General Violet. "You and I and Tom Oakes together ought to be able to get a cornet's commission. Eh, George?"

"I don't know that," replied the Commander-in-Chief, scratching his ear in a perplexed manner. "Both Dodger and his brother-in-law are very obstinate men when their backs are up. However, you know I will help you if I can, Ned; and if you take my advice you'll use private influence. Nothing else will do in these cases, half so well, depend upon it."

"Hang it, the Chief is a brick!" said General Violet as he and Colonel Oakes rode away from headquarters. "I am almost sorry he is going home, though

I must now in the ordinary course of things succeed him. But we have not done our work yet. How are we to get at Bodger? I don't know him well enough to ask a favour; do you, Tom?"

"Never saw him in my life, either in action or in a hunting-field, where most of my acquaintanceships have been made," returned the Colonel. "He generally happens to be ill on gunpowder days, and performs prodigies of humanitarianism among the wounded. He writes letters for them to their friends, and that sort of thing. I never heard of his doing it in peace time."

"You see these great characters take their own road to glory," laughed General Violet. "It does not much matter; they always get there."

"Then you think it is all U.P. about Young Brown's commission?" asked Colonel Oakes.

"I think it is something deuced like it, unless we can square Bodger," answered the General. "But there is Lady Laura Petty-Pells and her ponies. She ought to be able to do the trick, if she will, Tom. She keeps open house here, and nobody ever refuses her anything, on principle."

Her Ladyship bowed over her parasol whip to the two heroes of the latest great battle which had saved India.

"Hah hah ye, General?" she screamed in that highly pitched voice which delights the fashion. "Hah hah ye, Colonel? What do you both think of my ponies? Lord Hanaper has sent them out in exchange for the Ranee's shawls I took home last time I went to England."

"They are worthy of the Queen of Sheba," replied

General Violet, gallantly, alluding to the title by which her Ladyship was best known in the drawing-rooms of Calcutta.

"They are quite thorough bred," screamed her Ladyship again. "Lord Hanaper bought them of Lady Selina Bodger, whose husband you know is at the Mundane Office. Quite a charming person, who has the best horses in London."

General Violet, hearing the omnipotent name of Bodger, looked towards Colonel Oakes, as much as to signify, "Now then here goes;" and then he addressed himself to her Ladyship.

"We want to present a petition, great Queen," said the General, stroking the beautiful Arab which he rode at a smooth canter within an inch of her Ladyship's phaeton wheels.

"Then one of you must go away," screamed Lady Laura at the top of her voice. "It is sinful waste to burn two heroes at the same time. I shall want you to make love to me one after the other."

"When will my turn come, Lady Lo?" inquired Colonel Oakes, who was nearly related to the Calcutta beauty, though they had not met for a dozen years, whereas General Violet was one of her intimates.

"It will come whenever you can find your way into my house without leaving a card and running away," cried her Ladyship, shrilly. "I am at home every day at tiffin."

General Violet was a prime favourite with Lady Laura Petty-Pells. It was even whispered that he was one of those who sighed in her train. He was also extremely popular with ladies. He knew how and when to talk to them. Lady Laura was delighted to have the brave and kind-hearted exquisite escorting her carriage in the first flush of his great renown, and with all Calcutta looking on to envy her. Her face was all alight with triumph and pleasure. She determined to give a ball, two balls and a dinner (or two dinners and one ball, which should it be?), to show this illustrious paladin in her chains before the bloom of his valiant deeds wore off him.

As soon as General Violet, however, spoke of Sir Ajax, her Ladyship pinched up her lips, and evinced extreme annoyance. "To say the truth, General," observed her Ladyship in tones almost natural, and very much lower than usual, so that not even her miniature groom could hear what she said, "Sir Ajax Bodger is not a gentleman."

CHAPTER XVII.

Raised from the Ranks.

"How are ye, William Brown?" inquired a hearty voice of the young Sergeant as he walked rather disconsolately about the streets of Calcutta during the inexplicable postponement of his hopes of promotion. The next moment the young man's right hand was held in a grip of iron, while two kind, honest blue eyes looked out from a rugged old face at him.

"Ye'll just come and have a bit haggis wi' me, if ye're off duty," said the Scotch merchant whose acquaintance he had made on board the *Tanjore*. "I see that ye've already risen to the rank of Sargeant; and it's a grand credit to ye in these times, unless ye had some interest in that regiment, which I mind me now was the case through the minister boddy who came on board with your mother. Poor lassie, her face reminded me of my sister's when she laid down so pale and fainted. Mayhap, lad, it was that which first drew me on to take a fancy to ye."

William Brown, though dispirited enough, was glad to meet the merchant, because, when we are dejected and out of conceit with ourselves, any kind voice is welcome, and his was of the kindest. He went home with the merchant too, and found a plentiful lunch or tiffin, the name by which Mr. Brown disguised an early dinner, spread out. Very curious and characteristic was the half-concealed sense of degradation which the prosperous trader felt at asking a common soldier to sit at the same table with him, and he scrupulously called him "Sargeant," and spoke to him with an awkwardly assumed air of patronage before the well-to-do clerks who boarded with him. Had William Brown worn gold lace instead of worsted, the merchant would have been conscious of some inferiority, military officers being really the princes of all countries, and common soldiers the Pariahs of every people.

Young Brown, however, possessed the invaluable mental armour of what is called "a thick skin:" he was by no means sensitive or prickly-minded; probably because he was in robust health, and too honestly occupied with the business of life to be self-conscious. The Scottish merchant's dinner was excellent, and cooked by a Scotch cook, with as much Scotch material as possible. There was dried salmon and haddock, potted game, shortbread and marmalade, from the Land of Cakes, with amber ale of potent strength, and some extremely fragrant whisky, all of which things form refreshing diet in hot countries.

"I'll not ask ye to take any spirits, Sargeant," said the owner of these good things, helping himself, "because whisky is not good for the young; but I'll aye drink your health and success to you;" and he helped himself.

The taste of his native liquor seemed to open Mr. Brown's heart, and presently afterwards he said, "I've been thinking, Sargeant, that ye'll not like to bide for ever with a red coat upon your back and a musket on your arm; so if you would wish to enter my office, I'll see about buying your discharge one of these days. I can give ye a hundred pounds a year and your board and house room for a moderate amount of work daily."

"Thank you, sir," replied the soldier, straightforwardly, "but I like the army better than any other calling, and my superiors have promised to do their best to get me a commission." The Sergeant's hopes had revived after a good dinner, and he was now disposed to take a more cheerful view of his prospects than he had done an hour or two before.

"Whew!" exclaimed Mr. Brown, making a whistling sound peculiarly Scotch, and feeling an enormous increase of respect for his guest. "So-oh, ye have distinguished yourself so highly as that, have you, my lad? How comes it then that ye have not got your commission already? It is getting a long while now since the last battle was fought, and I imagine ye'll not get your commission out o' the parade ground."

The Sergeant then told his host as much as he

knew of the obstacles which had arisen in his way to advancement. He did not know much; but he was aware that General Violet and Colonel Oakes had both recommended him, also that the officers of his regiment had sent in a round robin in his favour to head-quarters, and that nothing had come of it. Moreover for the last few days Colonel Oakes had plainly avoided the subject, though formerly he had been very ready to talk of it, and had tried in various rough good-natured ways to make up for his disappointment.

Mr. Brown listened very attentively to all he said, and then answered, slowly stroking his chin, "I'll be thinking that ye have no friend at court, Mr. Brown, and that the true hitch lies there. Tell me now, do ye mind that ye ever offended any one who could put a spoke in your wheel, and prevent it turning round? I've often heard of such mishaps."

The Sergeant declared that he had never consciously given offence to any one; that he had been upon active service all through the mutiny, and that he was well considered by all his superiors, without exception.

"Still ye might like enough be hated by some of the officials without knowing it, though if ye have been kept out of their way, that can scarcely be. I apprehend, therefore, Mr. Brown, that it is pure wrong-headedness on their part. But are you quite sure of the General and the Colonel? They are, I am free to acknowledge, brave and good men, but in these matters ye will learn, if you live, that folks are not over trustworthy."

The Sergeant readily answered for both these

officers, and then a queer sort of smile broke over the Scotch merchant's face.

"Well," he observed, dryly, "maybe I might be able to serve you better than a bigger man. I am tendering for a contract for military saddles, and I have to see Mr. Toll Bodger, the storemaster, about it no farther off than this afternoon. He is related somehow to Sir Ajax, who has all British India under his thumb, and is as strong, through his connections in the Governor-General's Council, as he is in his proper department. I'll make ye no promises," added the merchant, "but if it's true that ye haven't given any personal cause of affront to the Bodger family, or their friends, I can see a short way to your epaulettes—though ye might do better, laddie, ye might do better if ye put a pen behind your ear, as I have done."

Young Brown then returned to barracks, thinking very little more of the merchant or his conversation. He had that easy creed which comes of sound sleep and a good digestion. The world was pleasant to him: everything seemed to him well as it was, and likely to become still better. There was nothing morbid—nothing of what soldiers call the "cocktail," about him. Certainly his ambition and self-esteem had been aroused by the chance of promotion so far beyond every reasonable expectation he could have formed on enlisting. He had thought of what the Curate would say at home there at Wakefield-in-the Marsh, and how his mother's fond eyes would kindle, and how erect his father would stand when they silently shook hands next time. And then he thought of what he would and could do for his brothers Jack and Gill, and Tom and Harry. It was an honest trait in the young fellow's character that his day-dream had not spoiled him, and that even when indulging it he never thought of denying his humble origin, or casting off any one of his poor peasant kinsfolk in the far Oxfordshire village away in the homeland, but that all his schemes of future happiness centred there. Even Susan Jinks was not forgotten, though he often wondered how little the remembrance of her seemed to move him. He recollected his child sweetheart, indeed, very much as a pretty picture he had seen long ago: perhaps in another state of existence. His own identity with the village boy of three years before was not quite clear to him. He was sitting alone in his barrack room on the evening of the day after he had dined with the Scotch merchant, and admiring the solemn beauty of an Indian night, with its large moon and stars looking so near and familiar, when he heard the voice of Lord Kinsgear faintly calling to him from an open window.

Hastening to his Captain's quarters in reply to this summons he found the Marquis propped up by cushions, as he had been ever since that day when the Sergeant had carried him at risk of his life from under the Indian fire. His Lordship did not seem to gain strength. The surgeons said he was a sickly patient; that he had inherited a bad constitution, and that he had not enough vitality to heal his wounds.

"Brown," said the Marquis, feebly, "you saved my life a few weeks ago, and the least I can do is to try and lessen your sorrow now. Prepare yourself, my poor fellow, for bad news."

"I must bear it, my Lord, whatever it be," returned

the soldier, looking very straight and stalwart as he stood upright, and prepared for evil fortune as firmly as he would have confronted an armed enemy; for he had not yet learned what terrible weapons there are in the hands of Fate, and had never once heard the fall of a thunderbolt from heaven. He heard it then for the first time.

"Why do you say 'My Lord?'" asked the sick man. "Come here; let me have you near me while you suffer. Perhaps I may find an antidote, though I must give you poison, poor fellow."

The Marquis fell back exhausted on his pillow, and closed his eyes before he resumed. "On my desk there, at the other side of the room, you will find two letters. The one came by the English mail this afternoon, under my father's cover. It is from Mr. Mowledy, the clergyman of Wakefield. He has also been so kind as to write to me, begging that I would prepare you for the contents of his letter, which is, you see, bordered with black. He must be a Christian gentleman, that country parson, and he is a good friend of yours, Brown."

"The other letter," added Lord Kinsgear after a pause which showed how painful a labour it was for him to speak, "was brought only ten minutes ago. I see it is official, and must bring you good tidings; though it came with 'Mr. Brown's compliments,' which I do not understand. You recollect the old Scotch contractor who hated me for being a Marquis?" The wounded nobleman smiled sadly, and took the Sergeant's hand in his, as if to keep him from the momentous news which awaited him a few minutes longer. He even gazed up into his face with some anxiety, and as he did so the one young man looked like the pale and wasted reflection of the other, seen through some distorting glass, which marred its attitude and fair proportions. Having satisfied himself that the Sergeant was calm-minded and stout-hearted enough to meet his sorrow steadily, "Read your letters now, Brown," he said; "but take the black-bordered one first, and let me hold the other for you till you have read the worst."

Then side by side, descending upon him from on high together, came, as they always come, suddenly, wonderfully, and without warning, the supreme joy and sorrow of his life. In a few short moments he had learned from a scrap of paper that his whole family had gone down at sea in a ship of which he had never so much as heard before. There was the paper in his hand, quite mute and silent, yet big with news. It had been pricked all over with holes, and fumigated, till the writing on it was almost unintelligible, lest it should be a messenger of evil, and yet it had stricken him to the heart.

As the young man stood, appalled and stunned by the tremendous blow which had smitten him, he felt the soft frail fingers of the Marquis close gently on his own. "Read the other letter now, Brown, pray. Read it at once, for my sake."

Sergeant Brown took the official envelope mechanically in his hand, broke the great seal of it, and took something out. He could not see what it was, and held the envelope with its contents before him, one in his right hand, the other in his left, as though he offered them for Lord Kinsgear's inspection, with military stiffness. He evidently did not know what they were, and all his thoughts were far away in his mother's grave, where the willows wept in the quiet church-yard, and beneath the troubled waves of Mona, where the *Royal Oak* and her living freight of human souls went down.

Fortunately he was a very young man. He was not yet seared by misfortune, so that it scars and dilapidates body and mind, shattering them with each successive stroke. The fountain of his tears was not yet dried up, and the merciful waters, which wash away so much of our early anguish, came to his relief. Two large drops, great as storm rain, coursed each other slowly down his ghostly cheeks, and fell with a dull sound upon the floor.

"Come, Brown, and sit down here beside me," said the young lord, with brotherly tenderness. "You need not go away, for we are comrades now. That despatch announces that you have been appointed a Cornet in the 1st Lancers."

CHAPTER XVIII.

Race.

WILLIAM BROWN felt much more at large and at his ease in his new position. He took to it naturally, much as a duck takes to water though bred in a hen-roost, or as a race-horse falls into his stride at a gallop as though he had never been forced to trot uneasily in the shafts of a butcher's cart or a hansom cab. The lad had the bearing and manners natural to a gentleman—the proud soldierly head, the upright mien, and clearly cut features, the white shapely hands, and well-defined nails. There is as much difference between men as between animals; and in all the inferior creatures there is a general appearance of stumpiness, coarseness, and clumsiness; whereas in the king beasts all is fine, cleanly made, and graceful.

While these lines are writing there is a bird-show at the Crystal Palace, and the strong point of the show is a collection of canaries, comprising no less than thirty-five out of seventy-seven of the different classes into which those little birds may be divided by observant naturalists. To one of these varieties, the original canary of the Canary Islands stands in the same relation as did William to his comrades in the rank and file of the army; or as the wild crab-apple stands to the finest fruit of the gardener's catalogue. The breeding even of so small a thing as a canary is a cunning mystery; and the gradations are infinite, beginning with the lizard-coated songster of the islands, and ending with those costly birds bred to the exact shade of yellow, and just marked with a dark feather in some appointed spot of head or wing. It takes many generations to produce the finer tints and markings, and of course the fanciers sometimes try to steal a march on time, as an enriched usurer buys a noble name; but there is a law of nature which no clipping, drawing, trimming, painting, or colouring of the bird's plumage can set aside; and the poor winged creature, however bedizened it may be, will neither sing nor look rightly if it is not thorough-bred. Therefore the great object of the canary breeders, who are a philosophical money-making class (at present much unconcerned with the government of this or any other nation), is to produce a bird of a fine shade of yellow; and it is certain that, as a matter of fact, it actually can be produced "ticked," or marked either on the wing or on the back, the breast, the neck, or the top of the head, as desired. Such birds practically may be bred to a single feather; though it is important to note that hundreds of eggs may have been laid and hatched before the exact plume makes its appearance.

So it matters little where or when a man may have been born; he is certain to rise up to his own level in every state of society which the world has seen; not perhaps in name, but in fact. Provided only he possesses the rudiments of education, he will come out of any dark and fiery trial whatsoever into the pure daylight of heaven the first time he has a chance if there is anything in him; and we all have chances enough and to spare—some that we spoil, some that we lose, some that we throw away disdainfully.

The first steps on the ladder of life are always a little difficult for a man who has to make his own way quite unaided up it. But then aid so soon comes to him in the ordinary course of things, if his footing is firm and his eye steady, so that he does not tumble down in the mud disgracefully at first starting. There is a natural instinct among the better class of people to protect and aid the young. A bold honest lad wins friendship and love without effort, and they smooth many difficulties over which their elders have to stumble painfully enough. Also the first gleam of success is almost certain to go on increasing till it becomes quite a halo, if not put out by any malevolent influence, and one honour is always security for more.

Thus, William Brown had been a mere village boy at seventeen years old; and, in the usual course of things, he could hardly have expected to culminate in anything higher than a farrier or a wheelwright. But in his veins flowed the blood of a race of kings, many of whom were of an indifferent sort, or had come to nothing, and some were fools, some rogues, some scoundrels of a deeper dye (just like the spoiled or addled eggs of the canaries), till at last here was a bird of the true feather, a man of the right stamp. His fate was uncertain till Mr. Mowledy had taught him to read, just as the canary would have no value if it could not sing and was lost in a hole where no one could find it out; but from the moment he had learned his alphabet thoroughly and could put pen to paper without difficulty, he might have been left naked in the streets in the morning, but he would have been found supporting himself creditably and winning kind opinions three days afterwards.

Moreover, as good luck never comes alone, Young Brown was presently appointed aide-de-camp to Lord George Wyldwyl, who had lately become Lord Punjaub with remainder to his daughter, the Hon. Miss Amabel Wyldwyl. That young lady was at present residing in England with the Marchioness (Abigail) of Newcomen, a rather necessitous peeress, of irreproachable character, who had consented to act the part of governess and companion to her rich and beautiful relative for such a handsome consideration as the great Indian soldier's means enabled him to afford without inconvenience. Indeed, there had been quite a public competition among the General's poor relations as soon as it was known she was to be sent to

England to complete her education; and the old soldier had been over and over again put to the blush by their rapacity and importunities.

Cornet Brown owed his position as aide-de-camp to this distinguished military man firstly of course to the warm recommendation of his nephew the Marquis of Kinsgear, who never rested till he had got the place for him; but he kept it and won the personal friendship of his chief by his own merits: for patronage and recommendations at best will only carry any man a certain distance unless there is very high rank to back them. Young Brown, however, was at heart a soldier; and as his chief was a soldier too—brave, single-hearted, simple, sincere—they had only to be once brought together to understand each other thoroughly; so that within six months of his appointment Lord Punjaub had given over the management of his stable, his household, his accounts, and the whole of his large hospitable establishment to his aide-de-camp, who accepted it with good-humoured readiness, doing all that was required of him and nothing more, in a quiet, easy way.

Among the things which should be noticed as most conducing to success in life is having the good fortune to serve under a congenial chief for the first time. There are many admirable people who cannot agree with each other more than oil and water, which are both good things, but will not mingle. Now William Brown and Lord Punjaub liked each other because they understood each other.

BOOK V.

CHAPTER I.

A Last Love.

WHILE the newly-made Lord Punjaub and Cornet Brown were gathering laurels in India, old age was gradually stealing over the Duke of Courthope and Revel. His Grace could not bear the thought of growing old, and put it resolutely away from him as soon as possible. He continued to dress like a young man when already near upon fifty. He did not choose a young man's colours; his taste was too well taught, his sense of ridicule too keen, to venture upon them; but his sober tinted clothes were always in the latest fashion, and so cut as to show the handsomest points of his figure, every one of which he knew with that perfect accuracy acquired by patient study of his own advantages over others. He rode very carefully-trained hacks too now, and avoided any horse which pulled or bored upon the rein, that his seat in the saddle might preserve its perfect grace and dignity. He felt that he could no longer bear to be seen hot or ruffled or disordered. He looked a picturesque and aristocratic figure enough, however, upon his favourite in the Park. It was an Arab mare, so gentle and docile that she might have been held by a silken thread, and with a canter so smooth that his Grace boasted he could carry a full glass of water unspilled at fourteen miles an hour on her back. He looked grand and distinguished too in his drag, or his phaeton, which he now preferred to a drag, finding two well-trained horses pleasanter to drive than four, which will want handling, however cleverly they pull together. He kept all the tastes of a young man. He was still seen at Epsom and Ascot, by the cover side, and at the great flower-shows. But he could very seldom be met in the streets on foot. He was conscious that time had begun to tell upon him when he walked, and there was a stiffness in his gait which is the first sign of infirmity, and which could not be quite got over. His step had lost its youthful elasticity, and could only have a firm spring put into it by persistent effort. It was as much as his Grace could do to stand quite gallantly and upright; and so he liked to have his hack or his carriage within hail. Over and above all these things, he became more a creature of habit than he had ever been before. He had his regular hours for doing certain things, and so ordered his life that he was punctually at the same place at the same time.

For the past three years he had always, when in town, paid a visit to Lady Overlaw between four and five in the afternoon, just before she took her drive down the Ladies' Mile. Then again his Grace paid another visit to her Ladyship after his dinner, at about nine o'clock in the evening, and took tea at a delightful house which she had overlooking the Park, in the best part of Seamore Place. She called it her dower house, though she had had no house property and

Lord Overlaw died notoriously insolvent. It was exquisitely furnished. Her Ladyship still remained a widow, though she was very pretty, kind to those she liked, very amusing, and only twenty-seven. The Duke of Courthope thought he looked handsomer and younger when reflected in the glass over the chimneypiece in her boudoir than he ever seemed anywhere else. Perhaps the delicate hues of the rose-coloured curtains, which tempered the light without excluding it, flattered his rather faded complexion, and was not too merciless in exposing the crow's foot imprinted at the corner of each of his eyes.

It was one evening about nine o'clock, his usual time, and in the very height of the London season, that the humming sound of the wheels of a well-hung carriage was heard in Seamore Place, and it stopped before Lady Overlaw's door, just as it had done almost at the same minute for at least three seasons, if not for four. Her Ladyship was also in her boudoir as usual, when she recognised the carriage by its steady, equal advance and gradual stoppage within just one half of an inch from the kerbstone. The door was opened with a discreet and muffled sound; her Ladyship's hall porter being as well trained as the Duke's coachman; then she heard her groom of the chambers with his wand of office go out from his private apartment to the landing-place of the greater staircase. She knew that her three footmen had ranged themselves to bow before the splendid noble as he passed up the steps, and his name was announced first from one footman to the other as he mounted higher and higher to her bower.

Said the first footman, at the bottom of the staircase, a gorgeous creature in the white and scarlet livery of the Plantagenets: "His Grace the Duke of Courthope and Revel," and he pronounced the name as reverently as though he were saying his prayers.

Said the second footman, posted on the first landing: "His Grace the Duke of Courthope and Revel." He bowed his powdered head very low, and held his hands straight down besides him, while his toes were turned out wide with awe.

Said the third footman, posted on the staircase top: "His Grace the Duke of Courthope and Revel," as though he were repeating some magic incantation on which his life depended very distinctly.

Then the groom of the chambers advanced, smiting the soft velvet carpets with his wand; and all along the vista of beautiful rooms which led to Lady Overlaw's boudoir, through mirrors and exotics, statues and the richest work of the upholder, the folding doors opened silently, and grave men in black breeches and silk stockings, and with heads artificially whitened, bowed before the Duke as he passed them, the chamberlain walking backwards staff in hand.

"Wet evening, Major," said the Duke pleasantly to the chamberlain, who had been a Polish cavalry officer, and was one of the best major-domos in Europe; "is her Ladyship at home?"

The Major made the same bow which he had made twenty years previously before the Emperor of Austria, as he replied in the affirmative. Indeed, the question was altogether superfluous; but the Duke of Courthope, like most great people, was fond of throwing a word to his inferiors, and he took the first that came uppermost.

Meantime Lady Overlaw seated herself before her boudoir fire, in the attitude of an invalid, though five minutes before she had been writing rapidly in her dressing-room. She seemed to have arranged herself for a purpose. She was wrapped in what ladies call a peignoir, which is a kind of dressing-gown, and looked to a casual observer as though she had only just risen from sickness. Beside her was a small table with some crochet needles and balls of coloured worsted, which she used as some men smoke cigarettes, to find employment for her hands. Her Ladyship was very pretty, with a little round mutinous face most winning. She was not lovely, but she was charming; a plump, wayward, childish little creature who was fond of lying down with half-closed eyelids in the daytime, and saying impossible things till she went to sleep—a lady of merry, innocent, playful ways, with a claw as sharp as a kitten's, and a tongue that could sting like an adder. She was a lazy, laughing, singing little thing, generous, naughty, rebellious, undisciplined, rash and wilful as a Plantagenet: very shrewd, too, very grasping, very lavish, very cruel and pitiless.

"Ah, Duke!" said her Ladyship, without moving or looking at him, and taking up her crochet work, "how do you do?" The tone of voice in which she spoke was rather cold and absent; his Grace felt it, and made no answer.

"Well," she continued presently, after working on in silence, "you have not told me how you are," and she put out two of her white round little fingers, still without looking at him.

"I am very well; I was never better in my life,"

replied the Duke a little stiffly, for he was pained, being rather sensitive where he loved.

"Ah!" returned her Ladyship; and there was in her voice the slightest possible tone of contempt, which could only have been seized and detected by a very fine ear.

"Yes," replied his Grace, who had caught the latent sneer in that undertone of derision, and was hurt by it; "I never was better or stronger in my life. I can do whatever any other man can do; and led the field with the Queen's hounds last Monday."

A sharp retort perhaps rose to Lady Overlaw's lips, which would have gone home like a barbed arrow to its mark in the Duke's morbid vanity, for ladies can generally find an answer if they are so inclined; but she seemed to suppress the unkind words by an effort, and she moved a little in her chair as she did so, as though she put the barbed arrow quietly by for future use.

There was a handsome King Charles spaniel on the rug of white Persian catskin at her feet, and she now called the dog to her, and put it on her lap.

"We want fifteen hundred pounds this instant minute, don't we, Beauty?" said her Ladyship, sportively, burying her small face in the long ears of her favourite, and pretending to be very much ashamed.

"Bless my soul!" exclaimed the Duke; "you had eight hundred only last week."

"Well," answered her Ladyship, looking up quickly; "pray how am I to keep house? There was my dressmaker to pay, if you must know everything—she had five hundred; and now I have all sorts of bills. The steward's account for the wages of all those servants you insist on my keeping; the coachmaker's bill. There, how should I know? you torment me. Go away! I have a headache, and you are making it worse," her Ladyship broke off petulantly.

"I suspect you have been driving about the streets again with Lady Trecorne, though I begged you would not do so. She is anything but a proper person," observed the Duke, who was a great stickler in his way for the moralities.

"Go away, I tell you. Go away," answered her Ladyship, as if she were spitting fire. "I do not ask you to come here. Why do you plague and bore me every day, every day, every day, at the same hour? I don't want you. Be off," and she made a face at him like a spoiled child.

The Duke smiled gravely. "Order your carriage round," he said with indulgent tenderness, "and go to my box at the opera. You will be in time for the last act of the *Traviata*, and then come on to Lady Palmerston's. I have been promised you shall be made a Lady of the Bedchamber, and you should thank the Minister."

"I won't!" said Lady Overlaw. "I hate tea parties; and the Palmerstons never give anything else."

"Then go to the opera. My carriage is at the door; and Lady Hanaper will go with you."

"'My carriage!' 'my box!'" repeated Lady Overlaw, mocking his stately mode of speech. "It is my box. I gave it away to my sister and her children. Are you satisfied? You may send your carriage for them if you like."

"I beg you to observe," said his Grace, drawing

himself up, for he was much annoyed, "that I have just come from the Palace, and am wearing the Garter. I cannot walk the streets in pumps and knee breeches."

"You have your cloak I suppose?" answered her Ladyship, rudely; and being ripe for mischief, she added:—"I won't have your carriage standing before my door at this time of night." She pressed the spring of her silver bell; and when her maid answered the summons, she ordered the Duke of Courthope's carriage to be sent home.

"I beg you will give no such message," remarked the Duke, dryly. "I cannot exhibit myself to the crossing-sweeper; and lately I have felt a very nasty twinge of rheumatism in my left shoulder."

"Ah!" sneered her Ladyship again in that contemptuous undertone, "I thought you were younger and stronger than ever. Poor old man! His carriage shall wait for him in Curzon Street, as he is too infirm to walk, sha'n't it, doggy?" and she bent down over the silken coat of the spaniel.

The rain beat fiercely on the boudoir windows which opened towards the Park; the fire burned very brightly; and there was that feeling in the air of the room which is produced by stormy weather without.

"Quite a tempest," observed the Duke of Courthope, desirous of changing the conversation.

Lady Overlaw looked suddenly up at him like sunshine, her baby face flooded and running over with laughter. "I want my money," she pouted; and it was all dark again.

"For the life and soul of me I can't give it you.

That is," added his Grace, quailing before the scowl which settled as he spoke on those small arched eyebrows beneath him, "not to-night."

He was standing with his back to the fire, and could not see her face, which was now turned away from him; but she could see every shade upon his countenance in a glass opposite, for her eyes were as keen as those of a young hawk. He looked very haggard and careworn. There were some deep lines on his forehead, and about his mouth, where she did not remember to have seen them before; and though he was carefully attended to by a consummate valet, the roots of his hair were visibly grey, and the rest of it was limp and straggling—the cosmetics he used having prevented it from keeping a natural appearance after he had removed his hat. She noted all these details with thoughts so hard that if he could but have divined them, or seen the expression they lent her face, he might have known she did not love him; known, perhaps, that youth *can* neither love nor pity age, as he wished to be loved and pitied in his poverty and sorrow. There was a profound silence in the room, and the rain could be heard pattering ceaselessly upon the window panes, as if it was keeping a running accompaniment to their talk, or filling up the pauses of it.

"You can get the money from Sharpe," resumed Lady Overlaw presently, in a decided way.

"I assure you I cannot. He has already got an assignment of my mines in Cornwall, and I am, as you know, insured in every office in London, so he says I can give no security."

Lady Overlaw went on working at her crochet as

some minutes more flew by, their silence only broken by the rain, which now seemed to the Duke as though it fell like human tears, and that all the winds which brought it were his sighs.

"Coutts will cash your cheque," said her Ladyship again from out the stillness, very clearly.

"I beg your pardon," replied the Duke, "circumstances have made me aware of the contrary." He could not get off his stilts even in his penury, and when he could not pay a servant's wages.

"They will cash the cheque if I take it myself; besides, you can send them the Revel jewels again." She knew every one of his resources; had appraised and valued him, and all he possessed, long ago.

"I *have* sent the Revel jewels," answered the Duke, huskily.

"I don't care," said the lady, passionately. "What are your affairs to me? You are growing stupid;" and she made another mouth at him.

"If the time has come," said his Grace, passing his hand for a moment across his eyes, "that you can no longer speak to me without using unkind language, I had better go."

"Yes, go," she answered, "Why did you not go to the opera with the Dowager Lady Hanaper to-night, instead of coming here? It would have been much better for you; and it is rude of you to ask her and not keep your engagement." She spoke indifferently, and seemed to say inwardly, "Why does he *not* go? He is not altogether such a bad person. Perhaps Lady Hanaper may like him, though I cannot; and if he goes to her I shall get rid of him half-an-hour-sooner." Those were her thoughts, and probably the

Duke was half-unconsciously aware of them. So wonderful a thing is animal magnetism that we may often understand the unuttered wishes of those we love. But he could not tear himself away from her. She might insult him; trample upon him; he was unable to resist the spell with which she bound him, or to forget his allegiance to that baby face and capricious temper.

She threw herself back in her chair, and kicked one of the balls of worsted which had fallen to the ground, playing with it, and tossing it a foot high with the point of her embroidered slipper. She did not seem to be thinking of him further than to wish that he was gone. She did not speak to him, nor look at him.

"From Mr. Roger de Beevor, my Lady," said the maid, bringing in a little twisted strip of paper. Lady Overlaw snatched at it, shrugging her shoulders at the maid, as much as to say, "Why did you not find an excuse for me to leave the room?"

"I am surprised," said the Duke of Courthope, very stiffly, "that you should condescend to hold any intercourse with an individual who has been warned off the course at Newmarket."

"I am to give up my own cousin next, to please you, I suppose," answered her Ladyship, scornfully.

"I think it highly improper and dangerous for you to be writing notes to a blackguard who has been turned out of society for failing to meet his debts of honour, besides cheating at cards," observed the Duke.

"How dare you insult my family? I shall do as I please, see whom I please, write to whom I please.

If you do not like it, why don't you go away, and never return?" answered her Ladyship, with something like positive ferocity.

Again silence fell between them like a curtain, while the lady kicked and toyed with the ball of bright-coloured worsted, as it bounded backwards and forwards on the point of her little slipper.

"Duke," she said, after a few minutes.

"Yes," said his Grace, tenderly; "what next?"

"Your conduct is not honourable," she continued, glancing up at him maliciously. "You promised me this money, and now you pretend you have not got it. I wonder you like to talk of Roger's debts of honour, poor fellow, after that. Your conduct is ten times worse than his, at all events."

"Who is Roger?" asked the Duke, wincing, as her shafts struck him.

"My cousin, Captain Roger de Beevor, the best and dearest fellow in the world."

"The greatest scoundrel in Europe," remarked his Grace, hotly.

"One excepted, at least," replied her Ladyship.

The Duke of Courthope took up his opera hat with some dignity, and rose to go. She did not seek to detain him. Still he stood irresolute, and after moving several times towards the door, he sat down at her writing-table. She watched him from the corners of her eyes, though she seemed so angry and disdainful; and she drew a short breath of relief as she saw him tear off the half of a sheet of note-paper.

"It is money which should have been paid into the Court of Chancery at twelve o'clock to-morrow, but if you send this to the bank before Mortmain's cheque is presented, you will get it paid, and the draft I gave the lawyers will be refused. I must say it is a mistake, and go to Paris for a few weeks till I can settle the business, or it blows over, and becomes among the by-gones."

The Duke sighed as he spoke, and the next moment he was gone. She got up briskly then, went into the next room, and watched his tall figure as it passed out of her house, and stalked stiffly away, past the garish lamplight into the shadow beyond. Then she clutched at the cheque. It was on a City bank where the Duke kept a trust account, and she knew at a glance what it had cost him; but there was only a gleam of satisfaction in her eyes as she put it hastily in her purse, and rang for her maid. Half-an-hour afterwards the two women might have been seen hurrying over Waterloo Bridge, through wind and rain, at midnight, in a street cab, upon their way to an obscure hotel in Stamford Street, where young Roger de Beevor, one of the most reckless spendthrifts in London, was in hiding from the sheriff of Middlesex.

"I'll marry him," she said to her maid, "if I have to follow him into beggary; and I would sooner share a crust with him than be twenty times Duchess of Courthope and Revel."

She, too, was a Wyldwyl.

CHAPTER II.

Lord Punjaub.

The famous Indian General and Administrator, long known as Lord George Wyldwyl, was a younger brother of the late Duke of Courthope, and consequently uncle to the present peer. The late Duchess, his sister-in-law, had remained so long without giving birth to a son that he had naturally expected to succeed to the title and estates, when an heir was so unexpectedly born in the presence of Countess Pencarrow. Then all his hopes had vanished; vanished so suddenly, so surprisingly, that many rumours went abroad upon the subject.

Among these reports there was especially one which obtained much credence with persons who are generally well-informed concerning the affairs of the nobility. It was therein stated that the newly-born infant was neither the son of the Duke nor of the Duchess of Courthope, but of the late Lord Alfred Wyldwyl and the Countess of Pencarrow, whom he had secretly married.

Upon the one hand it was said that the Countess could not avow her marriage without the complete loss of her fortune, under the conditions of her late husband's will; and it was equally impossible that she should acknowledge her own child without the entire forfeiture of her reputation and self-esteem, however innocent she might really be. Upon the other hand, the Duke of Courthope was known to be deeply and even dangerously embarrassed. Lord Trecorne and several of the Whig peers were talking loudly of an impeachment, hiding their party purposes (for that Duke was one of the pillars of the Tory party) under an affected zeal for the public good. Moreover, the Duke's creditors were extremely alarmed, because, in case of his death without direct heirs, they had no security whatever for their claims, nor was it possible they could ever obtain any. For the Duke alone, and without the consent of his next heir, was powerless over the entail; and there was something in the honest, unbending nature of Lord George Wyldwyl which would render it extremely hazardous to approach him with any scheme for raising money to pay off usurers at the expense of the permanent dignity and means of his family. If, however, a son were produced by the Duke and Duchess of Courthope, the wisest course which the creditors could take would be to wait patiently till he grew up to man's estate, and could be induced to make himself responsible for their claims. Then, and then only, by means of rent charges, life assurances, and a new deed of settlement, they might be paid every fraction of their due. It was urged therefore, with some show of reason, that the Duke himself, pressed upon all sides, and especially being under heavy pecuniary obligations to Lady Pencarrow, as well as surviving trustee and executor of her husband, had been induced to father the late Lord Alfred's son in order to save the Pencarrow estates for the Countess, and that the Duchess had consented to give a colour to the proceeding, in order to save him from utter ruin and ignominy.

Everything is known in this world, there being no secret in existence which could survive a properly directed inquiry for forty-eight hours; and what was thought by well-informed persons was very nearly true. Lord George Wyldwyl declined to set any inquiry on foot; but a family deed was shortly afterwards drawn up by Mr. Mortmain, the hereditary solicitor of the Courthopes, providing that the Marquis of Kinsgear should not marry, and that his line of the Dukes of Courthope should become extinct with him. By-and-by, however, it happened, as time passed on and Lord George had only one daughter to inherit his family honours, that the conditions of the deed above mentioned were modified, lest the great dukedoms of Courthope and Revel should die out altogether. It was then stipulated that the present Duke should marry forthwith, and that his son, should he have one, should be formally betrothed to Lord George's daughter. This arrangement was carried out, and the two young people, who were born within eighteen months of each other, were solemnly bound to love, honour, and cherish each other in the family interest before they could speak or hear for themselves.

Meantime Lord George had founded a new name and fortune for himself. He had consented to follow an Indian career at a time when very few men of his rank were disposed to serve at such a distance from home. He had therefore had the cream of everything in the East, and had risen with extraordinary rapidity. His pay and allowances for a long time had seldom been less than ten thousand a year, with free quarters, forage, and rations. He cumulated all sorts of high employments in his own person, and being a lord, and therefore in a manner born into high place, nobody was jealous of him or tried to upset him. So he rose step by step, sending home prize money in plenty, and getting twelve per cent. for all his investments in India, till he did not know what he was worth. Mr. Mortmain, a very discreet old gentleman, having a huge admiration for this calm-hearted soldier who had disdained a dukedom, managed all his affairs for him, and managed them very prosperously. It was said at Lincoln's Inn and about the parlours of Lombard Street, where people know a great deal of the property of their neighbours, that Lord George Wyldwyl's heiress would be one of the greatest matches in England, and that his Lordship's fortune could hardly fall short of three-quarters of a million sterling since his last great hauls of prize money.

The Indian General did not care much for money himself. He was a broad bluff-looking man, with a lion-like head, who kept his guineas in a bag, out of which his friends and intimates and all who came near him might help themselves. His aides-de-camp and secretaries, who all loved the open-hearted nobleman, were constantly occupied in protecting him from the importunities of beggars, and the moment his horse was seen in the street quite a flock of them seemed to start out of the earth to surround and accompany him whithersoever he went. He was enabled to save a city once because a Sepoy, who was quite willing to abolish the rest of the Christian race, could in no wise be persuaded to harm a hair of his head, and so warned the fine old soldier of his danger.

In his time life in India was such a very different thing to what it has now become. The world was altogether a better place for a gentleman to live in. The higher officials, especially if they belonged to illustrious families, enjoyed kingly authority, respect, and immunities. Lord George was very happy there, very prosperous, and very useful. In England he would have been lost among the crowd of Toms and Harrys who are entitled to call themselves lords by courtesy. At most he would have been known as a good shot on the moors, or perhaps as an enterprising salmon fisher in Norway. He must have played the part of Jock, the laird's brother, living at free quarters penniless, ignominious, and contented, till he was fit for nothing else, since he did not choose to assert his real rank at the cost of his kinsmen's honour. But at Calcutta he was a live authentic lord and something more; and very odd it was to see whole herds of middle class people copying the bluff nobleman's dress and bearing in the minutest particulars, so that one day, when he chanced to forget his cravat, all Calcutta adopted the fashion of going about barenecked till he was seen again with a stock on.

Only one event had ever disturbed the even tenor of his life. More than forty years before the Indian Mutiny broke out he had gone on furlough to England; and as soon as his arrival had been announced in the newspapers he had received a strange incoherent letter from a place called Wakefield-in-the-Marsh, and it was signed "Margaret Wyldwyl." The writer said that she was the wife of Mr. Odo Wyldwyl; and he knew that there was but one person of that name, who was his brother, now the Duke of Courthope and Revel, who had so lately succeeded to the title that his own patent of precedence as a duke's son was but just issued. If, therefore, the woman's statement meant anything it would signify that she was Duchess of Courthope, and that there must be two duchesses of that name in existence. Moreover, Margaret Wyldwyl declared she had a daughter, and if this were true, and she could prove that she was his brother's wife, that daughter would be some day Countess of Winguid—a title which descended in the female line, with some very large estates in Scotland, where the marriage was alleged to have been performed, and where it might indeed have happened without any publicity, or the slightest intelligence of the fact having reached England, considering that a Scotch marriage is merely a verbal contract between the parties concerned, which may be entered into at any time and place in the presence of witnesses.

Honest Lord George, therefore, was sorely puzzled. He had many doubts about his brother where a woman was concerned, and thought it quite possible that he might have gone farther than he intended before he had attained to such high fortunes. He saw him, interrogated him, and his answers were by no means calculated to set at rest suspicion. He prevaricated, cursed a little, and said he was very sorry he had ever been to Scotland, and "that it was all the fault of that canting old Majoribanks," with much to the same effect, which really meant nothing but that he was angry and alarmed. He was also suffering from some bruises about the face, which led up to the inference that he had been worsted in a stand-up fight with somebody.

Lord George, therefore, who was obstinate and pertinacious in his way, and quite incapable of countenancing any underhanded dealing, told his brother plainly that he would ferret out the truth, and that if there were two wives in the case, he ("honest George" as they called him) would stand by the first.

Down he went, therefore, in a yellow postchaise-and-four to Wakefield-in-the-Marsh, travelling all night to do so, and throwing his Indian outfit money about right royally. He arrived at the "Chequers" at about four o'clock on a summer's morning, making a great rumpus; and at five he had galloped away again, feeling convinced that there was nothing worth further notice in that business but what money could set right, bad as it was. The woman who called herself Margaret Wyldwyl still persisted in her story; she was pretty, though apparently far advanced in a consumption, and she had an infant daughter. That was all which she could make clear. She showed a box, too, which bore his brother's cypher and the family coronet; but there was nothing in it, though she maintained in a confused sort of way that there was, but that it had a secret fastening which she could not find. Her sister, however, or, as she seemed to say, her foster-sister, one Mrs. Giles, the wife of a publican who had been butler to old Dick Porteous, evidently did not believe the girl's story. She said there could be no marriage without a parson, as she herself knew, having been married only after having been called three times in church. She therefore told the poor young mother that she had merely come to the fate which had ruined many a pretty girl before her, and that she had better make the best of it.

So thought honest George, leaving her a cheque for £50, which he found next day sent back to his hotel without a word. But his conscience was at peace. He had done what he could to clear up a mystery which startled him; had cleared it up, as he thought, and there was an end of it, otherwise no considerations of expediency would have kept him quiet while a wrong was being done. With his own interests he had done as he pleased; he had given them up rather than that shame and misery should light on his brother, but he certainly would not have compromised the interests of others. The whole affair had long since passed from his memory, and General Lord Punjaub, Commander-in-Chief of Her Majesty's forces in India, little thought that his smart aide-de-camp, Cornet Brown, was a son of the shapeless infant which his brother's widowed wife had held in her arms on the summer morning when she wept to him in vain at the village inn.

CHAPTER III.

Peace.

By far the most precious gift which a young man can possess at the outset of his career in life is the faculty of attracting the good will of those who are placed in authority over him. It is a natural and not an acquired gift. Possibly it may depend upon causes too subtle for verbal analysis, words being as yet but clumsy and imperfect instruments. Like all natural endowments, however, it is of a better and higher quality than any of those which we can win by our own efforts—or prayers. It makes all the difference between success and failure in every profession. The men who rise rapidly, who attain distinction and honours at an age when they have a real value, are seldom clever; they are merely the men who are liked. Talent and even genius, though useful to the world, has never been well received by it; nor is good conduct by any means popular. All the valuable advice of friends, all the rules of moralists and philosophers, however scrupulously obeyed, never did much for any one. Probably it may be as well not to get into scrapes; but there is a notable difference in scrapes. If a young man who is liked gets into scrapes he will get out of them, or be got out of them, good-humouredly, and thought still more kindly of for having exercised the Christian virtues of his friends, perhaps. On the other hand, if a young man who is not liked gets into no scrapes, people will drag him into scrapes, shove him into scrapes, put him into other people's holes and wrongs, and leave him there.

William Brown was a favourite with everybody. The worst curmudgeons in the regiment—the Major who had a chronic toothache and a short temper, Lieutenant Highlowes who had great ideas of the respect due to him, and a light purse; Captain Skraype who was in difficulties with the authorities—all troublesome folk in their way—were equally ready to say a kind word for him. It is likely enough that he owed at least some part of these good wishes to the fact of his being just a little stupid. He had no perception of the faults or shortcomings of other people, no sense of humour. He could see nothing funny in the Major's hair-dye, or Lieutenant Highlowe's tall-heeled boots; and when allusions were made to these standard topics of mess-room merriment, his face did not depart from its handsome gravity. When he spoke of other men behind their backs he did so in such a manner as to convey the impression that he liked and esteemed them, or he said little. He never used flattering expressions, he never toadied any one; but there were tones of deference and consideration in his voice, extremely simple and winning. Perhaps he was innately kind-hearted, and therefore naturally polite.

So this young fellow had the best of all good things. He was to be seen at the Governor-General's balls, and in Lady Laura's pew at church when the Bishop preached. Even the right reverend prelate himself returned the Cornet's modest bow, when they met, with a half paternal smile; and Major-General Sir Ajax Bodger, a far more important personage than viceroy, lady, or bishop, deigned to give him a short grunt of recognition such as he seldom bestowed on anybody who had not at least one member of the House of Commons behind him.

Now among the innumerable ways in which it was possible a few years ago for well-disposed seniors to help a young man who pleased them up the ladder, was by sending him home with despatches announcing what every one knew long before. The case is somewhat altered now. The departments have grown sulky, or have given up this branch of business for the present; so that an officer coming home with despatches is very often left to pay his own travelling expenses. But not long ago it was a generally understood thing in the army that the bearer of news of victory or a treaty of peace received a step in his profession, with a gratuity of five hundred pounds. . Therefore, shortly after the Thanksgiving Day for the success of the British arms had been observed in England and in India; when peerages had been distributed to the victorious generals, and the storm of discontented pamphlets and angry disclaimers of those who had got nothing or not enough was beginning to subside, Lord Punjaub thought he might do something for his aide-de-camp by sending him home with a formal announcement of the cessation of hostilities.

"When can you start, Brown?" asked Lord Punjaub with his mouth full of tiffin, telling the good news to his aide-de-camp that "he had managed the thing with Bodger," and he was to be sent home officially.

"*Now*," replied the young soldier.

"Quite right, Brown," said the General; "just like me. When Ellenborough, who was a dandy, sent me to Somnauth, he asked Sir Mungo Barker what I should take with me for outfit. 'Give him a tin pot, my Lord,' replied Sir Mungo, and I took one; nothing else, I assure you, Brown." And the General blew his nose loudly in a yellow pocket-handkerchief, to give emphasis to his discourse.

"Baggage is a bore, unless it's the enemy's," observed Cornet Brown, sitting down to table and helping himself to a slice of York ham, which is a part of the ordinary cooling food we use in hot climates.

The General laughed till he was in danger of

choking. "Enemy's baggage!—damn the boy, he'll suffocate me,—loot, eh, you mean?"

"Yes, my Lord," replied the youthful hero.

"Ah!" ejaculated the General, suddenly becoming grave as an owl, after drinking a large glass of Madeira enough to drown a weak man's thoughts. "I sha'n't be long after you, Brown. Violet is to take my command in July, which is only a month off, and the Indian army is to be amalgamated with the Queen's service. This is what I have worked up to all my life," added the General, rolling his eyes and tongue about solemnly; "for the Company's officers were in a false position as to rank, and I am glad that my task has ended. They will not be quite so well pleased with the liberalities of the War Office as they were with large-handed 'Old John;' but they must make the best of it, and console themselves with the thought that gain and glory do not go together, or I for one should not be so well off."

"There are exceptions to every rule," answered the aide-de-camp readily, and he smiled so as to leave no doubt that he really thought his General had earned fortune and fame together. There was not much wonderful about the fact that a young man was liked who could imply admiration so delicately without giving it utterance. Lord Punjaub, who was very simple-minded, as most true soldiers are, felt the subtle tribute of the brave youth's honour, and colouring to the roots of his hair, began to bluster something about it being a hot day in the Hooghly; but the careless shaft at random sent had gone home to his breast, and he drew nearer to Young Brown, taking him affectionately by the arm.

"You'll go and see my nephew at his place, Beaumanoir. It is a very fine place, and perhaps should have been mine if every one had what belongs to them; but I am quite as well without it. I have made my own way in life, which is better than picking up other people's leavings."

The aide-de-camp nodded, as who should say, I should think so indeed; but he had the rare art of agreeing silently, an art most useful and pleasing when practised upon age and garrulity.

"Yes, Brown," spluttered Lord Punjaub, "you must see my nephew. He has all the vices and virtues, and is an accomplished nobleman." The General's lion-like face glowed with good humour, so that kind words bubbled out of him like water from a spring; and every sentence was flavoured with deep hidden thoughts, as water is charged with the properties of the soil through which it passes in its upward course to air, undergoing some such transformations as the voice when it rises into meaning.

"I have all your private letters with me, and shall never allow them to be out of my sight till they are delivered, you may be sure of that, my Lord," said Young Brown, showing an unfeigned sense of the importance of his trust. It was important, too, though only the loving scrawl of an old soldier to his only daughter. His pothooks could not have been very well formed, for his right hand had been maimed at Sobraon, but sweet girlish eyes would brighten when they saw them.

"Good fellow, good fellow!" blustered the General, patting his aide-de-camp on the shoulder as if he had been a horse. "I am sorry you won't see Amabel;

she is with the Dowager Marchioness of Newcomen in Ireland, but I shall present you as soon as I come home, and tell Missy to be on her best behaviour. Always call her Missy, Brown, you know, because she pulls my moustachios if she does not get her own way. You never saw such a tartar"—and "the dear old boy went off at score, being quite inexhaustible about that young person who was the pride and torment of his life," said General Brown, as he told this part of his story one day at Beaumanoir to the present writer, whereat his wife immediately pinched him, and ordered her hero to speak more respectfully of her.

There had been another parting previously between Young Brown and the Marquis of Kinsgear, who had never answered to the call of trumpet since the Nepaulese spear had struck him down. There had been consultations between the most eminent medical men of Calcutta about his state; but they could arrive at no other conclusion than that there was a lack of vitality in his constitution: and then it was remembered that his mother, the late Duchess of Courthope, had died early, and one of the Princes of Science declared that long life, like everything else worth naming which we either bring into this world or which takes us away from it, is hereditary. The wounds which he had received, though serious, were not such as would occasion any alarm in a healthy subject, being but flesh wounds, wherein none of the centres of life were concerned. Young Brown or Lieutenant Highlowes, or even older men—Lord Punjaub or General Violet—would have shaken them off by the sheer force of nature. The blood of the

Marquis, however, was more torpid than theirs. It was only when strongly roused, as he had been upon the field of battle, that he was capable of sustaining physical effort; so the Prince of Science shook his head, and although he maintained that those new forms of life which we call death should never display themselves in a young human frame, yet the feeling round the mess table of the 1st Lancers, as week after week left the Marquis's place still empty, was anything rather than hopeful.

Lord Kinsgear himself did not share these forebodings, for we are very seldom conscious of the nearest approaches of death. He thought that he should soon be well again when he got back to England, and could continue some experiments in electricity which interested him a great deal.

"Give my father the turquoises, Brown, that Meerza Ibraheem sent me from Persia, and tell him General Violet, who is a judge, says that these are of the purest colour from the old rock. I have been promised, also, the pick of the Begum's shawls, when the 'loot' is sold, for Lady Overlaw; and, Brown, try to like my father: I want you to make Beaumanoir your home."

"All right," returned his brother officer, briefly. "His Grace is such a swell that the best I can hope is that he will like *me*. No fear on the other side, you know. And now make haste and get well. That's the first thing to think about."

CHAPTER IV.

Coming Home with Despatches.

CORNET BROWN, travelling with despatches upon Her Majesty's service, and bearing official news of peace from India, was a very important figure on the homeward passage. His name and tidings were telegraphed from every station where he stopped, and he was abruptly introduced to newspaper readers as a European celebrity. Cheap illustrated prints gave his biography and portrait; the latter being a used up plate of the late Mr. Cobden, pressed into service for the emergency. The dashing Cornet was therein presented to an intelligent public as a spare person of middle age, looking not unlike an unprosperous shoemaker. But every one was satisfied; the intelligent public because it would as soon look at one likeness as another, and the proprietors of the illustrated prints,* which copied each other's novelties, because they sold their publications in great numbers throughout all the boarding-houses in British watering-places where Anglo-Indians resort.

Indeed, the soldier's return was more than a mere national event. When something happened to the P. and O. steamer off the coast of Egypt, and he was obliged to tranship his despatches and himself on board a vessel of the Austrian Lloyd's, she hoisted

* It is only fair to say that these remarks do not apply to such publications as the *Illustrated London News* and the *Graphic*, which produce portraits of rare fidelity and artistic excellence.

British colours and piped all hands on deck for him. They used to be naval officers when they were not Light Dragoons who commanded those Austrian boats, and they were exceedingly agreeable fellows, fond of clinking their spurs in salute to any celebrity who might take a passage on their vessel. But they were not expert sailors, and Cornet Brown—*mit Depeschen*—was almost lost during a four days' storm in the Adriatic, when they all took to their images and nearly got the ship pooped. However, they brightened up when the weather became calm, put on their gold-laced caps, and steamed into Trieste in grand style the ninth day after leaving Corfu.

A pompous man, whose head and shoulders were shaped like those of a cod-fish, then emerged from a cabin, where he had shut himself up with some bottles and a thin, faded lady. He walked upon deck as they entered the harbour of the largest of the Austrian seaports, and assumed an absurd sort of consequence, as if the ship belonged to him, and he was about to land in a conquered country.

"I understand," said this pompous man, "that there is a British officer on board with despatches from India." He addressed the engineer, who was an Englishman bearing the name of Onions.

"Praps thereriss an praps thereain't," returned Mr. Onions, hitching up his trousers without ceremony; for, like all Englishmen employed in foreign services, he fancied himself superior to all created things, because, indeed, he knew more of a ship's boilers than his assistant.

The pompous gentleman puffed himself out, and strutted up and down the deck as an owner should.

Being unable to obtain an answer from Mr. Onions, he desired to impress him with his importance, and, taking off a well-fitting glove to show a be-ringed hand, he drew out a handsome gold watch and consulted it.

"You hain't got such a thing as a quid about you, have you?" inquired Mr. Onions, nothing daunted; but the pompous gentleman pretended not to hear him, and continued his walk. His clothes were smartly made; his trousers had the neat cut of a racing man's tailor, and his long white hair, which hung far behind his hat, was scrupulously arranged. He seemed like a man of the world under a cloud, who had determined to thrust himself half way out of it.

Presently his eye was attracted to the neat bullock trunks and luggage of Cornet Brown; for officers' luggage always looks trim and shiny. The question, therefore, which he had asked of Mr. Onions was silently answered, for he saw painted in large white letters upon black oil-skin—

William Brown, Esq.,
H.M. 1st Lancers.

"Pleasure of speaking to the gallant officer whose name was mentioned in the last Gazette?" said the pompous man, speaking in a pompous voice; and then he added: "My name is Porteous—Sir Richard Porteous, late Coldstream Guards." *Very* late he might have added, for he had sold his lieutenant's commission forty years before, after three months' service; though he had ever since claimed a brotherhood with his profession, and it had not been disallowed. He was an honorary member of every mess and military club he could find, and the epaulette he had worn for a few days had served as a life-long introduction to him. It served him again now. Sir Richard Porteous of the Coldstream Guards seemed to the Indian soldier of fortune a vastly high and mighty military man; and his answer, given with perfect respect and good breeding, clearly evinced that he knew and understood the social value of a baronetcy, certified by a commission in Her Majesty's Household Brigade. This at once put things upon a convenient footing for the Baronet. Leaving the faded lady to take care of herself, he pulled up his collar and pulled down his wristbands, lounging over the ship's side as he had done long ago over the Park railings. He had met with a new acquaintance, a fresh mind which did not know him for a broken-down old gambler; and he could once more enjoy the luxury of speaking, acting, and feeling as a soldier and a gentleman.

"Have a cigar?" asked Sir Richard, putting himself at once upon a comrade's footing, the better to enjoy this treat of a new acquaintance.

Cornet Brown declined a cigar, finding whenever he had hitherto tried one that it acted upon the sockets of his eyes like a corkscrew. Then Sir Richard proposed pale ale and sandwiches, though they had just breakfasted, and finally a glass of Malaga, which he said truly enough was peculiarly good upon those Austrian Lloyd boats. The Baronet paid for those things out of a splendid gold purse, upon which a red hand was worked in rubies to act as a slide. He displayed this unnecessary piece of magnificence ostentatiously, and gave such a handsome gratuity to the steward, that the man, who was a brigand out of employment, from Ragusa, called upon all the saints to bless him.

"Dine with me, of course, Brown," said Sir Richard, whom the Malaga had made very friendshippy. "I always put up at the 'Kaiser von Oesterreich' here. Dayvellish good cook. Best woodcock in Europe, *and* best Steinberger."

"Thank you, I'm off by first steam," said Cornet Brown, not quite insensible to the dignity of his mission as the Messenger of Peace.

"Ha, to be sure you are; I forgot that. Hey, you flunkey there, when does the express start for Vienna? Hang it, I forgot the rascal can't speak English; can you manage their lingo?" The Baronet spoke first to the disengaged brigand and then to Cornet Brown. He was rather a flighty baronet, and he seemed to be trying to act a part he had played in his youth—that of a free-handed, free-spoken, thoughtless, careless cavalier. It was not so badly done, but he was a little stiff in the joints; and even the slang he talked was of a by-gone period. It would have been evident to any man in the 1st Lancers, save William Brown, that he had not heard the chaff of the "Rag" for many a day. But William Brown, who did not know this, was half amused and half awed by this semi-noble and warlike conversation.

"If you must go on at once I have half a mind to go with you myself. Lady Porteous is going to stay with her sister, the Countess Windischmagen, and joins me at Paris in the spring," said Sir Richard, indicating the faded lady, with a side movement of the head respectful enough; and it may be generally observed that all faded ladies of that type have a foreign countess for a sister. Even luckless marriages to poor pretentious scamps seem to run in families. Count Windischmagen, who spent his days at Monaco, was only an Austrian type of Sir Richard Porteous, and they had charmed two sisters who had once had comfortable fortunes and weak wits. It was a fine thing in those days—so near and yet so far—to be a British officer travelling on Government service. Under the mild despotic rule of the Austrian Cæsars, every gentleman who bore his rank and title about with him was supposed to have a free pass, which dispensed him from all the Custom-house formalities; and while merchants were detained for hours, and often roughly treated, Sir Richard Porteous and Cornet Brown had but to exchange salutes with the imperial officers, and then to pass on unquestioned. Only one pushing commercial traveller, junior partner in a Manchester firm, got through the wearisome business of examination as soon as they did; and it afterwards transpired that he had passed himself off as their servant, which caused the two gentlemen some anger and some amusement, for he was a candidate for a seat in the House of Commons, hurrying home for his election, and had committed a petty act of smuggling on the way.

Sir Richard Porteous having got rid of his wife by some occult proceeding, accompanied by brief verbal instructions, in which the last intelligible words were "send remittances to Baden," hurried with the Indian officer towards the railway station, and there learned that no train started direct for Vienna till next morning. Sir Richard Porteous was immediately for spending his substance in a protracted banquet at the Kaiser, to fill up the time, but Cornet Brown, having his instructions to make all speed and diligence upon his journey, coolly demanded a special train.

"Ya, aber nein," squawked the stationmaster, appalled by such a request. "Es ist gar nicht möglich, Herr Offizier. Du lieber Himmel! Aber wissen Sie was es kosten wird?"

Price made no difference to Cornet Brown. He had his orders, and acted up to them with military rigidity. So a telegram was despatched to Vienna, and the answer came as quick as thought that a special train should at once be sent after the express, which was only two hours a-head, and might be detained. They did things slowly then in Austria.

The British merchant who was soon to be a legislator, and other merchants, a noisy crowd of many nations, then clamoured for places in the special train, which indeed might as well have taken them. But the Lord under-Stationmaster, who was of baronial rank in a Bohemian village not mentioned on the maps, treated them like so much noxious dust, and very frankly calling them "ganayle," which was *his* French for doggery, shut the station gates on them, while he invited the two British officers to smoke a choice collection of meerschaum pipes with him, and hear a yoderl on the zither, while the steam was getting up.

Pushing commercial men had a bad time of it in Austria before the Constitution was heard of; and Cornet Brown was so impressed with the disdainful treatment which they had received from the Lord under-Stationmaster at Trieste that he asked him if his contempt for trade was a just feeling.

"It is a very old one," replied the Lord under-Stationmaster, who was a scholar as well as a baron.

"It had certainly existed long before the days of the son of Sirach, who has recorded a proverb that they must of necessity be rogues if they buy and sell at all."

"Rogues most decidedly they are," agreed Sir Richard Porteous, laughing. "Talk of usurers, no usurer who ever existed dared to take such profits as a fashionable tradesman; and so that fellow, who pretended he was our footman to smuggle a pound of tobacco, is worth half a million of money, while gentlemen like the Lord under-Stationmaster and myself—why, dammee, I say, Brown, we are often embarrassed; by the holy poker we are!"

The "holy poker" was often introduced into garrison talk forty years ago. What has become of it now? What does become of dead oaths? do they make part of the lurid atmosphere of purgatory?

The Lord under-Stationmaster and Sir Richard Porteous, being congenial spirits, were for keeping up the festivities. They esteemed each other so highly that they swore eternal friendship, exchanged meerschaum pipes, with their arms engraven thereon, as was then the custom in Southern Germany, and really preserved a respectful feeling towards each other for the rest of their days. Had either of them met the Lord Mayor of London, they and the Mayor would have separated with every sentiment of mutual anger and abhorrence. They would have really thought the Mayor a dull dog, however good a Mayor he might have been; and, in his turn, the Mayor, bred and taught in Cheapside, would have considered either of them offensive lunatics, or something worse, so completely is opinion the effect of birth and education.

Whosoever would be appreciated, and live a decently comfortable life, should associate only with his fellows; and it is for very good reason that birds of a feather flock together. Dick Porteous and the Bohemian baron would have drank, and talked, and sang in harmony with the utmost stateliness and formality till daybreak, forgetting all about the special train; but as soon as Cornet Brown heard the first snort of the engine he left his untasted glass of Rheinwein, which the Lord under-Stationmaster had brought out to do honour to his guests, and took up his despatch bags.

Then there was a gallant lifting of hats and clanking of heels, with oblique movements of the back, such as happen when officers and gentlemen take leave of each other, as officers and gentlemen should, and not with that silly familiarity which breeds contempt.

"Your humble servant, my Lord Baron," said Sir Richard; "your humble servant, my Lord Baron," replied the Lord under-Stationmaster, who knew nothing of baronets; and these were the last words borne on the breeze as the two noblemen bade each other good-bye, and the special train crawled slowly out of the station. Somehow or other, however, it happened that Cornet Brown, who was not a nobleman, was forgotten in the stately ceremonies which were performed at the last moment between the baron and the baronet.

The fact was that persons who were untitled were not considered born at all, just then in Austria.

CHAPTER V.

Sir Richard Porteous.

The Baronet whose acquaintance William Brown had made on board the Austrian steamer was not a very uncommon type of Englishman. He had inherited a fortune of about twelve thousand a year, and having nothing whatever to do he took to mischief. He was a strong, sanguine young man, full of high spirits, and he therefore did a great deal of mischief, mostly to himself. He had had a very long minority, during which his estates had been nursed by a parsimonious and somewhat narrow-minded mother, so that when he came of age he had not only a handsome income, but such large accumulations as made what seemed to him an inexhaustible sum of ready money.

Now a rich man who knows how to make a right use of his wealth has a power almost godlike of relieving human misery, and planting human hopes; but to spend money wisely requires a special education. And what can be expected from a thoughtless and ignorant boy who has come into possession of property without any labour or merit of his own, and is consequently devoid of all sympathy with those who toil and deserve? Having no knowledge of the beneficent employment of gold, he can but squander or hoard it. Sir Richard Porteous threw it away.

His mother, a rich grocer's daughter, did all she could to spoil him. She had exaggerated ideas of the rank to which she fancied herself elevated, and had never suffered her son to learn anything useful. He had run the usual profitless course at Eton and Oxford, living with men a great deal richer and cleverer than himself, so that he lost almost as much as he spent among them. Then he had got a commission in the Guards, and had held it pleasantly enough for a while, when a St. Leger race put a period to his military career. After this event he had been obliged to sell out and go abroad just before settling-day at Tattersall's. A score of hunters at Melton, half-a-dozen long-legged horses only fit to lose a steeplechase, an opera-box, some personal friends behind the scenes, a bachelor house in Curzon Street, and a villa at Fulham, with a yacht and a Scotch moor, had made quick work of his twelve thousand a year; and before he was twenty-three years old he had not a shilling he could call his own.

All, however, is never lost at the first throw in life. His mother put his character right at the clubs once, twice, and then provided for him by a marriage with one of her own people who had about fifteen hundred a year, well secured on ground-rents at Islington. Three weeks afterwards he had apartments at the Clarendon Hotel, with a new drag and a new betting-book. Nothing could save him. He did not know what to do with himself when he was not buying a horse or talking about it; and as he was not a sharper he seldom bought horses at saleable prices. He used to say he was "married" to these purchases, because he could not get rid of them. The time came when the Insolvent Court dissolved this queer kind of matrimony; and then he went abroad for the rest of his days, wandering about Europe rather a prominent figure among travellers with his shadow of a title. He could do no more to ruin himself, for he could not raise a shilling on his wife's settlement; and thus he had enough to live on creditably had he thought proper to do so. But the man had a demon of restlessness in him which would never let him remain long in any one place. His practice was to leave his wife with her relatives as long and as often as possible, while he lived in a large-handed way at hotels. She was an affectionate, insipid lady, of a pale faded brown colour. She wore limp clothes and ringlets. She had a vast admiration for him, and regarded him with much the same patient and unreasoning sort of affection as a house spaniel might have done. Perhaps she was a little puzzled at her lot in life, but she thought it grand. She was constantly receiving letters from places the very names of which made her relations gape with wonder. Sir Richard thought nothing of dating his communications from "The Hospodar's Palace, Moldavia," when he was really residing at a Viennese tavern; and now and then he really did pick up some Hungarian magnate or Russian boyard, who gave him a few days' shooting. Occasionally, too, at rare intervals, and especially when some small legacy dropped in from any one of his wife's kinsfolk, Sir Richard would promptly appear at Islington, and suggest that they should make a tour together till the legal preliminaries were arranged for its payment. She always consented, and she always gave him the money as soon as she got it, when he would immediately break out again in brief splendour at a foreign capital, leaving her at

Ems or Spa in small lodgings, or with her sister, the Countess Windischmagen, who was glad to see her, and who had much such a husband herself.

He was not a bad or an unkind man—he was simply raffish, selfish, and had gradually acquired a hatred of any settled residence. He found that three or four pounds a day had more spending in them at an inn than anywhere else. He lived about at inns, was a great man among waiters, and was known to all the crack cabmen in Europe, as well as to the Queen's messengers, who were proud of his friendship, his title, and his society. It was not an elevated conception of life, but it was by no means a disagreeable one. He enjoyed a good deal of air, change, and sunshine. He went about following the summer, shot crocodiles now and then in Egypt when it was cold and foggy in the North; and he was generally to be found at coronations, military spectacles, and all sorts of public rejoicings. He had met with strange adventures during these erratic courses, and had sometimes done wicked things, though not inclined to do them. But he had a fatal habit of good nature, which always moved him to render any service, at any risk, to others; especially if they were persons of rank, whose notice raised his self-esteem. He was very intimate with the late Duke of Courthope, and had been generally seen in close attendance upon his Grace when that gay nobleman had gone to Paris or Rome for a season in his younger days. They had played high stakes together—whist at five-guinea points, with a hundred on the rub, écarté, lansquenet, and what not. Sir Richard seldom won, for the Duke had the longer purse, and was one of the keenest players at all games of skill and chance when he chose to put out his strength. However, Dick Porteous was ready to pay anything for a duke's company, and be thankful. Besides, he liked the magnificent patrician, who had indeed many attractive qualities, and who was frank and kind with him, still calling him "Dick," both in speech and letters, to the last, as cheerfully as when his estates went to square the accounts between them after that fatal St. Leger day which had begun his life-long ruin.

William Brown, profoundly unconscious of his travelling companion's antecedents, was much entertained with him. He merely saw, seated in a negligent way, not without a certain well-bred air of distinction, a fresh-coloured gentleman in the sixties, extremely polite and well dressed. Sir Richard was quite delighted at the idea of their having a special train to themselves, and assumed all the honours of it, putting his head out of window and calling for the station-master, wherever they stopped, to communicate the important tidings which they bore, and to hear himself called "Euer Gnaden," and see the stationmaster bow to him with Austrian formalities.

So they went dozing along at a steady pace, leaving every station to the sound of a trumpet, which was then used instead of a bell throughout the railways of Southern Germany; and they often had a friendly gossip of some duration with the railway authorities where they tarried for ceremony's sake, while the express train bearing the Eastern mails was detained leagues a-head for their arrival.

"Monstrous pleasant way of travelling this," said Sir Richard, putting himself still more at his ease. "I do so hate all contact with cads. They should be shut out from carriages, and made to go in carts and on foot. Every fellow is a cad who is not a man of title or an officer," added the Baronet, decisively.

William Brown smiled with some gravity. "I have only just risen from the ranks," he was about to say, but on second thoughts his better taste told him that the remark would smack of self-assertion, and that his biography could signify little to a gentleman whom he had only met a few hours before for the first time, and whom he might never possibly see again.

The next words of the Baronet, however, drew the relations between them somewhat closer; for we live in a very small world, and few of the persons we see in it for the first time are such strangers as they seem.

"After all," resumed the Baronet, "I myself liked the old posting days better than this tea-kettle style of moving about; but I used to drive myself generally up to town from my place at Dronington. I do not know whether you ever heard of it—a very sleepy old market town in Oxfordshire."

"I am almost a Dronington man—I was born within sight of it," said William Brown.

"The deuce you are; then you must know the old Manor House, and I ought to know you, but I don't. It is nearly forty years ago since I lived there," observed the Baronet, with something like a sigh; but speedily recovering himself, without waiting for his companion's reply, he rode briskly away on his hobby.

"Well, I was going to tell you," said he, "I had a team of four tearing chestnuts, which Old Coper, or rather Old Sharpe, sold me. They could get over the ground at pretty nearly fourteen miles an hour, though they could not last. None of Coper's teams ever could, though they always looked in such high condition."

Sir Richard fell into the common error of thinking that what interested himself must interest other people, and he alluded familiarly to persons and things who had ceased to be in existence before William Brown was born.

"When I was a young man, Odo Wyldwyl and I used to walk a good deal during the 'long.' We were at Oxford together, and he was sapping for a living, though he afterwards became Duke of Courthope. I promised him my living of Wakefield, I remember, which is one of the fattest in England. My brother, Dr. Porteous, has it now, but he was then expecting a commission in the 1st Lancers; which, by the way, is your regiment. It used to be capital fun walking up to a tumble-down roadside inn, and then having our drags and servants come up to fetch us next morning. The bumpkins used to stare so!"

"I know Dr. Porteous, sir. He was very kind to me when I was a boy," observed William Brown, with a modest remembrance of how the affable old clergyman patted him on the head after he had been confirmed.

"So you know my brother, do you?" answered Sir Richard, a little crest-fallen. "We have both had our troubles; for, as the old song says—

> It's a very good world to live in,
> To spend, or to lend, or to give in:
> But to beg, or to borrow, or get back one's own,
> It's the very worst world that ever was known.

My property and his went the way of all properties that I ever heard of—that is to say, into the hands of the lawyers; still, I have managed to go through life on wheels, as you see, and my income is at least as big as that of most foreign princes." With this sage reflection Sir Richard drove dull care away. He would rather that the young officer had not known so much about him, because it was a circumstance which suggested moderation in his discourse, and clipped the wings of his imagination. It was fortunate, therefore, he began to think, that he had not given himself out as a millionaire, which was a frequent custom of his when talking casually with a new acquaintance.

"Yes," he said, gradually drawing in his horns, "I was monstrously fond of pedestrian rambles; and once I remember, after Odo Wyldwyl got his dukedom, we had a ramble together, though it was our last. He had just come home from Italy, and got married, but he was as sulky as a badger, and would not go out of sight of Dronington. He seemed to be looking for somebody; and had a very queer Neapolitan valet, who had been a bandit, with him. The fellow used to make us first-rate macaroni, and was quite hail-fellow-well-met with his master, though the Duke was as proud as Lucifer."

"You must be speaking of the grandfather of Lord Kinsgear, who is in our regiment," said Cornet Brown, who was an intelligent listener, and never let a conversation flag for want of fuel.

"There are two stories about that," replied Sir Richard; "but I remember seeing Lord Kinsgear's name gazetted a year or two ago, or three, which is it? He exchanged from the Household Brigade when the Indian Mutiny broke out. I myself applied for a command, but I had not so much interest at the Horse Guards as when Lord Hanaper, my mother's half-brother, was Military Secretary, so Sir Bodger O'Leary, the new man, refused my application. I got a spurt, however, with the Turks in Bosina last year, and they gave me the local rank of lieutenant-general slick off."

"That was good pay, sir," said William Brown.

"Yes, I believe you," answered the Baronet; "but as they did the same thing to a tailor and a saddler, I never take the rank till I get eastward of the Iron Gates on the Danube."

"It is a smart thing, though, to have about you, sir," remarked Young Brown, considerably impressed by his companion's military achievements, and taking them fully at his own estimate with the guileless simplicity of a well-conditioned youngster who has nothing of the cynic in him.

"I am not proud," replied Sir Richard, drawing down his well-starched wristbands till his massive gold studs gleamed beneath his coat cuffs. "I find my own title quite enough for me. It is a passport to good society everywhere."

The Cornet bowed, as who should say respectfully there could be no doubt of that, but he did not speak. He merely agreed with the baronet in that silent pleasant way he had.

"Well, I was going to tell you," continued Sir Richard, who was loth to let the impressive name of his friend the Duke of Courthope drop out of his conversation. "His Grace would keep on mooning about

Dronington as if he had some object in keeping in the neighbourhood, and it seemed to me as if he was frightened."

"'Hang it, Duke,' said I, 'let's be off out of this. I am bored to death.'

"'Can't you hold your confounded jaw with your Duke?' replied his Grace. 'Didn't I tell you to call me Mr. Thompson?'

"'Only you're not Mr. Thompson,' I answered, a little riled.

"'Yes, I am,' he replied, biting his nails; 'one of my father's names was Thomas, and if I must tell a lie, I like to do it cheaply.'

"I had nothing to say to that, and as no gentleman ever makes an advance to learn another gentleman's secrets, I tried to change the conversation; but he would not talk much, remaining silent even over his wine when we were not playing at écarté, as we generally were. He had taken, I recollect, the best room at the 'King's Head.' It was not a very good room, but it commanded a full view of four cross roads which met at twenty yards from it; and, whatever we might be doing, one of Courthope's eyes was always turned towards the window.

"We used to dine early, not well knowing what to do with ourselves, and one evening I remember we heard a fellow at the bar speaking in a broad Scotch accent, and inquiring the way to Wakefield-in-the-Marsh. I could not think what had come over the Duke. I thought he would have fainted. He turned quite blue, and clutched on to the arm of his chair like old death. When I wanted to assist him he waved me off, and called hoarsely for Giacomo, who was his Neapolitan valet. He spoke some gibberish to him rapidly, and presently the man slunk out of the house stealthily and took the road to Wakefield.

"'Nothing wrong, I hope, Du—, (I beg your pardon), Thompson?' said I; 'you are better now, I see.'

"'All right, Dick,' he answered, in a particularly hard, vicious way he had sometimes; 'but I ain't out of the wood yet, and if there's to be a scrimmage you must stand by me. You can play with your fives, and so can I; besides, Giacomo knows a trick or two; and I received a letter from my lawyer this morning to tell me there is danger in the wind.'

"'I don't advise any bailiff to look us up, Thompson,' said I, doubling my arm, and feeling my biceps, for I was in capital training, and always ready for a fight in those days.

"'Ah, the confounded bailiffs!' said the Duke, apparently seized with a sudden idea. 'They can't touch me as they could a few months ago, because I am a peer; but that infernal Scotch fellow I fancy is on the look out for you or Giacomo.'

"'The dickens he is!' said I; 'let us stop his game. I am up to anything from marbles to manslaughter, in such a case.'

"'That's right,' said the Duke, getting up; 'for there's going to be a row presently.'

"Just then Mr. Scotchman, who was a large-limbed, gawky fellow, not at all like a bailiff, shouldered a bundle he carried at the end of a stout stick, and strode away at five miles an hour, toe-and-heel walking, after Giacomo.

"'I won't have my servant mauled while I am

within hail of him; would you, Dick?' asked the Duke, with a flushed face, and taking up a heavy loaded riding-whip he had with him, though I had never seen him carry such a murderous thing before.

"'I say, Duke,' I remarked, putting my hand on his arm, and stopping him; 'hang it we are a match for one man; put that thing down, or you'll crack his skull, and besides it isn't fair play. Leave him to me; I'll punch his head: and he won't feel very cheerful afterwards.'

"Courthope was ghastly pale. I never saw a fellow in such a state, and he wanted to shake me off and make for the door; but I was the strongest man, and at last he chucked the whip down in a corner and gasped, 'We shall be too late, Dick, if we go on squabbling.' I did not much care what he did to the bailiff with his hands, so I let him go then, and we both set off running after the Scotchman. We had not gone very far when we heard a yell as if a monkey was being flayed alive, and presently Giacomo bounded along like a scorched cat, with the Scotchman's ash stick playing on his hind quarters.

"'Come, now, none of that, you confounded bumbailiff,' said I, meeting him with a straight blow between the eyes; which half-blinded him, I suppose, for he reeled and put down his head as if he was going to toss me. I had the science however, and polished him off in style, sending him into the middle of next week every time he butted at me with that bullock's front of his. Still, he would not give in, and had closed with me after the wrestler's fashion, so I might have got an awkward fall, when I felt that tremendous hold of his round my loins relax, and he reeled to the ground stunned. The cowardly Italian had stolen up behind him, and hit him a blow with a life-preserver behind the ear.

"'You'll swing for that, you dog,' said I, very angry.

"'Never you mind me, Sa; yes, Sa. Better me swing than Duke he swing, Sa. Yes, Sa,' said the man in his vile gibberish. "He no see my master at all, Sa, and I save you very bad fall, Sa. Yes, Sa, knock um down, Sa.'

"'Sure he did not see me, Giacomo, before he dropped?' inquired the Duke, anxiously, without noticing me.

"For reply the Italian lifted the head of the Scotchman, who was quite stunned and insensible. I had bunged up his eyes with my first blow—'Dimmed his peepers,' as they say in the ring.

"The Duke of Courthope drew a deep sigh of relief. 'Come, Dick,' said he, 'let's be off. It won't do for us to be found here in a wayside brawl; we shall have the constables after us, and that might be a bad thing for you, as you have so much stamped paper about.'

"'No,' I replied, 'that won't do. We have knocked the man down and must pick him up, whatever comes of it, and whether I go to the Bench or not. He may go off the hooks if he is left here.'

"'Well, then, stay with him, Dick, if you like, till we send him help,' said his Grace, coming in his quick way to a resolution; and so I did, when in about half-an-hour two of the parish constables came up with my brother's warrant, and took the stunned Scotchman into custody for assaulting Giacomo Scampavia, body servant to Mr. Thompson. The bailiff was just beginning to open his eyes, for I had unloosed his necktie, sponged the blood off him with my handkerchief, and done what I could for him. I never saw a fellow look so astonished in my life as when the constables took him; and I'll be hanged if I wasn't half sorry for the poor devil, though he was a bumbailiff. However, the Duke told me afterwards that it was only a lark, and that Giacomo was not a valet at all, but an Italian nobleman in difficulties, whom he had felt bound to assist; and that the Scotch bailiff got nothing worse than a few weeks in the County Hospital."

"Wir sind angekommen, meine Herren," said the guard, opening the window and saluting the travellers in the special train.

CHAPTER VI.

Beaumanoir.

LIEUTENANT BROWN was well received by the Duke of Courthope when he presented his letters of introduction. His Grace had lived more and more in the country of late years, and his place though very stately was somewhat dull. The arrival of a stranger properly introduced would have been welcome therefore at any time, and the visit of an officer from the seat of war was an event which interested all the county.

The Duke of Courthope, like most provincial magnates, was fond of early news and exclusive information, and he generally contrived to obtain it, for the world is very eager to convey both verbal and epistolary information to a nobleman of his rank. No one was sooner acquainted with the changing events of current history. He knew the very latest movements in party politics, and as they were often false movements, made by persons who had to retrace their steps, he had a rather less accurate idea of the state of affairs than the outside public. He was present at all the false starts for power, so that when the race was run and won, nobody was more surprised at the result than himself. He had around him when Lieutenant Brown arrived the usual party which assembles at ducal palaces when pheasant shooting begins. They were mostly good shots, for his Grace, who sold his game by contract to a London poulterer, could not afford to let his birds be knocked about, and did not like to have them made wild by random firing. There was a brace of Parliamentary colonels, who always killed with their right and left barrels. There was a local banker, who had an absurd resemblance to the Duke in dress, manners, and whiskers. There was a sprinkling of minor barons, a few official dependents who had prospered under the shadow of the great house, an Italian singer and his wife to amuse the evenings, and Lady Overlaw with her aunt the Countess of Clanmore to do the honours.

The Duke took a fancy to the young Indian soldier from the first; perhaps because his manners were perfectly free from either embarrassment or self-assertion. The Lieutenant never made his presence felt oppressively, for he had the secret of amusing himself without getting in other people's way. His voice was never heard at unseasonable times, and he was cheerful without being boisterous or brilliant.

"Come, Captain Brown, and shoot beside me," the Duke would say to him in high good humour, and giving him brevet rank by courtesy. His Grace liked a young man who never missed his bird, never fired first, and picked up the outsiders with unerring aim. The boy's silent, pleasant laughter and deferential manners won him, and while his Grace was amusing himself, he thought he was paying off his son's debt of gratitude very handsomely, so that his conscience approved him not a little.

There was also, however, a subtler influence than either of them could have explained, had they been interrogated, which drew those two together. That splendid peer and the village lad who had shown such unusual qualities when put to the test had many thoughts in unison, and the speech of either found a natural echo in the other's mind. They both felt as soldiers, and despised trade; they had both an innate love of grandeur; they had even some physical peculiarities in common. Both were straight and tall, with a chest rather deep than broad, and admirably formed for exertion; but the face of William Brown was one which had not been seen in the Courthope family for nearly two centuries. It was frank and open during an ordinary conversation and when he was engaged in the common concerns of life. His smile was almost as innocent and winning as the Duke's own, and made all his countenance sparkle when lit up with it. But in moments when his thoughts were concentrated upon any serious subject, his heavy brows closed like a horseshoe, and his look was earnest and intense. A very grave face it was too in repose, very fixed and determined. The lips, neither so full nor so delicate in their outline as the Duke's, were firmly shut, and the massive jaw seemed to lock them in with a clasp of iron. The Duke's eyes were of an uncertain colour, changing in the light, and had naturally a mournful, almost an appealing look, though they had latent fires in them. The eyes of William Brown were deep set, steady, and passionless, rather unforgiving eyes, with gleams like the flash of steel in them when he was roused to anger. But his feelings were not upon the surface. It was not easy to offend him; and in any quarrel he would be likely to have right on his side, whereas the Duke was for ever in the wrong. They would not have made bad types of success and failure. An observer would have at once perceived that the Duke of Courthope was unlucky, and the Lieutenant fortunate: a little experience of the world would have revealed the causes which made them so. A phrenologist would have gone farther, and shown in what respects the nobleman was superior to his guest. His Grace had large perceptive faculties; he was a man eminently skilful in debate, very ready and sagacious, clear-sighted in his view of present things, but not far-seeing. The soldier's perception was defective or undeveloped; he might be deceived and misled, having a simple faith in those around him. His mind was reflective and far-sighted, not acute.

His Grace was fond of prosing to his guest—most dukes are—as the intimacy increased between them, and his discourse very much resembled extracts from an autobiography. He was not a bright or a witty man, and his idea of conversation was to record events that had happened to himself, with his reflections upon them. His ideas had little novelty. He was indeed a Conservative, and liked to think backwards, so that whenever a new thing was brought before him, his first impulse was to meet it by a negative. He could hardly have said the word "yes," without some qualification which neutralised it, ten times in the course of his existence since he had attained to years of discretion. Nor was the reason far to seek for this reticence. All his life long, sharp persons had been setting traps to catch his promises, and quoting his own words against him, so that he had, like many grand and powerful people, adopted a vocabulary which had no meaning at all; or he was shrewd enough to talk in his most unguarded moments upon subjects which had no connection with any matter of business by which he could be compromised.

One of his favourite topics was blood and race. He used to say that he could tell a man or woman of rank by the first inflection of their voice in speaking, and that there was something distinctive and beautifying in mere birth. He had a marked contempt for women, mentioning them as toys and playthings. They belonged, he observed, to no definite station, and beauty was their only title to consideration. One might have thought, to hear him, that he had never known what it was to love, and it seemed to William Brown, as he listened, not surprising that there should be so little sympathy and affection betwixt him and his son, Lord Kinsgear, seeing that the Duke considered family ties as a troublesome, if not an ignominious restraint.

"Women," said his Grace, as he shot a pheasant, and brought the bright-plumed bird to the ground without breaking a bone or ruffling a feather, "are the proper amusements of gentlemen. Never marry, Captain Brown, if you can possibly help it. Women make admirable mistresses, sublime mothers, and abominable wives. You might as well sell yourself into slavery, as have a petticoat tied round your neck."

Then, having killed another pheasant with a side shot, as who should put a comma to his talk, he resumed, "I remember the prettiest girl I ever saw was at an inn at a village in Oxfordshire one day when I was thrown out with the Cloudesdale hounds, which used to be hunted by old Dick Porteous: a famous fellow he was once, I have heard my father say."

"Egad," the Duke added, handing his gun to a keeper, and cutting himself a blackthorn, for he had many of the ways of a country gentleman, and had an eye for a straight stick when he saw it—"Egad! the girl was so pretty that I gave her a ten-pound note when I drove away next morning, to smoothe the way for seeing her again. But I went abroad soon afterwards, and when I came back I put myself in double harness, and did not care to canter abroad as I used to do in my bachelor days." The Duke showed those white teeth of his gaily now, took his gun from the keeper, shouldered it, and the next moment another pheasant had fluttered and fallen, while William Brown picked off two birds, one after the other, at his left.

"Well shot," said the Duke, approvingly, for neither of the Lieutenant's birds fluttered after they fell, any more than his own did, and not one of their gorgeous hues was stained. "I told you that gun would carry straight;" and then he went back to his autobiography again.

"I recollect," observed his Grace, as though he were recalling a fact of importance to the universe, "that I had a skittish grey mare in my team, and I thought she would have upset the coach at starting, so that the girl would have had to nurse me, which wouldn't have been such a bad thing; but she tore away at last; though she had me into a shop in Pall Mall three weeks afterwards, as I was tooling down some pink bonnets to Richmond. All the ladies wore pink bonnets then."

"Bless my soul," exclaimed his Grace again, presently, "why that's Stubbs's farm. I vow and declare it is nearly six o'clock already. That fine sunset out there has got the better of us, and we shall only just have time to get home and dress for dinner." Time had passed agreeably with him that afternoon, as it commonly does to a man who has all the talk to himself, and about himself, and chooses his subjects.

Lieutenant Brown liked this conversation amazingly. He already thought himself one of a privileged class, being received on equal terms by such good company. He was proud of his epaulettes, proud of his rank in the army, proud of his grand acquaintances. Having succeeded so well in his profession, the boy was something of a soldier pedant, and was beginning already to look down upon the world in a way amusing enough to a philosopher.

CHAPTER VII.

The Lost Letter.

It was late when the Duke of Courthope and Lieutenant Brown returned to Beaumanoir, for they had been on the outskirts of the Home Park when the evening had overtaken them. The company therefore had already met in the noble drawing-room that looked towards the quiet lake and solemn woods, on which had been bent the gaze of so many generations of nobles and statesmen.

It was rather a numerous dinner-party, for the Assizes were going on in the chief town of the district, and the Duke was Lord-Lieutenant of the county, so that it was among the duties of his office to receive the Queen's Judges and some of the leading barristers on the circuit. He did so the more readily because he had many reasons for wishing to stand well with the lawyers; and therefore he lost no opportunity of making friends among them. His Grace moved about very grandly in his ancestral halls, and enacted the part of a courteous and high-bred host to perfection. No one present was denied the gracious welcome of his smile and cordial words; and he was never seen to so much advantage as upon such occasions.

But William Brown was for the first time since the commencement of his visit a little out of his element in that fine house. Lady Overlaw, who liked handsome young men, had always been particularly kind to him, and had made him feel at home among the gentlemen and ladies of the county when they had come to dine at the palace in couples, of only half-a-dozen at a time. Now she was sitting between the Attorney-General and one of the Judges. There was a group of black coats and strange, shrewd faces round each of the Parliamentary colonels and minor barons; and even the local banker, whose dress and whiskers so oddly resembled those of the Duke of Courthope, was absorbed by the High Sheriff, while a portentous bevy of provincial dames, in full plume and full feather, sat in state upon the ottomans, like majesties too august for speech or movement. The young fellow was just beginning to feel the light irksome to him, and that his own hands were in his way, when his attention was attracted to the spare, bent figure of a gentleman in the evening dress of a dignitary of the church. He was talking to the Under-Secretary of the Post Office, who was attending the Assizes on some Government business, and had been staying for the last few days with the Duke.

The clergyman's back was turned towards him, but there was something in that bowed head and placid demeanour which seemed familiar to Lieutenant Brown. While wondering who this person could be, and yet unwilling to intrude upon a conversation which might not be intended for his ear, the Under-Secretary suddenly turned round and addressed him.

"Had good sport, Captain? There is no need, however, to ask you that, for I saw you go out with the Duke, and he never brings home a light bag. Here, allow me to present you to Dr. Mowledy, the new Dean of Drowth."

"Brown and I are old friends already," said the

Dean, affectionately taking his late pupil's hand; and so the prosperous soldier stood again in the presence of his best and earliest patron, whose lessons had first opened to him the gates to Fame and Fortune. He had paid his first visit to the Curate upon his return to England, but had found that he was away on a visit to his relatives in the North, whither he had not felt authorised to follow him; then he had written a letter very full of respect and gratitude, asking permission to see him on his return. Meantime, wealth and honour had at last found out the village priest, and he too was an honoured visitor at a Duke's house.

"I am glad to hear of your promotion, William," said Dr. Mowledy, kindly. "My thoughts have often followed you in India, and no one can have rejoiced more heartily in your success." The mild, earnest eyes of the Dean expressed far more than the mere words he spoke.

"May I presume also to congratulate you, sir?" answered the young man, respectfully; and he wrung the parson's hand in huge delight.

"Thank you, William," replied the Dean, in his simple, unassuming voice; and then he added, with that far-away, dreamy look which had become habitual to him, "It came very unexpectedly, and when I had long ceased to hope, or even to desire it. But I am grateful, and the more so because I owe it indirectly to your excellent mother."

"Yes," continued the clergyman, observing the mute surprise in his old pupil's face; "just before you went to India your mother had some business in London, which I never mentioned to you, thinking it needless at the time to do so. It is still more needless now, for it was of a painful character. My presence in London was also necessary, and I went. While there I was induced to call upon my cousin, Sir Dowdeswell-Mowledy, whom I had not seen for many years, and I have reason to believe that I owe my deanery to the kind offices of Lady Selina, his wife, with her brother, Lord Hanaper, the present Premier."

The second dinner bell rang just then and separated them—Dean Mowledy having been selected in a whisper by Lady Overlaw to take down the High Sheriff's mother, while to Lieutenant Brown was apportioned a partner of forty-five, who was descended from Hengist, and looked like it.

The dinner was stupid and heavy, as such dinners mostly are, and nothing but the princely arrangements of the Duke's household could have prevented it being tedious, if not ridiculous. No one whose establishment is not regulated on an expenditure of a hundred thousand a year could have ventured to dine so many pompous personages without a calamitous failure; but his Grace had a consummate major-domo, and everything went like clockwork—the dinner being really divided into messes of four, as royal dinners are, each served by two servants, one of whom presented the dishes of burnished gold, and the other poured out the proper wines to be taken with them, never turning aside to the right hand or to the left for any other concern.

It was over at last, and at a mystic sign which passed ·between Lady Overlaw and the lady of most ancient creation among the peeresses, the sea of plumes and laces rose and surged away. Then the gentlemen, much relieved by their departure, drew up their chairs in freer fashion to the table, passed the bottle briskly, and talked politics or something better, or something worse, in accordance with the ancient usage of the kingdom.

Under this new dispensation, William Brown was seated next the Under-Secretary of the Post Office who soon began to hold forth *ex cathedrâ*, as officials will, on the business which had brought him to the Assizes. He was a well-informed man, and spoke to the purpose. His immediate objects were two—the one being to watch the trial of a local postmaster for embezzlement, and the second being to establish better postal communications between the two principal market towns of the county; for those towns could only exchange ideas on paper through the instrumentality of two donkey-carts, whose owners had a vested interest in the public injury, and were the holders of a contract to carry Her Majesty's mails, which contract would not expire for a considerable period yet to come. Neither of the two people who had a vested interest in a nuisance which afflicted about forty thousand of their fellow-subjects could be compelled to give it up by legal methods, and therefore the Under-Secretary had felt constrained to attempt that dearest of all things to the British official mind, "a compromise." He had come down from his office at St. Martin's-le-Grand to negotiate with these vested interest holders, and to ascertain if they could not be induced to take more equitable views of the general welfare—for a consideration. His terms were handsome: he offered prompt payment, besides promises, and he was able therefore to express a hope that his mission would be crowned with success.

"Very stubborn old man, Krorl, though," observed the Duke, doubtfully. "You will find it tight work to get to windward of him." His Grace smiled; he knew the owners of all the vested interests for twenty miles round, and he had never known any one of them to be moved by public considerations.

"There are, Duke," replied the Under-Secretary sententiously, "ways and means. We have other mail contracts at our disposal, and I have held out hopes to Mr. Krorl that if he behaves himself we will bear him in mind, and put his name, and the name of his son-in-law who holds the other contract, down on our list. Those are our ways. If he objects to these terms, we shall bring the thing to a wrangle, and Mr. Attorney will have to deal with him. Those are our means. The first are pleasant, and the second strong. We always like to pat people with the palms of our hands before we close our knuckles; but when it comes to fist work we hit hard. It is our policy to do so—a good policy. It would never do to let off a man who makes himself troublesome, because if people once found out that it paid, everybody would begin to bother and assault us."

"Please do not cut out any more work for me, Bodger-Wyvil," interrupted the Attorney-General, addressing the Under-Secretary across the table; "come, a glass of wine, and let us hear no more of it."

"We have submitted the case to the solicitors of the Post Office," replied Mr. Bodger-Wyvil, "and they have already prepared a brief for your consideration, respecting those two donkey-carts, in order that we may be in readiness to answer questions upon the subject in the House of Commons. I am happy to inform you that *this* brief only weighs *one* hundred weight and a half, avoirdupois; *but* mark me, we have another in reserve for you."

"I shall then," said the Attorney-General, decisively, "throw them to the devil—that is, my devil, who is very much like the other, as most defendants say in cases where he is for the plaintiff."

"You must have very odd things pass through the Post Office sometimes, Bodger-Wyvil," observed the Duke graciously to his namesake, for he had not spoken before to him during dinner. "A glass of wine —port or claret?"

"Claret, Duke," replied the official, colouring slightly with pleasure, at this public recognition of the family name he had assumed in right of his grandmother, by the head of the house of Courthope; and then he added, "We have indeed strange things; but that which I think affected me most was a little crumpled bit of paper which fell into my hands more than twenty years ago, when I was in the Dead-Letter Department. It might have been scrawled with a skewer, it was so ill-written, and was almost illegible, for it had been blistered by tears. The words it contained were very few, but touching, and I have remembered them ever since. They ran thus:—

"'Come back, please. Dear, kind gentleman, O, do come back, or I shall die. Come back for the love of God. I am with child.'"

"Very romantic," said the Duke, dryly. "Pass the bottle. That old East India Madeira is with you, and the Judge drinks nothing else."

"Did you never know to whom it was addressed?" enquired Dean Mowledy, with interest.

"O yes," replied the Under-Secretary. "It was directed in rather a scholarly hand, in strange contrast with the writing inside, and bore the postmark of a place you know very well. It came from Wakefield-in-the-Marsh."

"Indeed," said the Curate, much moved, and bethinking him which of his parishioners could have loved so unwisely, and have been so cruelly abandoned in her trouble. "Can you remember the name of the person to whom it was directed?"

"I can," replied the Under-Secretary, "for the whole thing made an impression upon me for which I cannot account. Moreover, the address, though well written, appeared to have been penned by some one who lived out of the world, and was unaccustomed to direct letters, or at least letters of business to commercial people. This was the superscription of it:—

To Mr. Marmaduke Walker,
Dealer in Fermented Liquors,
Upper Street, Islington.

"There was no such person as Mr. Marmaduke Walker living at that time in Upper Street, Islington, and therefore the communication to him was returned in due course to the Dead-Letter Office, where it came into my hands, also in the usual way, and I opened it. There was neither date nor address inside, and consequently, after the usual lapse of time necessary to provide for possible inquiries, it was destroyed."

"And was there no signature to it?" asked Dean

Mowledy, who now spoke very faintly and turned extremely pale.

"I am afraid I am telling you Government secrets, Mr. Dean," answered the Under-Secretary, "but it is so long ago that, at all events, I cannot be accused of selling early intelligence. The name inside was simply 'Madge.'"

"What's the matter, sir?" said William Brown, starting suddenly up, and making towards the Dean, whose head had fallen backwards on his chair.

"Here, Buffet! Walters!" called the Duke to his servants. "Throw open the windows, and ask Dr. Bridgeman to step downstairs immediately. The Dean has fainted, I suppose," added his Grace, turning with real concern to his guest, who slowly revived to consciousness as the cool air flooded into the banquet hall. "I suppose it must be the heat of the room."

CHAPTER VIII.

The Heir of Courthope.

NOT long after the return of William Brown to England, Lord Punjaub and the Marquis of Kinsgear came back also; the one having been raised to the rank of a full general, and the other to that of lieutenant-colonel, promotion always travelling by special trains for the nobility. Both of them had, however, well earned their advancement. The Marquis, having risen chiefly by death vacancies, owed but little on this occasion to the accident of his birth, while Lord Punjaub had only been treated according to the usual rules of military precedence. It had been a fine thing for him at the outset of his career to be the brother and then the uncle of a duke, and many a stepping-stone had been put in his way to help him over dangerous places in consequence; his position, indeed, had given him opportunities of acquiring distinction which are denied to meaner men. But having once attained a certain rank by these means, favour was no longer of much use to him. He was surrounded by competitors as noble and high born as himself; and whose connections were quite as influential. Moreover, the eyes of the public were on him, and it would have been impossible to bestow honours upon him if he had not more or less deserved them. He could neither have obtained a command of importance, nor have held one after the loss of an ill-fought battle, or the commission of any signal blunder. Upon the whole, therefore, Anglo-Indian notions were very well satisfied with the rewards bestowed on the two noblemen; and it was said and printed in many places that they had only been fairly dealt by when their services were handsomely and promptly acknowledged.

But the time had come when nothing which this world has to offer could be of much value to the young Marquis. His health had steadily declined since he had received that wound in the Indian battle, and at last the physicians who had attended upon him at Calcutta had reluctantly consented to his return homewards.

"It will exhaust his strength, and he would live longer if he were not moved from here," objected one medical man of a very ripe experience. "Patients whose vitality is already low are often killed by the exertion of changing from one place to another, whereas they would have weeks, perhaps months of life in them if they were kept quiet, and taught to spare the small quantity of strength which remains to them."

"Ah!" answered a more courtly colleague, "that is true; but the Marquis of Kinsgear is a nobleman of the highest rank. He will die in any case, and I would rather the responsibility of treating him rested on others than upon us. His connections might make a great noise about it, and I have known the reputation of very eminent practitioners compromised by such a death."

"Humph!" ejaculated the first speaker at one of the numerous consultations which preceded Lord Kinsgear's departure, "my conscience is not quite easy. The voyage home will exhaust him completely, and he will only reach England to look his last upon it."

"Exactly," replied the other physician, "but the principal thing is that he should be able to reach home at all; and if he remains here only a little longer, that is extremely problematical. Now there must be family arrangements and interests of great consequence to settle in the case of such an important death as his; and therefore our duty is to restore him to his friends as soon as possible. I hear, by the way, that the Marquis received his wound from that famous French renegade who was in the Begum's service— Malvoisin I think they called him. He was recognised by Highlowes, who knew him when he was Vice-Consul somewhere."

"It is," observed a third physician, without paying any attention to the last remark of his professional colleague, "taking from him his only chance of a precarious existence for a few months; nevertheless, I agree with the opinion that he should be sent home at once for the reasons just stated."

So Lord Kinsgear, to the great scandal of the Radical newspapers, which cried out against favouritism, obtained leave of absence upon sick certificate, and some weeks afterwards arrived at Beaumanoir with Lord Punjaub; not being even permitted to live his natural and appointed time because he was a marquis. His title and great fortunes had always been unlucky to him. He had never enjoyed their possession, and yet he was summarily sent home to die because of them. Had he been a cheesemonger like his ancestor by his mother's side, whom in constitution and mental endowments he most resembled, he might have been a useful and happy man and have attained a good old age; as it was, he had always been misplaced in the world. It cost him a persistent effort to fill the position which had been assigned him in it, and constant calls had been made upon his energies which his nature could not answer. Few and rare had been the times when the faint strain of Wyldwyl blood had manifested itself in him; at all others he had been lymphatic and indifferent; and the splendour with which he had been surrounded had only wearied him.

He was brought down in an invalid carriage to the palace where his family had kept high state for centuries, and not a footfall was suffered to be heard about the gorgeous chambers of his home, after he was carried up-stairs and laid upon the bed from which he was never to rise again in mortal form. The hand of the destroyer was quite visible upon him, and those who looked upon his livid face and wasted limbs could cherish no illusions as to his possible recovery. The light in his eyes was nearly extinct, his lips were white, and there was that tightening and glazed appearance of the skin over the upper part of his face which announces approaching dissolution. He seemed to be nearly dead already, and only rallied for a short season when he saw William Brown. He appeared to feel under some restraint in his father's presence, and though his manner was respectful and becoming to the last, he only answered the questions put to him, and voluntarily said nothing. It was as though he felt himself a being apart from that splendid and haughty race which claimed him as its representative, and considered himself an unwilling intruder upon it. He had been very happy as a boy in his mother's dower house, with his scantily furnished room and his mechanical occupations. He had never been altogether at his ease after he was removed from them.

The hopeless condition of Lord Kinsgear was a cause of terrible anxiety to the Duke of Courthope, all of whose plans were upset by his son's illness. He earnestly pressed William Brown to prolong his visit, because the Marquis only revived in his society, and would not hear of his going away.

"Don't leave me, Willie," he said, faintly. "I shall not trouble you long; you must make this your home as long as I am here, and I hope afterwards."

So an extension of the Lieutenant's leave was obtained from the Horse Guards, and William Brown stopped on at Beaumanoir.

It might have been evident to any one better acquainted with the ways of the world than this young soldier of fortune, that the Duke of Courthope had far other and deeper causes for anxiety connected with his son's death than even the sorrow which parental affection must have inspired for the loss of his only son and heir. Though all the guests but Lady Overlaw and some near relations of the Wyldwyls had departed from Beaumanoir in presence of the grief which had descended like a pall upon the great house, flys and carriages were hurrying backwards and forwards through the Park to the station all day long at intervals, and generally they deposited a lawyer, or a lawyer's chief clerk, who would remain often for many hours closeted with his Grace, and then hurry away with sheaves of paper and parchments in blue bags. Not even the express trains which sped to London thrice a day could keep pace with the hurried rush of legal business consequent upon the expected demise of the Marquis; and messengers and telegrams were despatched hot foot with supplementary instructions, or answers to interrogations from Lincoln's Inn.

Mr. Sharpe had now his own apartments in the palace, and had been there for days, drafting documents, which his clerks took away and brought back upon sheets of lambskin with large seals and gaudy stamps attached to them: narrow silken ribbons bound them together. Lawyers are very neat in their instruments of torture. The Duke of Courthope would sit with haggard eyes in the great Gothic library with its carved oak sculpturing and oriel windows, while these things were doing, and pore painfully hour after hour over the papers which his solicitors sent to him.

It may have been fact or fancy, but late one evening, when the household were gone to bed, and Lady

Overlaw went into the library for the last volume of the last new novel which had arrived from London; she dreamed that she saw the splendid noble, to whom life had hitherto been one long festival, with his head bowed upon his hands, and moaning grievously. Before him were whole reams of foolscap fresh covered with the drafts of legal documents, and on their margins were annotations in the Duke's own hand. On either side of him were two tall candlesticks, which had been burning so long that the lights flared in their sockets and gave a gaunt unearthly aspect to the apartment as they flickered and blazed by turns. The first beams of a moon which rose late, streamed in through the oriel windows and touched the dark colouring of a portrait by Vandyck as it hung stern and silent amidst the hard carved oak around. It was the picture of the Lord Chief Justice Wyldwyl—an upright judge, who had redeemed the fortunes of Philip Wyldwyl, Earl of Allswon, in the time of Charles the First.

The beautiful lady stopped, with the silver lamp which had lighted her from her dressing-room in her hand, and looked at him. She might have stood for a picture of Pity watching over Sorrow, and she made a hesitating step towards him; for her heart, light and frivolous as it was, had been touched by that supreme agony in one so proud and great. But the Duke—if her fancy, overwrought by some romance, had not deceived her altogether—lifted up his head instantly at the sound of her footstep, and rising with the knightly grace which belonged to him, came towards her with a gallant smile and lofty courtesy.

"Belle Cousine!" said he. "What, eyes unclosed so late! I shall have some of the park-keepers taking them for stars, and telling marvels to his neighbours of how my place is haunted by heavenly visitors. Stay," he added kindly, "let *me* look for your book;" and then, when he had found it, he conducted her to the door and held it open for her as she passed through, and bade her a chivalrous good-night. He was so grand a prince of manners that perhaps she loved him then, and she went onwards with footsteps which seemed to hesitate. For a moment—it was when she reached the foot of the private staircase which led to her own suite of rooms—she turned and looked back. But the massive door of the library had been gently closed when she retired beyond it, and the Lord of Beaumanoir was alone again with his anguish. He toiled on with those papers all through the night, covering every inch of blank space on them with his marginal notes, and his features looked sometimes very shrewd and keen as he did so. The morning broke dim and grey, and the air, chilled by showers, was very bleak in the lofty room; but still he worked on with knitted brows and close attention, as one who fought for his life with an invisible enemy who must be combated upon paper. If there was any lawyer who was trying then to take advantage of him the case of that lawyer was not hopeful. Some of the acumen of Judge Wyldwyl's mind was showing itself, struggling out of the superincumbent load of idleness and pleasure which had weighed it down so long. Old men who had passed half a century in the law courts would be amazed and puzzled by that night's work; for the Duke was brought to bay, and defending himself like a stag of ten who turns upon his hunters.

At about nine o'clock he rang for his valet, bathed

himself, dressed entirely afresh, and ordered coffee; then he sent to ask if Lord Kinsgear was awake, for Mr. Sharpe was with his Grace again, and had brought a parchment deed ready for signature.

The Duke showed no outward trace of his vigil, but he looked very anxious till the answer came from his son's sick-room, pressing his lips together and drawing down one side of his mouth in a way he had when he had determined to act with resolution, or, if needs must, with harshness, and to stifle his natural feelings, which were considerate and amiable to all who were immediately about his presence.

Presently the servant came back with a message from the Duke's domestic physician, saying that Lord Kinsgear was awake, but very feeble, and that Captain Brown had been sitting up all night with him.

"I had rather he hadn't," said Mr. Sharpe, coarsely, when the servant was gone. "Captain Brown is always with him in business hours—and out of them."

"What's Captain Brown to you?" answered the Duke, sternly. "You want to have the thing signed, and I will take care *that* is done." He touched the deed scornfully as he spoke, and Mr. Sharpe, bully as he was, perceived that he had struck some chord with a sharp note, and that it would not be safe to touch it again.

"It *must* be done, I suppose, Sharpe?" asked the Duke, after a pause.

"It *must*," answered the lawyer, "certainly, your Grace."

"Nothing from me or Lord George will do, instead of disturbing the dying boy in his last moments with this trumpery? It is a ghastly practice yours, to hunt a man out of the world with a pack of bonds and assignments after him."

"Nothing else will do, your Grace," answered Mr. Sharpe, decisively, "because his Lordship is his mother's heir, and the latest securities touched her property."

"Well then, sir, follow me," said the Duke, coldly, and he led the way with an unfaltering step to the chamber where the dying Marquis lay.

CHAPTER IX.

Amabel Wyldwyl.

WHEN the Duke of Courthope and Mr. Sharpe entered the sick-room of Lord Kinsgear, they found him talking feebly to William Brown, who was seated by his bed-side. The young men were going over their Indian campaign again, as they used to do when together, and recalling many a stirring scene of battle and of bivouac. There was even a faint flush upon the faded cheek of the Marquis which half resembled a sign of returning health; and perhaps, so strong is life before grief has sapped its sources, he might have then revived had he been left at rest. His native air had done something for him, and the companionship of his comrade seemed to have given him new strength, or, perhaps, a new interest in existence. William Brown, who had a creative mind, was showing the Marquis the model of a new pontoon bridge upon which he had been engaged for some time past, and had brought to great perfection; for he was always thinking of his profession, and devising something which might be useful in it, having reflected that behind every difficulty there lurks an invention. He had, therefore, put together, upon a new system, a number of flat-bottomed air-boats, very strong, very portable, and very easily managed. The Marquis, who was fond of mechanics, and understood all things relating to them extremely well, had dropped off to sleep on the previous night with his mind pleasantly occupied about this pontoon bridge, and had slept soundly, so he woke refreshed. The two officers were busy with their plan for facilitating the transport of troops across rivers. The Marquis sat propped up by pillows, and his wan hands held the soldierly toy, pointing out where it was defective and might be strengthened, or made to fold into a smaller compass.

He closed his eyes wearily when the Duke entered, and the transitory look of restored vigour faded out of his face. His head fell back upon the pillows, though a minute before it had been bent eagerly forward, and a petulant expression flitted over his countenance.

"What do they want of me now, Willie?" he muttered. "I signed something yesterday, and the day before, and the day before that. When will it be all over? I wish we were back in India under canvas again. It was so pleasant."

"It will all come right," said Young Brown. "You are ten times better to-day, you know. There's the Duke speaking to you. Come, cheer up."

Meantime, while the young men exchanged these words, his Grace had entered the room, and stood in the place of William Brown, who had risen respectfully to make way for him. He was too fine a gentleman, however, to disturb his guest without an apology, and courteously laid his hand for an instant on the Lieutenant's arm, as though he desired to detain him, and took his place at last only with a deprecatory bow and polished word. "I beg," said the Duke, kindly, "that you will not move, Captain—that is, unless you prefer the society of Lady Overlaw to that of the lawyers. You will find her in the breakfast-room, a little jealous of your deserting her levee so often." Then, and not till then, the Duke sat down in the chair which his guest had occupied, and William Brown discreetly retired; feeling, but neither seeing nor hearing, that he was in the way.

The room was nearly full when he left it. Not only the Duke and the lawyer were there, but Mr. Senior, the steward of the household, and Eaves, the head footman, as well as one of Mr. Sharpe's clerks, who had been sent for to attest the deed which the dying man was required to sign that day. They were in all five persons, and their presence seemed to overpower the Marquis, as though their robust vitality oppressed and was too much for him.

Leaving them there Mr. Brown took his way through stately corridors and storied picture-galleries, away to the breakfast-room, which was a delightful apartment surrounded by conservatories, and opened on to a flower-garden with a view of the lake. It had a southern aspect, and was so sheltered that it was possible to breakfast there with the windows open even in the finer winter days. It was quite at the farther end of the house, and was one of those quiet pretty dwelling-rooms which are sometimes found, even in palaces, as a refuge from splendour.

William Brown walked with noiseless footstep over the velvet-pile carpets; and his mind was still too newly in possession of the good fortune which had come to him to be quite at rest. He was vain of his epaulettes and commission as an officer in Her Majesty's service. He was still more vain of his regiment, and had a lurking contempt, though he was considerately careful not to show it, for every one who was not a cavalry officer who had seen service in India.

Presently he heard the voices of Lady Overlaw and Mr. Heriot, who had just arrived on business at the palace by the morning mail train.

"I am glad to inform your Ladyship," he heard the lawyer say, in that bland punctilious tone peculiar to the princes of his caste, "that I have satisfactorily concluded the little affair between your Ladyship and the late Lord Overlaw's executors. I intimated to them that I had myself prepared the settlements when your Ladyship had consented to marry the late Lord Overlaw; and—ehem!"—here the lawyer raised his forefinger to add emphasis to his words—"and with a view to possible contingencies, and considering that his Lordship was a nobleman of somewhat advanced years, I had—ehem—with due regard to my professional obligations towards your Ladyship and the illustrious family of Courthope, which I had professionally represented for a considerable period—I had provided that they should be extremely stringent. Briefly, therefore, I am rejoiced to acquaint your Ladyship that I have required that the executors shall purchase a Government annuity for your Ladyship before any part of the late Lord Overlaw's assets are distributed among his creditors; there being no legal proof whatever that his Lordship was insolvent at the time when his marriage was contracted."

"Heigho!" sighed Lady Overlaw; "my husband was the best friend I ever had, and his death was the only thing that ever cost me a tear."

"Ehem!" coughed Mr. Heriot politely, for he had heard different accounts of her Ladyship's domestic relations with the deceased peer: though she spoke quite truly; and such little trifle of a heart as she had ever had, had been really given to the dead lord, who indulged, spoiled, amused, and protected her with an inexhaustible and patient tenderness, such as none ever could or would show to her again.

"And pray," inquired the great solicitor, "may I ask your Ladyship who is staying at the palace— ehem, under the present melancholy circumstances? Are Lord George and his beautiful daughter here?"

It was always a grand day for Mr. Heriot when he came to Beaumanoir, and he liked to sun himself among the grand company, and hear the fine names of those whom he was about to meet in the confidential capacity of the most deeply trusted adviser of the ducal house.

"Lord George, that is to say, Lord Punjaub, and his daughter, are expected to-day," replied Lady Overlaw; "for the rest we have only my aunt, Lady Clanmore, whom you know; a few people who are always here, and—oh yes—there is a Mr. Brown, who I understand was a charity boy, and is now a sort of companion, or man-governess, to the Marquis; he is very stupid, and talks to me about 'field telegraphs,' I think. But, dear me, I declare there he is, coming through the conservatory."

"How do you do, Captain? See, I have kept some peaches for you,"—and her Ladyship was all smiles and gracious gossip directly.

The young fellow did not sulk, though he could not help hearing what had been said of him; and she knew that he knew it, but was no more embarrassed than great ladies usually are when they have said or done something rude. Moreover, the Lieutenant had the instincts of a gentleman, and behaved well under punishment; but he felt it keenly, and therefore it did him good, for it cured him of consequentiousness for the rest of his life, and taught him that there was upon earth something which commanded more universal admiration than a lieutenant's commission; that it would not quite do to show himself a military pedant before ladies, unless he expected to be laughed at; and that fine society is not given to over-estimating those who suddenly obtain access to it; and that it finds out about them rather more than they know themselves, whatever the specious nothings of good manners might indicate to the contrary notwithstanding.

Still the young man had received a severe, though a wholesome lesson, and he smarted under it. He felt almost ashamed to go back to his friend's sick-room, lest he should be marked by the servants as a toady and a sycophant who gave his companionship for wages and succulent food. He wandered through the great rooms when he had quitted Lady Overlaw and Mr. Heriot after breakfast, becoming every moment more dejected. He no longer liked to order a horse for a ride in the park, or to send for one of the keepers and a couple of dogs, as he would have done yesterday; he who was looked upon as a charity-boy, and an upper servant. He was degraded in his own esteem; he felt himself to be an interloper and an intruder, who had no right to be among all that marble and carved oak, and gilding, and suits of armour, and pictures, every one of which was probably worth more than he could ever expect to win: —a poor soldier of fortune raised from the ranks to a place where he was only despised by those born to fill it; he had better, he thought bitterly, have remained a private, or at most a non-commissioned officer, and been content to associate with his equals, since there were barriers to intercourse with gentlefolks which no exertions or merits of his own, if he had merits, could surmount; and very likely he had no merits: no, it was quite certain that he had none. Had not Lady Overlaw sneered at him for being stupid? She was a great lady, and must have judged him better than he judged himself. He was a fool, an idiot,— yes, a pretentious donkey—that was the best description of him. He would go back to barracks again. Colonel Oakes liked him, and if he resigned his post as aide-de-camp to Lord Punjaub, as he would do, some day he might be made adjutant of his regiment, and then he would have enough to do; and, meanwhile, he could forget the baseness of his origin in the call of the trumpet to stable-duty. He was perhaps good enough to associate with a horse if not with dukes and marquises and fine ladies.

He had wandered into the library while in this

contented frame of mind, and looked listlessly out of window, thinking of how he should take leave of the Duke that day. The weather was gusty and sad; great lead-coloured clouds rolled up heavily from the west, and now and then a shower seemed to sweep scornfully over the landscape. A travelling-carriage-and-four, piled high with imperials, came galloping up the avenue, arriving from the station, which was a good way off, owing to the great extent of the park; the late Duke would not allow it to be cut up when the railway was making, so that he and his guests were obliged to use post-horses; and the Courthope arms at Revel was one of the few posting-inns still in existence. Doubtless the carriage contained some more of the relatives or dependents of the noble family whose heir was dying. He had come from the station in a fly; and the lowest menials of the place must have made a mock at him, he fancied now.

He was still torturing himself, and might have imagined that he had committed the unpardonable sin, or that he was a leper, before he had done, so deeply had Lady Overlaw's contempt stung him; but while he was honestly trying to hurt his feelings a little more, the library door was suddenly flung open, and a radiant vision, all joy and laughter, came bounding up to him on feet of air, looked archly at him for a moment, then dropped a demure curtsey, and threw her arms round his neck and kissed him.

"Thank you for getting well, Cousin Kinsgear. I am so happy; and it is so nice. Come out into the garden with me. I want to see my golden pheasants again," said this young person.

"Hallo, Brown," cried the deep voice of Lord

Punjaub, who now entered the room; "I told you I would show you my daughter when I could get her back from Ireland. Missy, Lieutenant Brown, one of the finest fellows in the army, and a member of my family."

The General spoke in Indian fashion of his aide-de-camp, but Lieutenant Brown looked as if he had just dropped from the clouds, and was wonder-stricken at what had happened to him; while Miss Wyldwyl had disappeared, and was not seen again till dinner-time, when she was so entirely absorbed in a conversation with the Dowager Marchioness of Newcomen that she did not even see Mr. Brown, which was at least extraordinary after her conduct in the library; and the General scolded her for being "uncivil to one of the finest young fellows in the service, you minx."

"I hate fine young fellows, Pa," answered the young lady, with much spirit. "They are always in the way when they are not wanted. They ought to be put to death."

Somehow or other it happened that after this remarkable incident in his biography Lieutenant Brown had no desire to leave Beaumanoir that day, or for some time afterwards. Had he not his duties as aide-de-camp to Lord Punjaub to attend to? He was on leave of absence; but what of that? The General was staying in the same house with him, and the first duty of a soldier was obedience. The General had always plenty of employment for him, for his Lordship was accustomed to be surrounded by young men who were ready to gallop forty miles before breakfast at his nod, and liked it. He could not do without them, and it was, "Here, Brown, just step up to the village, will you, and get some sweetmeats for that girl of mine;" or, "Brown, that tyrant of ours wants a new sash from Howell and James'. Bring it down with you this afternoon." Indeed it appeared as if the young lady herself insisted that these commissions should be executed by the handsome young aide-de-camp, evincing upon every occasion a passionate eagerness to get him out of the way; yet never failing to ask when he would come back again. But she would not speak to him or look at him, or even be introduced to him, saying, pertly, that she knew a great deal too much about him as it was; and the General, who had hitherto found her always the charm and darling of his "family," as they call aides-de-camp in India, was surprised and a little hurt at her capricious behaviour towards his favourite. "A Victoria Cross too, Missy, think of that. Ho! ho! think of that," remonstrated the old soldier, who had a mighty idea of military distinctions, as it was right and becoming that he should have. But nothing would move Miss Amabel Wyldwyl from her entrenchments, and when her father pleaded very hard with her for Young Brown, by-and-by she got into a way of putting one of her small hands before his mouth, and pretending to stop her ears with the other. Yet, when he said no more, it was she who began to talk of the soldier.

He seemed to be never out of her head and she was constantly mocking him. At dinner, when Lord George Wyldwyl one day carved the roast beef in the old fashion, the Duke being obliged to attend the quarter sessions, of which he was chairman, Miss Amabel left the contents of her plate untouched.

"What, no roast beef, Missy?" roared the General.

"Ho! ho! no roast beef. I never heard of such a thing in the whole course of my life!" The General was fond of large language, and had a certain amplitude in his talk as in everything else. There was always something to spare about what he said or did.

"I don't like it, Pa," she answered, with a wry face, all make-believe.

"Not like roast beef, Missy!" exclaimed Lord Punjaub in extreme astonishment.

"I like *some* of it, Pa," said Miss Amabel, "but you have given me the outside, and I cannot *eat* Brown, though you are so fond of it, you know, Pa."

It was girlish talk, and not very wise or very witty, but then Miss Wyldwyl was only a girl.

"There is a bullet gone the way of my aide-de-camp again!" said the General, looking at his daughter with his honest eyes full of something that was half laughter and half displeasure.

"Lieutenant Bro—, I beg your pardon, papa, but I meant to say that the Lieutenant will not mind it, Pa, because he is so *bold*. I think you said something about the Victoria Cross? What is the Victoria Cross, Pa?"

"Finest thing in the army, Missy," answered the General, briefly, with his mouth full. "It is the reward of valour."

"Is it brown too, papa?" inquired the young lady, innocently.

Now the Lieutenant was absent during these conversations about him, having been despatched hither or thither in hot haste. Miss Wyldwyl was never tired of discussing his demerits when he was absent; nevertheless, when Lady Overlaw brought up the story of the charity-boy in her hearing, her eyes lighted up with a pretty enthusiasm.

"Brave men," she said, glowing with the warmth of her praise till her beauty became a marvel, "have no need of ancestry, and my father says that Mr. Brown is a hero."

"Take care, Belle!" smiled Lady Overlaw, arching her eyebrows, and just then the young lieutenant entered the room, having returned with a box of sugar-plums from London. His countenance was quite radiant; he never felt the shafts which the wayward girl threw at him after that. A few days later, too, when he was sent for to attend Lord Punjaub in his afternoon ride and found Miss Wyldwyl already mounted on the other side of him, the ice was broken henceforth between them.

"Ho! ho!" laughed the General, as he observed the Lieutenant assisting his daughter, with a fine sense of discipline, to dismount, as they halted upon their return before the noble terraces which rose flight upon flight before the grand entrance of Beaumanoir. "Ho! ho! Missy, you have taken possession of my aide-de-camp as usual, I see. He will never find time to do anything more for me."

It was her father's turn to tease her now; and he did so everlastingly without truce or mercy.

CHAPTER X.

The Anglo-Indian.

VERY many years before the date at which this story has now arrived Lord George Wyldwyl had returned to England on furlough. He was then only a Captain of Hussars, and the law, or rather the custom of entail and primogeniture which gave everything to the eldest sons of great families and nothing to the younger ones, had made him a very poor man. Although after the early death of his brother Alfred there was only one life between him and the hereditary wealth of the Wyldwyls, he had not a shilling beyond his captain's pay. But there was a general opinion in high places that he had behaved extremely well in some settlement, rendered necessary by the birth of an heir to his brother, the Duke of Courthope, and both the Court and the Ministry entertained a strong feeling that "something should be done for Lord George." Now this is generally the beginning of a great fortune in England. There are young men, and even young noblemen, against whom there exists a prejudice at the palace, and about the public offices. It is a tacit, obstinate, and often an inexplicable thing, but whenever it makes itself felt the name of the person whom it affects seems in some occult manner to be put out for a generation; often, indeed, to revive under a series of favours which take the guise of atonements in the next. In the case of Lord George, however, it was understood that the family influence was to be reserved for him, and concentrated in his person. He was made one of the royal aides-de-camp; he was put into Parliament, and he was promised a post of under-secretary at the Horse Guards as soon as there should be a vacancy or one could be made. Then all the ladies of the great house to which he belonged took him up and determined that he should make a rich marriage. Lady Trecorne and Lady Pencarrow both prepared two Cornish heiresses for him. He might have become one of the largest mine-owners in the country if he had hearkened to Lady Pencarrow, and Lady Trecorne would have provided him with pilchard fisheries and jetsam and flotsam without end. Lady Hanaper and the Lady Overlaw of that day were equally active. The one presented him to the only daughter of a defunct loan contractor, to whom her husband was guardian, so that there could be no doubt about a property which was chiefly in the public funds; the other introduced him to the young widow of an unreformed bishop, who had died worth nearly a million sterling.

But Lord George had disappointed all their efforts to make him rich; he seemed to be quite contented with his own means, and even lived within them. It required no great sacrifice to do so. His sole expenses were his horses, his uniform, and his tailor's bills, which were not large, for when Lord George dressed in plain clothes, the bucks and bloods of the period were accustomed to say with a smile that they were "very plain clothes." No wonder; they themselves were accustomed to wear cravats of great height, and to slide down an inclined plane into moist buckskin breeches, that no wrinkle might appear in these garments to mar the perfect symmetry of their legs. They had portentous wigs, and silver buttons as large as hand mirrors on their coats; while Lord George cared for none of these things. For the rest, twenty houses were always open to him in town and country, where he might live at free quarters and was welcome as healthy weather. He might have passed his existence in this way had he pleased to do so, at less cost to himself than it takes to keep a lawyer's clerk; for he was "born invited" everywhere, and the chimney-piece of his bachelor lodging in St. James's Street was never without engagements for three weeks at least upon it. It was somewhat difficult, however, to get hold of Lord George. Dinner-cards and three-cornered notes went on accumulating till they formed quite a heap, and his servant was at last induced by much persuasion to sell them at a high price to a family in Russell Square, which loved to boast of titled visitors and to take high names in vain. Meanwhile, the young nobleman mounted his horse every day at three o'clock, and rode briskly down to a little cottage by the river-side at Walton-upon-Thames, where dwelt an old sea captain and his daughter. Abandoning the fashionable world of London, with all its greed and hungering ambitions, he took tea and water-cress, and heard ballads sung in a sweet bird-like voice by the river-side. So to him said the sea captain at length, "My daughter's happiness is at stake; you must come to us no more."

"How now, sir?" answered bluff Lord George. "She accepted me for her husband yesterday, and I am come to ask your consent to the wedding. Kate might do better than take a penniless beggar like me, but she has given me her word, and I have saved five hundred pounds to rig us out."

So the two men shook hands, and London learned with sneers and some astonishment that Lord George Wyldwyl and Katherine Howard, only daughter of Captain Ralph Howard, R. N., had been married in Walton Church, without more ado than ordinary mortals; and that they probably had not four hundred a year between them.

Lady Pencarrow was the only person of quality who did not give up Lord George after that. It is one thing to have a young lord who may be useful, and who is at least ornamental, to dinner, and another to have a married man with an ill-dressed wife arriving on foot from a suburban lodging. Marriage fixes the position of a man, and as Lord George's wife was unknown beyond the parish of Walton, polite society had no desire for her acquaintance. The beautiful widow of Lord Pencarrow—now widow of Lord Alfred Wyldwyl too, had truth been known—never withdrew her friendship from him. She obtained an offer of the secretaryship to the Embassy at Vienna for him from Lord Hanaper, for diplomacy was not a regular profession then; and finding that he would not leave the army she lodged the price of his majority in the hands of his agents, and she gave the Pencarrow jewels, which were the finest in the kingdom, to his wife. She was for ever sending him costly presents, now a charger, now a collection of rare arms; and she presented him with the Parliamentary qualification of £300 a year in land, which was then needed, in the shape of a considerable estate she had purchased from a part of the splendid fortune bequeathed to her, and

which she had scrupulously put aside for some years.
But Lord George had declined to receive any of her
bounties, and returned them all. The money lodged
at his army agents', Messrs. Cox & Co., was paid back
to the bankers of the Countess; the Parliamentary
qualification was re-assigned to her Ladyship immediately it had served its purpose; Lord George per-
sisting upon looking at its presentation to him only as
an ordinary courtesy usual at the time between the
friends and relatives of considerable political personages, and by no means as a gift which he could
in anywise accept for himself. Horses and jewels were
declined likewise. When Lady Pencarrow died, a
portrait of the honest and single-minded soldier was
found next her heart; and she willed her whole property in trust to him for the Duke of Courthope, after
having vainly entreated him again and again to take
at least a life-interest in it for himself. But he would
not; and all through the long second widowhood of
the Countess, whenever she heard speech of worth and
honour she thought of George Wyldwyl, and cherished
for him a feeling which was like hero-worship. For
forty years she had never appeared in public but once,
and then she had only taken her place in the gallery
to hear the thanks of Parliament voted to the famous
Indian General.

"I have not dared," so the high-descended lady
wrote to him, in the excess of her admiration and
humility, "I have not dared to subscribe for the sword
of honour which I hear is to be presented to you,
since you forbade me years ago to restore you any
part of that which I and mine have taken from you;
but I have planted another laurel on your lands of

Pencarrow, that you may see how I have gloried in your glory, whenever you come to claim possession of the poor place which is all your magnanimous soul has left you in lieu of Beaumanoir and two dukedoms."

It so happened that Lord George did not make such a bad marriage after all, and society might have looked better on it could society have seen into the future; but when did society ever do that? Captain Howard was a man of good family, who had preserved the records of his genealogy very carefully, and they stood him in good stead before he died. A distant relative of this poor naval officer had emigrated to America in his youth, and returned in his old age to the home country to seek for an heir of his own blood to succeed to one of the most colossal fortunes of the New World. Captain Howard, happy in his cottage on the banks of the Thames and his daughter's letters, which reached him every post from India, referred his kinsman coldly to the Heralds' Office, and shortly afterwards was surprised to hear that he was declared sole legatee and executor of one Mr. Silas Howard, of New York and South Carolina, whom he had never seen but once, upon the condition that he could establish his descent from a Sir Rupert Howard who fell at Naseby, and who was supposed to be their common ancestor. The proofs being readily forthcoming he entered into possession of a large property, minus only the duty or tax to the Crown upon it. But he never left his cottage, and when he died Lord George Wyldwyl's wife received it all, with the accumulations of a huge capital placed out at American interest, untouched. The Indian soldier was amazed to hear one day at tiffin that he owned a railway, and a plantation well stocked with slaves, and that he kept an hotel, and a manufactory for small arms, a ready-made clothes' shop at Washington, and a store at New Orleans. He handed this perplexing acquisition, body and bones, to Mr. Mortmain. He and his wife laughed over it, and never gave two thoughts to the subject, except that he teased her and called her the "Begum" now and then.

They did not want the money; he was acting-governor of Madras at the time, and had quite enough to do to attend to some races which were going on under his patronage. He had more money than he could spend; he did not play, he did not care for magnificence, having seen enough of play and splendour in his youth. He lived merely in the midst of a rude plenty; kept open house for all comers, and threw rupees about to every one who wanted them. Money was always pouring in upon him; he was deluged with it. There was his general's pay, his pay as acting-governor, and then his allowances, and the salaries of four or five sinecures he had in India and in England. He lived rent-free, always had lived rent-free as long as he could remember now; ever since he gave up his lodging in St. James's Street, and moved into the Walton cottage just after he was married. His horses were all foraged for him, and stabled and groomed. They never seemed to wear out, and he got many of them as presents. His very plate, off which he ate, and the table linen it was put upon, and the chair on which he sat, were all found for him by "John Company." For many years he had neither chick nor child, and he and his wife seemed to have opened their hearts and adopted the whole army.

It was a sad day for the Indian General when a daughter was at last born to him; for her mother, the very joy and sunshine of his life, died in childbirth. It was long before the helpless little thing she had left behind her could take any place in the affections of the bereaved widower; but when the motherless girl had once entered into his vacant heart, she reigned supreme there.

Lady Selina Petty-Pells brought the child up among her own offspring, and she soon budded into as fair a flower as his own poor lost Kate had seemed when first Lord George had seen her. As soon as he could bear his anguish he had called on Lady Selina, and thanked her. She was a good woman, though she turned the light and frivolous side of her mind outwards to the world. But there was no better-ordered house than hers; and the Queen of Sheba, as they called her, though bent on receiving half Calcutta every evening she did not go abroad herself, was always to be found in her nursery, primer in hand, till two o'clock in the afternoon, when she dined with her children and their governesses.

Amabel Wyldwyl became a great favourite with her; and if ever there was a family fight in the nursery, Lady Selina always allied herself with Amabel. She was a charming, wayward girl, all laughter and high spirits; she was for ever dancing and singing and romping. Lady Selina often wondered how it was that her own daughter looked rather lumpish beside little Amabel; but then Mr. Petty-Pells was an official person, and rather lumpish too perhaps, so it was better not to think of that; only when her Ladyship took Amabel out with her in the barouche, she always came back amused and inspirited, whereas, when she had either of her own girls with her, she returned from her drive just a wee bit bored.

There was indeed a reason for this, of which possibly her Ladyship did not take sufficient account; for Lord George Wyldwyl and his staff were always on the watch for her, and directly her two iron-greys came tossing their rosettes along the road, one of the General's aides-de-camp, remarkable for his keen sight, reported whether Amabel was or was not with Lady Selina in the carriage that day. If not, the General only saluted her with the knightly homage he paid to all ladies, and trotted away upon his ride somewhat sadly. But the moment Amabel's small face and bright impudent eyes peeped out beside her foster-mother, the whole party advanced, and capered round the carriage, forming an extremely brilliant procession of gay uniforms and gallant cavaliers. They escorted her for hours, if she liked to stay out so long, and the child had fun and frolic for them all. When they drew up in the shade, Lady Selina felt like a queen receiving her court; the General paid her such abject service. His tall, burly form lounged over the arched neck of his charger till his arm rested far into the carriage; and those wide open honest eyes of his would look at his daughter as if they could never get their fill of that most lovely vision. She was very demure, and had a comical sense of her own dignity with him, ruling his big generous heart as children will, while the General's staff, which was the most brilliant then in India, clustered round Lady Selina and paid her compliments; for to do so was a sure way to the General's friendship, though not to his favour: he was too upright a chief to have favourites. Only his aides-de-camp lived with him like his own sons; every one of them got on, because he was always ready to help them forward; and therefore they were glad to please him.

Lady Selina owed half her reputation as a leader of fashion in Calcutta to her good deed in having been a mother to the motherless. Perhaps she was conscious of it, and being pleased with herself was pleased with her charge. Certain it was that she and the General became fast friends. The first thing in the morning the General's orderly galloped up with a gift and a message for Amabel and her. The last person who left her Ladyship's house, after the children had been put to bed, was Lord George; and if he was sometimes admitted into the nursery, and passed hours on all fours, with a bit of stick and a bobbin in his mouth, while half a dozen young urchins rode upon his back by turns, why that was a secret between his Lordship and Lady Selina Petty-Pells. She was half-sister of the Countess of Pencarrow, and both these ladies admired the old soldier too much to talk of anything he did otherwise than with respect and good feeling.

So all went on delightfully till Amabel was nearly five years old, and then suddenly the little maid began to droop. The climate of India seems always unfavourable to Europeans in the second generation, and if she had remained there she must have died. Both the General and his friend were quick to notice the change in her, and long experience of the country had prepared them for it. They knew also that there was but one remedy, and that the child must be sent forthwith to England, while her strength lasted. It was very hard to part from her, and Lord George would have accompanied his daughter home, could any good have been effected by his doing so. But the physicians set their faces against his being with her on the voyage. She must, they said, be kept from all excitement just then, lest hectic fever should set in, and close attention would have to be paid to her diet and regimen. She would require attendance and care, such as only a woman, perhaps a mother, could give her, and he was a rough soldier who could not nurse her, however prayerfully and anxiously he might try to do so. Then the General appealed once more to Lady Selina, and besought her to undertake the voyage home. She consented, for it has been said that she was a good woman; and Anglo-Indians still talk of the manner in which her cabins were fitted up by the lavish father, and how he chartered all the best part of the great ship which was to convey them over the seas. Mr. Petty-Pells, in after life, has been heard to date a considerable addition to his fortune from this event, and Lady Selina's shawls and diamonds were much remarked during the season which she subsequently passed in London. It was certain that her journey could have cost her nothing; for Mr. Mortmain took the house which she occupied in Grosvenor Square from Lord Trecarne, who was of course absent on the Continent in consequence of his domestic differences; and Mr. Mortmain also remitted the rent of it in two equal halves, the one going to his Lordship at Baden, and the other to my Lady at Naples. Even

15*

the carriages which Lady Selina used during her stay in town, and her Ladyship's opera-box, were also provided by Mr. Mortmain, who insisted on relieving her of the entire expense of her establishment, and opened an unlimited credit for her at Drummond's for that purpose. Now as the lawyer would not have presumed to do such things himself, nor could Lady Selina have accepted them from him, it is fair to suppose that they were done by Lord George's order. He would have given all he had to bring back the roses to his daughter's cheek; and a thousand pounds each would have seemed a small sum to him for Lady Selina's letters announcing, first, that she was better, and then, after a brief interval, that she was quite well.

Not until little Amabel was safely placed with the Dowager Marchioness of Newcomen did the Anglo-Indian lady return to her husband and family at Calcutta; and the first person she met on landing was Lord George Wyldwyl, who said to her simply, "God bless you," and kissed her hand, having provided for her return as munificently as for her going.

CHAPTER XI.

Wooing.

THUS Amabel Wyldwyl had been brought up in England, and was now just eighteen years old. She was very beautiful, and very much accustomed to have her own way in everything, having been spoiled all her life. She had been the darling of the Dowager

Marchioness of Newcomen, whose children were all grown up and had left her, so that the bereaved lady was glad of that bright young presence in her lonely dower house. She resided for the greater part of the year at a fine picturesque castle on the coast of Ireland, but she came to London occasionally, and was not unknown to the world of fashion and politics; being herself by birth one of the ancient family of the Townshends of Tynedale.

Miss Wyldwyl had lived with this excellent person much as the beauty of a fairy tale lives with her godmother; and there had been always the best possible understanding between them. Amabel had learned to ride with great courage and skill, for the Tynedales had ever been leaders of the turf. She had also become an accomplished musician, for the Townshends were hereditary patrons of art. She could draw and paint too with no common cunning, and the Dowager having a very sound taste for books, because she had had too much experience of life to tolerate a false representation of it, Miss Amabel was familiar with a class of authors who do not often come under the notice of young ladies. She was indeed that most precious product of nature and of education, a beautiful girl, who had many of the best qualities, and much of the intellect, of an honest man. It did not prevent her from being graceful and womanly; it did not save her from being extremely capricious. But her caprices were all harmless and innocent: they came merely of youth and high spirits; there was never anything cruel or calculating in them, and when her feelings were touched she was as docile as a child. If she plagued her father it was because she knew that he liked to be plagued by her, and teased her into reprisals. If she had been wayward and aggressive towards Lieutenant Brown it was because their first introduction to each other had been of an unusual character, and the girl had lain awake of nights crying and laughing and hiding her blushing head in her pillow dozens of times when she remembered it. She thought that she could never bear to see Mr. Brown, still less to speak to him any more; and then she found herself watching for him, and wondering about him, talking of him, dreaming of him, and she grew angry with herself.

It was not till she learned how brave and good he was, how simple-hearted and unassuming, that she began to forgive herself, and then she resolutely determined to look upon him as a brother. He was her father's aide-de-camp, and it was the custom in India for Generals to consider their aides-de-camp as members of their family. There could be no harm in her following so time-honoured a practice; and so the maiden lulled her troubled heart to rest, and sometimes slept the tranquil sleep of self-approval. Mr. Brown's manners were so reserved that it was clear he must have forgotten how forward she had been in having kissed him by mistake for her cousin; perhaps he had not noticed what had happened; or, if he must have noticed it, he must have known that it was all a dreadful, shocking, tragical event for her. These later considerations followed her into her doze and brought her back to broad wakefulness again; and once more she hid her pretty head in her pillow and felt so angry, oh, so angry, and so ashamed, that she could have died, if something had not whispered to her that it might be sweet to live; and so, when she had cried a little, and laughed a short reluctant laugh, followed by a plaintive whine, she lost consciousness, and awoke at sunrise, while all the birds of the garden were singing their matins, or perhaps chirping out to each other in merry couplets that she had been naughty, and her slumbers were broken in consequence.

It was worse still in the morning. She was afraid for days and days to go downstairs to breakfast for fear of meeting Mr. Brown; and the Dowager was much edified to see Miss Amabel come demurely into her dressing-room, to share her dry toast, when there were such very nice things prepared for her elsewhere, and the girl had a fine appetite.

She got a little more self-assurance after breakfast, for even dry toast, accompanied by hot coffee and boiled cream, such as the Dowager's maid combined, has invigorating qualities. "Why," she then argued with herself, "should she torment herself about a stupid person—well, perhaps he was not stupid, it was only Lady Overlaw who said he was stupid, and Lady Overlaw never liked anyone who did not pay her compliments; but why should she torment herself about a *person* who could never be anything to her?" "Why, indeed?" said some internal voice, which seemed to mock her slyly; and all the morning, as she walked with the Dowager and her poodle, or as she sat with her pencils and Bristol boards before her, sketching under the beech trees, she thought of William Brown, till she drew caricatures of him in a grotesque and petulant despair at being quite unable to get him out of her head for a moment, and then she drew knights and paladins and troubadours, who one and all resembled him. Even King Arthur, portrayed by her pencil, sat his fabled steed like William Brown; and had the same steadfast look in his royal eyes as when last she saw the young soldier, as he rode away from Beaumanoir to do an idle errand for her, leaving all the palace and the park behind him uninhabited, and without the soul which made them stately and fair.

Yet still, now pleaded graver conscience, what if he were a hero and a gallant gentleman, as she owned he was, what could he be to her? A friend whom she could never see—nothing more. She might follow him in her imagination, indeed, where brave men win their bright renown; she might sometimes pray for him when he was in sorrow or in danger; and when they were old, old people, who had done with life, she might meet him again with eyes which would not burn and ache and weep by turns, as hers did now.

Why had they talked of him to her so much and so often? Why had she seen for herself how fearless and gentle he was? Why was his name for ever on her father's honest lips, but another word for valour and goodness? Every one liked him, from the under-gamekeeper, whom she heard praise his shooting to her own groom, up to Dean Mowledy, who treated him as if he were his own son, and whose language took more than its usual grave sweetness when he spoke to the young soldier. Why had they all joined together to steal her heart away from her, when perhaps she might have kept it fancy free, or lured it back again from its first tremulous flight? They all knew that she had been engaged almost from her cradle to the Marquis of Kinsgear, and that they were betrothed as man and wife. If he were dying, as the physicians said, she would remain a widow for his sake, as a noble lady should do. But only a few hours ago the Marchioness of Newcomen, her last refuge from persecution, had put up her glasses to look at him when he had offered her Ladyship some ordinary token of respect, and had remarked that he was the handsomest and best-bred man she had ever seen; "except the late Duke of Courthope, my darling, whom, by the way, he resembles in a manner which is quite astonishing," added the Dowager: and moreover the likeness which the Lieutenant bore to the Wyldwyl family was generally noticed. It was that which had deceived Miss Amabel when she first saw him and had she ventured to admit any excuse to herself it lay there quite ready for her acceptance. He was but a taller and finer resemblance of her affianced husband, and as she had not seen her betrothed for three years she had been the more easily misled.

The girl had no idea of breaking her engagement if her cousin could have lived to claim it. She had been brought up to look upon Lord Kinsgear as her husband, and she did so. The ties of relationship are very strong among the Anglo-Indians; and her father always wrote to her and spoke to her as if a duty were imposed upon her from which she could in nowise depart. She was aware also that there was a mystery in her family, though she did not know its precise nature, and that many things would be set right when she married the Marquis. She had tranquilly accepted her lot in life also, without question and without repugnance hitherto; for the Marquis was very kind and pleasant, though so silent, and sometimes, as she thought, a little awkward. They had not seen much of each other; but whenever they had passed a few months together she had liked him, and taken possession of him, in her girlish way, as something which was to belong to her by-and-by. If now the doctors barely gave him another week to live, that did not seem to her to loosen the bond between them. On the contrary, she felt that she should love him better now, and mourn for him worthily.

Meantime, William Brown rode with her and her father daily; and Amabel became too sad to avoid him, as she had hitherto done. She no longer spoke of him with pertness or mockery, and the conversation, as they wound slowly through meadows and woodlands in the autumn afternoons, was very pensive. They could hardly be gay while the young lord was dying; and even the General's bluff good humour was not proof against the melancholy circumstances which surrounded them. The good old man was grieved to see the hope of his race smitten down so early; but the feeling scarcely amounted to a personal sorrow. His rough soldierly nature had little sympathy with the taciturn Marquis and his sedentary pursuits. They had never understood each other, and although they had preserved the outward forms of kinsmanship when they met, they had met but seldom. The General's house had always been open to the young man, but he had rarely gone there; and if they had a cold mutual respect for each other, there was no affection between them. Young Brown was far more to his mind. The Lieutenant was silent and reserved too, and studious, which Lord George had never been; but he could back a horse and take a joke, and sit steadily behind a bottle as long as any youngster he had ever known. His Lordship was glad to get out with him from the stifling air and hushed whispers of Beaumanoir, and generally prolonged his ride, upon some pretext or other, from two o'clock, when lunch was over, till nearly six, when it was time to dress for dinner.

They wandered along through the home park, where the deer browsed and the timid hare flitted across their path, and the partridges called to each other from their cover, and so on out into the open country, amidst the lovely English landscape, with its village church steeples and old manor-houses half-hidden in ancient oaks and ivy. The General rode between them, with one of the young people on either side of him; and both of them would have thought it treason to say a word which he could not hear or comprehend, and yet, unconsciously to themselves, no accent passed their lips but had some hidden meaning.

They conversed chiefly about India; and the young soldier said that when the General's present command expired he should return thither, having neither interest nor desire for a career in England.

Miss Amabel answered that he would do well, though her cheek paled slightly as she spoke, and her horse showed signs of uneasiness.

Then the General asked what he should do when they had both gone away from him, and seemed to class them together as though they had been his son and daughter. He thought that Lord Kinsgear might still recover, and that then she would be soon lost to him.

Miss Amabel said that she would never leave him now; and Young Brown added that he should never go while the General, or any one near or dear to him, desired his presence. The young lady rejoined that England must be dull and spiritless to one who had seen so much of camps; and the soldier replied that he had never found it so. It was not dull, he deemed, but sorrowful—a place where vain, ambitious, hopeless fancies grew. It was only for the rich and highborn to aspire to live there. It was an abode for happiness, not for disappointment.

"Disappointment, Brown!" observed the General, bluntly. "Pray, how the deuce can you be disappointed?"

"Papa," replied Miss Amabel, with a woman's ready tact, "you speak as if there was nothing in life beyond the army regulations and the rules of the service."

"Stuff, Missy!" retorted Lord Punjaub. "A young fellow has no right to be discontented who has got a captain's commission in prospect, and is well and strong. He may be anything he likes, do anything he likes, and have half the girls in the kingdom breaking their hearts for him, if he likes. Look at me. Egad, I might have married a dowager bishopess and a lovely west-country heiress at the same time, if I had not preferred your mother. They both set their caps at my red coat."

"Captain Brown will choose a lovely west-country heiress, I suppose?" said Miss Wyldwyl, dryly; and she appeared to have just caught a slight cough.

Captain Brown winced as the sharp little shaft struck him, and it was some time before he found words to answer that he should never marry.

"Quite right, quite right," said the General, putting spurs to his powerful thoroughbred, and pounding along the road at a thundering trot, while the light horse on either side of him broke into a canter. "It won't do to marry till you become a field officer, and can get good quarters for your wife, and buy her a smart turban now and then."

"Turban, papa!" exclaimed Miss Amabel, horror-stricken, yet laughing, as she breasted a south wind, which brought back the colour to her cheeks, at a hand-gallop. "Who upon earth wears a turban?"

"Everybody did in my time, Missy. A turban made of an Indian shawl, with a bird-of-paradise feather in it: most becoming, I assure you," replied the General, with perfect gravity; his notions of the fashion being dated about forty years before this present writing.

"If Captain Brown makes his wife wear a turban, papa, she will never speak to him again," observed Miss Amabel, decisively.

"Why, you small firefly," returned her father, "do you mean to command Brown's wife as well as himself?"

"Oh, dear, no, papa; I am sure I shall never see the lady," said Miss Amabel, as they checked their horses after a burst over the turf.

"What next? Are you going to shut your doors upon Brown when he gets married, as all the fine ladies did upon your mother and me, because we had not got ten thousand a year? Ho! ho! ho! If you do, I hope he will laugh at you, as we did at them," remarked Lord Punjaub.

"I shall never put Miss Wyldwyl's hospitality to the test for a wife, my Lord," said Young Brown. "It is enough honour if she will condescend to receive me when next I return home. I shall live and die a bachelor."

"You will do as other young fellows have done before you," observed the General, with rough good humour. "You will become the slave of the first pretty girl who thinks you worth catching."

"A fish cannot be caught twice, my Lord, if he is once safely netted," said Mr. Brown.

"Oh, that's the way the cat jumps!" exclaimed the General, slyly. "A dead man cannot be killed over again."

"Of course, if Captain Brown is engaged, the case is altogether different," observed the young lady, adjusting a button of her glove.

"Who is it, Brown?" inquired the General, maliciously. "One of the Dashwood girls, or Miss Swan? I do not think that you visited anywhere else in Calcutta, except at the house of that cantankerous old Scotchman, who looked as if he had never seen a petticoat."

"You forget, my Lord, that Miss Swan has married Major Gosling—and the two Miss Dashwoods—well, I had better, perhaps, say nothing more about them."

"Garrison hacks, eh? Ah, I daresay you are right. You youngsters are always hard upon girls who have been long in the market. They are good girls, too, Brown. They were the belles of the room at a ball I gave; let me see, when was it? In 1840, I think."

"They must be very interesting young ladies indeed, papa," said Miss Wyldwyl.

"Very!" returned the General, seriously. "One of them talked to me about botany, I think it was, or astronomy, I forget which, the last time I saw her at Government House. Brother a very good fellow too; made a Member of Council just before I left Calcutta. But who the deuce is your flame, Brown, if you have not caught fire from the Dashwoods? Somebody down Dronington way, eh? Famous places for pretty girls those Oxfordshire villages round Dronington and Wakefield-in-the-Marsh."

"It is some one whom I am never likely to see again after I have left England, and therefore I do not presume to pronounce her name," said Young Brown, despondingly.

"That is a bad business," remarked the General, with twinkling eyes, as though he saw some humour in all love affairs. "But faint heart never won fair lady. Have you asked her?"

"I might as well have asked for the moon," said Young Brown; "and it would not be fair to laugh at me, because I could not get for the asking."

"Yes, it would," observed the General, curtly. "You may have anything worth winning in this world if you try for it, and go on the hunt with a bold heart and a clear conscience. If the girl's got a father send him to me, and I will say a word for you in the right way. You must win the lady's good graces yourself. I cannot plead for you there. If she has got a mother, by George, Missy will ask the dowager to help you, won't you, my girl? I have seen this young dog under fire," observed the General, turning to his daughter, "and now he tells me he is afraid, because he is lovesick."

Lord Punjaub struck his hand with bluff affection on his aide-de-camp's shoulder as he spoke. "I won't stand by and see your life's happiness marred if I can help it," he resumed; "and if you are very hard hit by a pair of bright eyes we must win them together. It will not be the first time we have ridden out to a victory."

George Wyldwyl had always taken pleasure in the happiness of those around him, and had a ready-made theory of his own, that his life would be worth little if it could not contribute to the advancement and the good of others. He was a candid old man who had seen the world, and he had no doubt that if there was any obstacle to the love-making of a handsome youngster, money was more likely to be the thing really in the way than any other. Then he thought of his Indian strong box, and how little anything that could be wanted in the present instance would diminish it.

"My Lord," said the young man, "I am quite overcome by your goodness. You cannot help me. I think I am in love with a dream." He laughed and turned away his head; but for the first time since he had become a man there were tears in his eyes.

"How you do tease everybody, papa," whispered Miss Amabel, shaking her little forefinger, and she stooped over her saddle bow, till her lips just touched Lord Punjaub's white moustache.

CHAPTER XII.

The Heir's Death.

THE Marquis of Kinsgear grew rapidly worse. The physicians now said that his malady was pulmonary disease. There is always a name for everything, but all that they knew was that his brief life was drawing fast to a close. Many learned things are always said about the death of a Marquis, and doctors dispute over it.

Reputations are made and lost, as the medical men who attend upon him may be popular in their profession or otherwise—the honour remaining with him who can state his case the best in print; though print has but little to do with the healing art. Perhaps there was truth in what they said, that the wounds which he received in the Indian battle should have been cured, or should have killed him long before. But nature is a poor student of logic, and they had never healed satisfactorily, or grown much worse. They were always breaking out afresh, as though he had some radical vice of constitution. There may have been a poison, too, which works slowly, upon the renegade's spear, or he may have received some internal injury which none could detect or guess at. When a pin's point is sufficient to produce death it is but waste of time to wonder that the immediate cause of it cannot always be detected with complete accuracy. This much was clear, and no more—the Marquis of Kinsgear was dying. He had a cruel cough—he was wasted to a shadow—he could not eat or drink, or sleep, as the healthy do—his eyes lacked lustre, when they were not all aflame—his cheeks were livid, when they had not a hectic flush upon them. He was like a fire of straw, which flares when the wind smites upon it, then falls into an unsubstantial heap of ashes.

So many hopes were centred in him, it seemed hard that he should pass away from the world thus early, leaving no memorial to show that he had been here. There is a verse in the hundred-and-ninth psalm —it is the twelfth verse, and it probably explains why the young man died in the dawn and promise of his career: but no one thought of that at Beaumanoir. They only marvelled, and some wept, because he drew to his end as a post that hasted by, or, as when an arrow is shot at a mark it parts the air, which immediately comes together again, so that none can know where it went through.

Ever since the day of his birth numbers of grasping people had speculated upon what they might gain by him; and ambitious people had planned how he should further their interests, or those of their children when he grew up; and plots and combinations without end were making in which he played some part involuntarily.

The next heir of the Courthopes was Lord Punjaub, and he was old; after him there was nobody, and the two historic dukedoms, which had been united for three generations, would become extinct. Some of the Scotch peerages in the family descended in the female line; and so, if the last two Dukes of Courthope both died without issue, Miss Wyldwyl might claim to be Countess of Winguid in her own right, and would succeed to those great estates in the North, now forming the chief property which maintained the hereditary splendour of the dukedoms; for the English estates were overhoused and unproductive; it cost more to keep them up than their net rental. Although the present Duke had made enormous purchases in land since he succeeded to the title, not an acre which he nominally possessed was unencumbered, and he had mortgaged every inch of ground he acquired on the day he bought it, or he could not have found the money to feed his passion for adding field to field. Title-deeds and mortgage-deeds had both changed hands at the same time. Every estate which he had bought would be sent to the hammer when the Marquis died, and his Grace would have to live henceforth abroad, a ruined man, with no means of existence but what could be saved out of his son's life insurances. So Mr. Mortmain had told him plainly: the splendid noble now stood face to face with poverty, and executions for debt were being daily threatened. The bailiffs were in fact waiting to seize his very furniture and the bed upon which his son was dying, under bills of sale for seventy thousand pounds, and collateral heirs in all parts of the kingdom were starting up, and rushing to the Court of Chancery with moth-eaten wills and testaments, to show that some of it might, or could, or would, or should belong to them.

Moreover, all the money-lenders were in arms. If the Scotch estates were to descend to Miss Wyldwyl, they would come to her without a charge upon them; and all the securities based upon their rental, which had been given by the present Duke and his son in virtue of their life-interest, would be waste paper.

Then the old stories came up again, and the newspapers teemed with advertisements for poor Madge, who was dead and gone; or for some proof of the late Duke of Courthope's alleged marriage with a Scotch lady, whereby the succession to the vast estates of Winguid might be changed; lawyers were ferreting out the records of every village and town in Scotland to find what they sought, working as actively and stealthily, in silence and darkness, as ferrets or moles. Even their advertisements were discreet and lawyer-like; for it would not do to put Mr. Mortmain, the family solicitor of Lord Punjaub, upon his guard upon the one hand, and upon the other it was inexpedient to say too much at once. What the money-lenders wanted was to discover a needy heir, whose case might present an aspect formidable enough to serve their turn, and then to make their own terms; or to effect a compromise in which everybody's interests should be sacrificed but their own. The unsecured debts amounted to about four hundred thousand pounds, as far as the real state of the Duke's affairs could be known, and the money-lenders might well make a desperate effort to save themselves from such a loss as that.

In this fierce conflict of interests there was little time for the home affections to make themselves heard, had they been better known at Beaumanoir. But the Duke had always looked upon his son rather as a part of his grandeur than of his heart, and there were only two persons who mourned for him. Miss Wyldwyl did all which a young lady could do under such circumstances; it was but little, for she was necessarily excluded from the sick-room. Young Brown was constant in his attentions, and sat up night after night by the side of his comrade and brother officer, taking only brief intervals of rest when the Duke of Courthope came to replace him; and the intricate web of business which the lawyers continued to spin round the dying man required the latest remnants of his strength to unravel it.

Although there was little love in the great house among the young heir's kindred and connections, the servants liked him, for he had never been rude or uncivil to them, and had wanted little waiting on while he could wait upon himself. So the under-housemaids might be seen crying on the stairs while the under-footmen comforted them. Without too, among the public, and wherever the honest heart of England could be heard beating, there was sympathy for the young soldier lord, who was heir to such illustrious fortunes and would never own them. Thousands of good and gentle people read the daily bulletins which were issued of his state with emotion, and remembered how a few short months before his name had been mentioned in gazettes and newspapers; and they said with patriotic pride that the highest of their nobles still knew how to die for their country. Royalty also telegraphed daily for news of him, and cards and letters of inquiry poured in by hundreds every hour both at Whitehall and Beaumanoir. Simple people living in country towns and remote hamlets sent their family recipes and remedies, hoping that they might do something to ease the young lord's sufferings, or by Heaven's blessing to prolong his days. For we are not an evil or an unfeeling people.

Then occurred one of those passages of low comedy which will intrude into the saddest drama; though some say that Shakespeare would have better represented life had he left out the part of the gravedigger from Hamlet. Mr. Sharpe, in abject fear for his securities and bills and bonds, brought down a quack doctor who had faith in tar-water, and came with a quart bottle of it in a gig. They were obstreperous and argumentative; they would not go away, till William Brown, hearing a scuffle outside the door of the chamber where his friend had just fallen into a fitful slumber, came forth and forbade their entrance.

It was nearly all over then. When the Marquis awoke after his last conscious sleep, he appeared calmer than he had done for some days, and spoke hopefully of his recovery.

"Do you remember, Willie"—he said, as the two young men talked together over their campaign once more—"Do you remember the evening I found you reading under my tent, when I came in from dining with General Violet?"

"Yes, well," replied Young Brown; "I was reading Macaulay's account of the battle of Killiekrankie. You asked me, 'How goes the day?' I answered, 'Well for King James',' which you know is in the book," observed the Lieutenant, gravely. "Is that right?"

"Quite right, Willie; and I answered, 'Then it matters the less for me.' I wonder why I should think of it all so clearly now? Yes. It matters the less for me."

Suddenly the Marquis started after he had spoken,

and was seized with a fit of coughing, followed by a slight convulsion. William Brown supported his comrade's head upon his breast, and held him there till the shock seemed over.

"I am better now," the young lord murmured faintly, and a peculiar light passed over his face. He sunk gently backwards upon his pillow, sighed very softly once, and so died.

"His Grace has sent to ask if the Marquis is awake?" said the groom of the chambers, opening the door gently and looking in.

CHAPTER XIII.
Humbled in the Dust.

YES, the young lord had awakened to a new life, and in a few minutes his father was standing by his bedside, alone. He did not mourn. He looked at the motionless form of his son with a pathetic surprise, like a man who is unaccustomed to grapple with great afflictions and does not understand them. Young Brown had retired that the father might give way to his grief unrestrained; but the Duke could feel no grief. He twirled one of the massive rings on his fingers, adjusted his high shirt collar, and at last, moved by unconscious curiosity, laid a timid finger on the still warm hand of his late heir. Then he paced the room with a heavy step, and thought of the overwhelming ruin which must come upon him through this heir's death. The boy's slender life was the thread on which hung all the honour and fortune of the

House of Courthope; it was snapped, and now that house must fall to the ground. Yet even this thought did not succeed in biting deep into the callous egotism of the Duke. His luck had always been so great that he could not realize the prospect of its deserting him; ruin presented itself to his eyes as no more than an unpleasant difficulty which would bring him a few days' worry and necessitate exertion, but which could be overcome by finessing. It caused him a momentary depression, nothing more. After an hour the Duke walked out of the room without drawing the sheet over his son's face; and, addressing his servants in his grand quiet way, which seemed to them the very voice of crushing sorrow nobly borne, said, "Let everything that is proper be done."

So women took possession of the young lord's body, all the blinds in the house were drawn down, a groom set off for the village to have the church bell tolled, and telegrams were despatched to a grand undertaker in London. Soon the carriages of the county gentry swept up the avenue of Beaumanoir, and cards were heaped up in a great pile on the table in the front hall. During two days the tide of condolence flowed in unabated, and preparations were made on a large scale by the household in view of a sumptuous funeral. But these preparations were to be unceremoniously interrupted by the Duke's creditors.

So long as life remained to the heir of the Courthope property, these creditors had been willing to show some forbearance; but now, losing all expectation of payment, they evinced no respect for the bereaved nobleman. Before the Marquis had been dead forty-eight hours, half a dozen executions were put into the house; and men in greasy coats were to be seen taking inventories in all the chambers. They intruded even into the death-room. Stretched out, with the simple majesty of eternal sleep on his white features, the young Marquis lay dressed in uniform with his sword by his side, a ring on his hand, and a little assortment of his favourite trinkets lying on a cushion between his feet, for burial with him. The men seized these trinkets, they unbuckled the sword, drew off the ring, and debated whether they should strip off the scarlet tunic also for the gold lace on its facings. Meanwhile the London undertaker arrived, but only to say that he could do nothing without ready-money or a guarantee. This man's name was Tholegiddle, and he had an extensive acquaintance with the aristocracy from having measured so large a number of them for coffins. His ideas of their greatness, too, being somehow blended with his recollection of the space which they occupied underground he would say innocently, "Lord Yardtwain was the greatest man of modern times—six foot six was the length of his inner coffin."

Mr. Tholegiddle was shown into the Duke's presence, with a book of funeral designs bulging out of his breast-pocket. This book had been brought with a purpose, for before preferring his pecuniary request, Mr. Tholegiddle wished to show of what great things he was capable when sure of his money. He displayed designs for a hearse with twelve horses, four-and-twenty crests of plumes, and a church catafalque eighteen feet high. Then he exhibited patterns for hatchments, not painted crudely but by competent artists with an eye for shading. "The shading on a hatchment is a great point, your Grace," said Mr. Tholegiddle, anxious to gain time. "I have no opinion of an artist who makes the leopards on a quartering look like Manx cats."

"Let everything be done in the most becoming manner," said the Duke, in that magnificent tone which never became him so well as when he was ordering, regardless of expense, something for which he could not pay.

"Certainly, my Lord Duke," answered Mr. Tholegiddle, whipping back his book into his pocket; "but I wished to say that our firm are not prepared to risk the Marquis's funeral without some guarantee."

"A guarantee!" and the Duke of Courthope turned with a haughty glare on Mr. Tholegiddle, who was a small man cased in black, with a wrinkled, sallow face like the kernel of a walnut.

"It is not I, but the firm that wants a guarantee, your Grace," expostulated Mr. Tholegiddle, sidling by easy but nervous stages towards the door; "I myself would esteem it a happiness to bury the Marquis, or your Grace himself, or all your noble relatives, for nothing—but the firm, your Grace—the firm has heard you are insolvent."

At this moment Young Brown burst into the room almost without knocking, so great was his agitation. His face was flushed and he spoke in a trembling voice:

"There are some men in Lord Kinsgear's room, your Grace, who say that I must surrender the watch which Lord Kinsgear left me as a keepsake, and which you gave me with your own hands."

The Duke made an impatient gesture:
"You will receive my orders," he said sharply to the undertaker, who vanished. "And now, what is it, Captain?"

"There are some ruffians who are desecrating your son's corpse," exclaimed the young man with his whole frame on the quiver. "They have taken off his sword; I found one of them wrenching from his finger a ring which has a lock of Miss Wyldwyl's hair in it, and when I wanted to fling them out of the room they set upon me all together, and said that if I did not give up Lord Kinsgear's watch I might be indicted for theft."

The Duke sat down. Then it was, and not till then, he understood the depth of utter poverty into which he had fallen. He dismissed Young Brown, saying he would see him presently; and it was with an aching footstep that he sought the apartments where Lord Punjaub and his daughter had kept themselves secluded, so as not to trespass on his sorrow. The General knew nothing of the executions. He had seen the greasy men about the house, but had taken them for servants of the undertaker, and such is the consideration sometimes shown even by domestics, that Lord Punjaub's valet—an old soldier—had concealed from him the news, which was keeping the servants' hall in a ferment. Singular to add, Miss Wyldwyl's maid had observed an equal discretion; though to be sure she was French, and would have needed an hour's tutoring before she could have comprehended what an execution meant.

Amabel was not in the room with her father, so Lord Punjaub came forward alone to meet his kinsman, and uttered a few feeling words. The Duke grasped his hand silently, and sighed, preparatory to telling his pitiful tale.

Once face to face with a pressing difficulty, however, his inveterate habits of dissimulation recurred to him. There was no need to tell the whole truth just yet, and so it was actually with something of the air of an absolute sovereign conferring a favour upon an honoured subject, that he asked his uncle for money, alleging that his rents had not come in. "Certainly," answered the old soldier, kindly; "I will go to London and send anything you require, immediately after the funeral."

The Duke coughed slightly. That solution of the case would hardly meet his requirements; so he replied, with a melancholy shake of the head, that he should have no need of money then, but merely wanted some till his rents came in.

"Why, there is my prize-money which you drew for me and lodged at the bankers," said Lord Punjaub; "I will sign you a cheque for that."

Now this prize-money, which the Duke had drawn, was alluded to in a previous chapter relatively to a transaction with Mr. Sharpe. The Duke, instead of lodging the money at the bankers had appropriated it, calculating on his ability to repay it at one of those convenient dates which he was continually scoring down on the ledgers of his imagination. There was no evading the truth now: it must all come out, and it did come out—a dark torrent of wretched ignoble avowals. Perhaps the Duke felt relief at unbosoming himself of all the secrets which had weighed so long upon his peace; perhaps the consciousness that he was speaking to a man whose chivalrous mind would surely come to his aid, emboldened him to discard even such euphemisms as might have served to cloak his degradation. Anyhow, once he began to make his confession, he poured out a story which might well have humbled a more unscrupulous man in the dust.

Lord Punjaub stood horrified. The honour of his name was so sacred a religion with him, and he had been so far from dreaming that any member of his family could stoop to a base thing, that the avowal of miserable acts committed by the man who above all others, was charged to keep the family escutcheon spotless, struck him aghast. Blasphemy from a priest, ribaldry from a child, the shame of his own daughter, would have appalled him less. As the first self-accusing words were groaned out by the Duke, the old soldier's face turned crimson; but when the Duke, frightened by the expression on his relative's features, ended by throwing himself on his knees in his utter abasement, and gasping a prayer for help and forgiveness, Lord Punjaub recoiled with an exclamation—

"Good God! Are you mad, or are these facts?"

"They are facts," sobbed the Duke: "I am a ruined, fallen man, and if you do not assist me there will be nothing left for me but to die."

"Would to Heaven you were dead, instead of that boy upstairs!" exclaimed the General, hoarsely: and disregarding the Duke, who scrambled to his feet again, he strode to and fro with a brow black as storm. Then he suddenly turned, moved by the first and last gust of incontrollable anger that ever possessed him: "Great God, why did you do this? Are you a real Wyldwyl, or some puddle-blooded bastard that has been palmed off on us? Do you know that it is my name and title that you are bearing, and that I can be disgraced by your misdeeds? What did you want—money? You had it. Power? All England cringed to you. Pleasure, sport, men's friendship, women's love? All these things were at your beck. You are one of those whom the world sets high not because of their own worth, but for the honour of their fathers; and all that people asked of you was to remember that you sprang from gentlemen, and to be yourself an honest man. But no; that even is too much for you: you must play the black-leg, pawn your honour to hucksters; do things for which a private soldier would be flogged, and for which, not long ago, a lower born man than you would have been hanged! If it were not that by Heaven's providence I am rich —and God knows when I got this gold I never guessed it would help me to clean a tarnished name —if it were not for this, there must have been an exposure which would have forced me to hang my head for ever after. If you are a madman I pity you; but if you were in your right mind when you thus dragged your name and mine in the mud, then scoundrel is the only title I can find to fit you."

"Forgive me," groaned the Duke, cowering under this scathing denunciation; "forgive me; you are my only friend now."

"Don't talk of friendship between us, sir," replied Lord Punjaub, waving back the Duke's proffered hand, and he left the room.

But he had not gone far down the passage before he remembered that the man on whom he had so sternly laid the weight of his anger, was a bereaved father whose only son was lying dead under this roof. He called to mind, too, that this only son was the gentle, high-souled young soldier who was to have been his own daughter's husband, and whose bravery he had seen tested beside him in the field; and at this his generous heart smote him. His anger fell in a moment. It would have been a study for a painter to see the grim expression of the features abruptly relax, and give place to a look of woeful compassion, deepening into self-reproach. All-humbled by the quick change in his emotions, the General retraced his steps.

The Duke had sunk into a chair near the window, and the grey light of evening was beating on his bowed head, buried in his hands. He was prostrated, not by remorse for his offences, but by the abject humiliation which exposure had entailed on him. Lord Punjaub noiselessly crossed the room, and laid a hand on the Duke's shoulder.

"Courthope, that boy upstairs has been whispering to me. He is asking pardon for you now where we shall both have to kneel for it some day, and he sees us both. For his sake—here is my hand."

CHAPTER XIV.

Requiescat.

So Mr. Tholegiddle received his guarantee, and the greasy men were compounded with for the present, and left. They put back on the young lord his sword, his ring, and the golden spurs he had worn once at a levee. Young Brown stood by whilst this pious office was performed, and laid at his comrade's feet a large wreath of white camelias and violets which Amabel Wyldwyl had given him to place there. Other wreaths and bouquets, the gifts of county neighbours, farmers, and humbler dependents, abounded in the death-chamber, and made it fragrant: for it seemed as if this young nobleman, who had filled so small a place in the thoughts of mankind whilst he lived, had left a gap, not only in their thoughts, but in the hearts of his countrymen now that he was dead. One English nobleman, who thus dies in his country's service, blots out the follies of a dozen of his peers who extinguish their nobility under a jockey-cap, or train themselves for the work of legislation by acting as theatrical managers or stage-coachmen.

They gave Lord Kinsgear a splendid funeral. That half-barbaric pageant which surrounds the mighty among us who are borne to their last homes, was performed completely in all its details. An army of mutes invaded the house, and three coffins, of oak, lead, and maple-wood velvet covered, were carried down the long array of staircases and corridors. The hearse had twelve horses, and the pall was decked with the plumed hat and second sword of the young warrior. Behind came his charger with empty boots in the stirrups, and then followed an endless procession of mounted tenants in trailing cloaks, members of the hunt, and mourning coaches so far as the eye could see. At the village church wherein was the family vault of the Courthopes, a circle of clergy, in the simple but striking vestments of the Church of England, met the body in the porch. There were crimson hoods from Oxford, furred hoods from Cambridge, and a bishop stepped out as the coffin was drawn from the hearse, and read in an impressive voice the opening words :—

"We brought nothing into the world, and we can take nothing out. The Lord gave, and the Lord hath taken away: blessed is the name of the Lord."

The Duke of Courthope followed the coffin into the church, and stood behind it during the service, joining audibly and reverently in the responses. He was a man who could be touched by the externals of mourning, and all this show impressed him, causing him to sorrow more devoutly for his lost heir than he himself would have thought possible. Then, none knew better than he how to enact the part of a great noble in any ceremony, festive or funereal, and to many who gazed on him with impulsive sympathy, he looked the very picture of a broken-hearted father. Yet was his heart not broken, nor had his grief deeper roots than the flowers that spring up and bloom for a day on a rock. As the service was long he fell to musing, before the end of it, that Lord Punjaub was going to clear him from all his embarrassments, and to revive his credit. If the truth must be told, he thought with complacency that he had once more outwitted Ruin, and that he should be able to obtain more loans from Mr. Sharpe. And in this he was not blameworthy, for a tree can only bear the fruits peculiar to it.

Very different was the attitude of Young Brown. He stood with drooping head as near the coffin as his lowly rank would permit; for there were peers at either side of him, and two dukes had held the pall. Every word of the beautiful Anglican Burial Service fell on his ear with its full sense of awfulness or divine consolation, and he clung yearningly to such texts as explained death to be but a brief parting. He was not unmanned, and he shed no tears, for the courage of the soldier and the strong faith of the Christian sustained him; but when the coffin was lowered into the vault and a handful of clay rung on its lid; when the bishop said, "We commit his body to the ground, earth to earth, ashes to ashes, dust to dust; in sure and certain hope of the resurrection to eternal life," then his eyes did fill with a mist. The promise of an immortal life was too grand and holy to be heard with formal impassiveness, and he clung to a pew rail for support.

Young Brown was the last who lingered in the church when all the other spectators had returned to their business or their pleasures, and when none but workpeople tarried. The sexton was removing the draperies from the pillars, an architect, rule in hand, was measuring a space on the wall for a marble monument, a couple of workmen, with trowels and mortar, were preparing to brick the vault over and to put back the outer flagstone in its place. After hovering near the vault for a few minutes, and taking a last look at his friend's coffin - a look he would have prolonged for hours if it had not been for those workmen—Young Brown issued out of the porch into the churchyard, where birds were chirping and sunbeams were playing over the rows of humbler tombs. He felt a hand laid in his, and saw Dean Mowledy, whom he had not before noticed in the throng of clergy.

"I sympathise in your grief, William," said the Dean, gently linking his arm in the boy's.

"I feel, sir, as if there were an injustice in my being alive when he is dead. My life is of such small account beside his."

"That is for God to judge," said the Dean, with grave kindness. "His ways are inscrutable, and the lives He spares are spared for a purpose."

"Mine is such an insignificant life. If I lived to a hundred and did all the good I could, I should never perform a tenth of what *he* would have done. His life would have been a blessing to thousands. I never felt it as I did to-day, seeing all those tenants mourn for him sincerely as for a friend."

"Lord Kinsgear's death is certainly a loss, but do not treat any human life as insignificant, William. You, too, may become heaven's instrument in doing good to thousands; but if not, if your sphere of usefulness remains narrow, remember that to one man the Lord gave ten talents and to another only one. Make the best use of your one talent, and you will not have been an unprofitable servant."

They had now reached the park, and Beaumanoir broke upon them majestically, tower by tower. The flag on the keep was still flying half-mast high, and carriages, circling round the gravel sweep before the state entrance, were bearing away guests who had returned to the castle after the funeral. It looked as if these guests, whose presence had lent a day's animation to the house, were forsaking a home which would never know animation any more; at least so it seemed to Young Brown, who glanced at the façade of the now heirless manor house and heaved a sigh.

"One would think it must be hard to leave all this wealth and state, but Kinsgear seemed to be wholly indifferent to it; his rank and possessions gave him no joy; and I can partly understand it, judging by myself. Once I should have thought it impossible I could ever be better off than I am now, and yet I am not contented. It is very ungrateful of me; but my rise has brought new longings which must remain unsatisfied."

"That, again, is a merciful law of Providence," answered the Dean, with affectionate earnestness. "If man could be too well satisfied with his lot, he would cling to the things of this earth and forget the Giver of them. Every one of our desires accomplished brings with it a wish for something higher and better, until, having obtained all that this world can yield, we discover that the higher things towards which we have been tending do not belong to this world at all. Then we fall back upon God, and turn all our hopes to the life beyond this, which knows no disappointment."

"I suppose it is so, sir," murmured William Brown, submissively. "Well, I will look to that distant future. Whether my hopes here be realised or not, it must be all the same a hundred years hence."

"Nay, but heaven often fulfils some of our dearest hopes here below, and may it be so with you," replied the Dean. "God bless and prosper you, my dear boy. God guard and sustain you."

They parted on this blessing; the Dean turning away from Beaumanoir, William Brown returning to it with a slow step and moist eyes. He had crossed a lawn, and was entering the house by a private door, when a brisk man in black flashed on his path, and he was accosted by Mr. Sharpe. This gentleman had of course attended the funeral, and had just been refreshing himself after it. The crumbs of some eatable were on his mouth, and his lips were still bedewed with sherry. He glanced curiously at the young officer, and then smiled with a queer twinkle in his eyes.

"Mr. Brown, I believe. Well, this has been a sad affair, has it not? It's odd for such a fine place as this to be going begging for an heir."

Young Brown made no response, and Mr. Sharpe proceeded, laying a hand coolly on his arm:

"Look up at those walls, Mr. Brown, and now in front of you at that park. How should you have liked to be born heir to all that? There's a difference between a Brown and a Wyldwyl, ain't there? and yet I'll be bound you'd have made as good a dook as any of 'em. Aha!"

Mr. Sharpe's strange laugh followed Young Brown as he entered the house, where he was but a stranger without recognised kin or title.

CHAPTER XV.

In the Picture Gallery.

THE Duke of Courthope was frequently closeted with Lord Punjaub during the following days, and men who came down from London with blue bags took part in the interviews. There was an indefinable air about the house as of something important being done, as if the tragedy just concluded by Lord Kinsgear's death were being followed by a long epilogue. The gentlemen in blue bags ate copious luncheons after their interviews, and returned reinvigorated to further closetings, which sometimes trespassed far into the evening. Lord Punjaub wore a pale look, and his voice had settled into a tone of saddened gentleness; but whenever he appeared in the Duke's company he strove to be cheerful, and paid his relative the same affectionate deference he had always shown him in the past.

All this time William Brown was left much alone, and had the house well nigh to himself. He wandered about the park, and when indoors might generally be found in the Armoury. During Lord Kinsgear's lifetime he had constituted himself custodian of this Armoury, and the thought that his comrade would some day own all the treasures—for to him they seemed treasures—which it contained, lent loving zeal to his care about the old helmets, breastplates, and battle-axes. He could have no further interest now in things which would probably, at no distant date, be dispersed by the hammer, and yet he came back to his self-imposed work all the same. It had grown into a habit; he had got to like the study of armoury, having picked up much lore about it in dusty books out of the library. There were old Milan breastplates inlaid with gold, Damascus blades with carved hilts, and suits of rare English chain mail worn in the wars of the Roses, and which had been proof even against the cloth-yard shafts of Kentish yeomen; and all these things could only be furbished by a man who had an artist's eye for good work.

One afternoon Brown had stolen up to his favourite haunt, and was busy there, when a girlish head peeped through the door, and Amabel Wyldwyl, in her black dress, and with her golden hair and blue eyes rendered more golden and bluer by the contrast, glided in.

"Am I disturbing you, Mr. Brown?"

Young Brown blushed. He was tricked out in a baize apron; there was a bottle of oil in one of his hands, and a piece of wash-leather in the other, and some smudges of plate powder had got on to his moustache. "I am cleaning a morion," he said; "excuse my strange dress. Did you want to look at the armour?"

"Yes, I have never been up here. What is a morion?"

"An iron hat," answered Young Brown. "They wore them in the sixteenth century. They were more serviceable than handsome."

"I call that thing you are cleaning very ugly."

"It is of beautiful workmanship though. See these arabesques, steel on steel; I believe this one went to the New World on one of Drake's followers."

"Here is a helmet broken right through," said Amabel, rising on tiptoe to look at a panoply on the wall. "It reminds me of that knight in Scott, Sir Henry de Bohun, was it not, who was killed by Robert Bruce?"

"Yes," said Young Brown, kindling a little:

> "High in his stirrups rose the King,
> And gave his battle-axe the swing.
> Such force upon the blow was put,
> The helmet crashed like hazel-nut." . . .

He stopped short in his quotation, for he remembered that Lady Overlaw had called him a pedant.

"Ah, you are a clever man, Mr. Brown, you know everything," laughed Amabel. "I have no sympathy though with your Sir Henry de Bohun, or with any other of those gentlemen who put themselves into iron casing, and called that chivalry. You had no iron on when you fought the Sepoys."

"It would have been of little use to me if I had had any."

"Is that a modest way of saying that you were always so close to the cannon's mouth? But I am not going to teaze you; I want you to show me your portrait."

"My portrait?"

"Yes; papa says that strolling through the picture gallery the other day he saw the picture of Lord Charles Wyldwyl, who is the exact image of you? Do you know the story about Lord Charles?"

"No, I do not," said William Brown, astonished but interested.

"Well, if you will please put down that washleather and come with me into the gallery, I daresay we shall find the picture between us."

Young Brown took off his apron, wiped his hands on the chamois skin, and followed Amabel into the long gallery, where all the worthies of the house of Courthope were painted. The canvases were not all portraits merely; on some of them scenes were depicted, and that one for which Amabel was looking represented a military execution. They were not long in finding it, for it hung apart, and was a striking picture which could not but attract the eye. In the foreground was a firing party of English soldiers in the uniform of the latter end of the eighteenth century; and in the background a man stood in civilian's dress, with a bunch of shamrocks in his buttonhole. With a skilful effect the painter had thrown the face of this last figure in the shade, the red coats of the soldiers standing out in the red light of a lantern held high by the sergeant in command; for the execution was taking place at night. Amabel, who had tripped along the gallery, stopped before this painting. The colour rose slightly to her face, and she said:

"See, that is Lord Charles Wyldwyl, and those soldiers are going to shoot him: they take him for an Irish rebel."

"How is that?" asked William Brown, standing close to her.

"Ah, it's a touching story, which made me cry when I heard it, and I shall cry again in telling it to you. It seems that Lord Charles Wyldwyl was in command of troops in Ireland during the rebellion of 1798, and he fell in love with a young Irish lady who herself loved a rebel. This rebel, however, was a gentleman, something like Emmett, and he was very brave—so brave and dangerous that they put a price on his head. Well, one day he was taken prisoner, and after trying him by court martial the English ordered him to be shot at nightfall. Lord Charles sat on the court martial, but hearing that the prisoner was betrothed to the girl he himself loved, he got admittance to the cell two hours before the execution, changed clothes with him and gave him a passport and money—merely asking him to promise that he would not bear arms any more against the King, but marry the young Irish lady and sail for America. The rebel of course never suspected that his escape would bring any great trouble on Lord Charles; he thought he would be reprimanded, perhaps, or slightly punished, and nothing more. But Lord Charles felt that in having helped a rebel to escape, he had forfeited his own life; so he took great pains to disguise himself—which was easy to do then, you know, for they all wore wigs, and it was night. He disguised himself, and was shot in the rebel's stead. They only discovered the mistake when he was dead, and that sergeant there turned the lantern on his face."

"What a noble story!" exclaimed William Brown, much moved.

"It's the noblest, most generous thing I ever heard of," said Amabel, wiping some tears from her eyes. "But look, now: papa says Lord Charles has exactly your features, and he says you would have done just the same thing."

Young Brown felt all the blood rush through his veins in quick pulses. He was a little behind Amabel, but so near to her that a lock of her hair, stirred by the breeze which came through an open window, kissed his lips. He looked at the picture, and there beyond any doubt stood his features reflected to the life. It was the same serious brow, the same thoughtful look in the eyes; even the attitude of the body was one which Young Brown felt to be familiar to him. Passing through the picture gallery at other times he had often noticed his resemblance to some of the other Wyldwyls, but this resemblance had something almost supernatural in it. Amabel looked round, and having disposed of her tears now, inquired archly:

"Is it true you would let yourself be shot for a girl you loved, Mr. Brown?"

"Yes, I should," answered the young soldier, with an emphasis quite solemn.

"What! even if she did not love you, but was going to marry some one else?"

"Why should anyone love me?" answered William Brown, bitterly. "I am the son of a poor man, having no name and fortune, and nothing to expect but from the benevolence of patrons. Men like me are born to be shot for the first person who has anything to gain by their death."

"Come, you talk quite melodramatically," pouted Amabel. "I ask you a question for fun, and you answer me as if you were going to die this evening. Who talked of shooting you, I should like to know?"

"Nobody, Miss Wyldwyl."

"Nobody did, I am sure, and it's quite unreasonable of you to believe they did. I sha'n't speak to you again if you try to make me miserable; but in any case we shall soon see whether Irish girls can make you devote yourself like that, for it seems you are going to Dublin."

"To Dublin? I was not aware of it."

"Oh, I thought you knew. Papa says he is going to send you with some letters to the Commander-in-Chief in Ireland; because he thinks a little of the society of Phœnix Park will do you good after all this trouble in the house. There are pretty girls still in Ireland, Mr. Brown, and rebels too, I believe."

"No rebel will win his liberty through me, Miss Wyldwyl, for the Irish girls will be as indifferent to me as I shall be to them."

Amabel did not seem altogether displeased at this statement, though she chose to smile mockingly at it. They were standing now at the top of the staircase, and Amabel said she would wish him good-bye in case he started before she saw him again. "You soldiers are off with such speed that you have no time even to take civil leave of your friends; but mind, I expect you back soon, for I shall have no one to teaze whilst you are away."

"If I consulted my own wishes I should not go away at all," sighed the soldier.

"Ah, but you must obey orders, Mr. Brown."

She held out her little hand to him, and turning away with a demure pretence at curtseying, contrived to drop the handkerchief which had served to dry her tears. William Brown picked it up and quickly pressed it to his lips. He was not so quick, however, but in turning to recover the handkerchief she caught sight of his movement. Strangely enough she did not claim her property, but ran downstairs with her cheeks all in a flame.

CHAPTER XVI.

The Soldier and the Lady.

A YEAR had passed, and once more William Brown and Amabel Wyldwyl were at Beaumanoir seated together on the banks of the lake, both still clad in mourning. He had come to say good-bye to her before starting for what he meant to be a long journey, yet could not find the words in which to bid her farewell fittingly. It was more than twelve months after the Marquis's death, but the great house reared its stately fabric as haughtily as ever amidst the ancestral-woods of the Wyldwyls, and all was outwardly much as it had been. Lord Punjaub, who had an honest sense of the becoming, had cleared off the most pressing claims on the family property, saying simply that he could not wear a tarnished name; so the men in possession had been paid out, and the collateral heirs, who trembled for the old plate and pictures, had been unable to advertise their high birth and claims by law-suits; which was a sad thing for the Inns of Court, and several rising young barristers had put down their broughams when it was known in the clubs that the Duke of Courthope's affairs were settled.

Settled?—well, perhaps Mr. Sharpe could have told a different story. No man likes to tell all his liabilities, and the Duke had only mentioned those which immediately disquieted him, and something fresh was always turning up. Still the outward dignity of the ducal house was preserved, and the gentlemen of the county were assembled there as usual that year to shoot the covers of time-honoured Beaumanoir.

Captain Brown dropped pebbles absently into the lake, and watched the cygnets sailing over its placid surface. Miss Wyldwyl was sketching; and the Dowager Marchioness of Newcomen was taking her usual airing in a bath-chair near them, being pushed slowly from behind by a black servant in livery. Her poodle barked beside her, and now and then she watched the soldier and the lady through her keen eyes furtively, knowing or suspecting more of them than they knew or dreamed of themselves.

It was Miss Wyldwyl who first broke silence. "Why should you go back to India?" she said, gently. "The Duke tells me that you have been offered employment at home, and surely you have done enough for fame?" They had become almost as intimate as brother and sister now, having seen much of each other during the past year and having of late lived daily in the same house.

"I go," he answered, "because I am restless, and discontented, unworthy of my good fortune and kind friends; dissatisfied most of all with myself."

"And why?" she asked; "Why can you not stay with us? My father has urged you so often to remain with him; and I," she added, somewhat mournfully, "am I such a dull companion for you both?"

"My place will be soon filled up," replied the soldier, with a sad smile, "and I shall leave no regrets which will not be forgotten in a week; though I shall take with me memories which will endure as long as I."

"What memories?" she said; "since you have no ties to England strong enough to detain you."

"It would be truer to say that I shall carry my chains with me, because they are fastened to no other heart but my own," he answered.

"You do injustice to your friends," returned Miss Wyldwyl. "My father said but yesterday that he had never known the Duke speak so warmly of any one, and you know his own feelings towards you. We have all lived together under one roof so long, that it will be a hard parting for him, for all of us."

"Yet it is better I should go, Miss Wyldwyl." replied the soldier, dejectedly. "I told you long ago that I was in love with a dream. I think it is the dream of your goodness. And so farewell. I was not a charity boy, as they say here," he added with a blush, "but I was a peasant born and bred—a mere soldier of fortune, who has been raised above his sphere and looked upwards till he grew giddy."

She did not answer him; but still he lingered, though he had said good-bye, and bade God be with her now.

"Can you ever forgive me?" he resumed. "I can never pardon myself. But I could no more resist your loveliness than I could have withstood the powers of Heaven. Think of me sometimes as of one who would willingly have died for you; who dared not ask to live; and who had nothing, not even hope."

He turned with a sombre grace to leave her; but she had risen and stood before him in all the radiance of her youthful beauty.

"Is not my heart enough for you?" she said, and placed her hand in his. Then her head drooped upon his shoulder, and she hid her face.

An hour afterwards Miss Wyldwyl's arms were round her father's neck, and she told him of her happiness; and asked the General's blessing on her.

"You have chosen me one of the finest fellows in the army for a son-in-law. Mind you don't spoil him," said Lord Punjaub to her, fondly.

And that night it was told at dinner that Captain Brown, a person whom nobody knew, had carried off the greatest heiress in England; so that everybody must know him now.

CHAPTER XVII.

A Discovery.

WHEN many persons had remarked the extraordinary likeness which existed between Captain Brown and the Courthope family, and it became the common talk of the palace, the Duke at last had observed it also; and it had rendered him pensive. He was old and childless now, as far as he knew; he had few interests in life, and he began to feel a kind of lazy curiosity in this Indian soldier of fortune, who was so like himself. He set himself to remember if there was any event in his past career which could account for the astonishing resemblance between them, and he could recollect nothing. His Grace interrogated Captain Brown in his own shrewd way, apparently so careless and polite, yet so searching; but he could only find out that he was born at Wakefield-in-the-Marsh, on the borders of Oxfordshire; a fact which threw no light upon the subject. The Duke had lived a great deal in that neighbourhood when he was a young man at the University, and had afterwards hunted the country.

Then he set inquiries on foot, but conducted them in a discreet way, mostly through Dean Mowledy and the local gentry, so that he obtained no precise information. The Dean was especially reserved for reasons of his own, and the Oxfordshire squires could only say that young Brown was the son of an innkeeper, that had enlisted and done well in the army, as the Duke knew, and that his family had died in the wreck of the Royal Oak as they were about to emigrate; which circumstance touched upon a fact he did not care to remember, having resolutely forgotten some proceedings which had been taken at that time against a possible claimant on his father's estate. Of course, if Captain Brown was connected with those people, his likeness to the Courthope family might be only too well accounted for, and the less said upon the subject the better.

Still he was not sure about that, and if there was the remotest chance of this young fellow becoming troublesome, it might be well to keep him in hand. Upon the whole, his Grace thought it would be as well to consult Mr. Sharpe, who knew everything, and would be certain to have it in his power to clear up the mystery, if it were worth his while to do so.

Meantime, the Duke had taken a very strong liking to the young man. He was very frequently at Beaumanoir with Lord Punjaub, being still the General's aide-de-camp, and in constant attendance upon him. He had been sent frequently with confidential messages between the Duke and his uncle; and the General, being an indifferent penman, conducted all his correspondence through Young Brown, who wrote a straight upright hand, the characters of which were as stiff and plain as a regiment of soldiers. In all these circumstances the aide-de-camp had behaved himself with perfect good taste, and shewn himself peculiarly straightforward and unassuming. The Duke himself was not a straightforward man at all, and therefore liked those who were, because his own habits of subterfuge made him prompt to see through all kinds of deception and trickery. Gradually Captain Brown had come to fill the post of private secretary between the two noblemen, and many intricate accounts and complicated questions of business had passed through his hands. He seemed naturally to encourage confidence without inviting it, or thrusting himself into it. He never shewed a vulgar astonishment at anything, however strange, but did what was wanted of him without remark; paying little real attention to it, if the truth must be told, for he was perpetually thinking of Miss Wyldwyl: he would have done anything, however dry or wearisome, which kept him near her, and she, with the Dowager Lady Newcomen, was now installed at Beaumanoir; Lord Punjaub, indeed, having been legally placed by Mr. Mortmain in possession of it, and the Duke's life-interest having been formally ceded to him, though his Grace was still permitted by his kinsman's courtesy to be master there to outward seeming.

"Sharpe," said the Duke of Courthope one day,

entering the lawyer's office in Argyll Street, "I want you to guess a riddle for me."

Mr. Sharpe no longer came to Beaumanoir since it had belonged to Lord Punjaub, who had an Indian soldier's hatred of money-lenders: but the Duke and he kept up their old intercourse, and often did business together without the General's knowledge, some promises which had been given by the Duke to his uncle notwithstanding.

"To guess a riddle, your Grace?" echoed Mr. Sharpe. "With all the pleasure in life, if I can; and I think I may go so far as to say that there are few that I can't guess. What's the figure this morning, your Grace?" inquired Mr. Sharpe, blandly, having been recently paid many of his claims, and having little anxiety about the others, because he had received their value many times over in the shape of interest already.

"What are you good for, Sharpe?" asked the Duke, who could never refuse the offer of money. He liked even the crisp rustle of new bank-notes in his pocket, and it literally soothed his fingers to handle sovereigns.

"Anything your Grace likes under five figures," replied Mr. Sharpe, cheerfully; "shall we say three thou.?"

"Nine will do better," observed the Duke, reflectively, pushing his credit to the last limit indicated.

"Well, then, nine let it be—minus commission—minus commission, in course, your Grace?" observed Mr. Sharpe, taking up his cheque-book and a bundle of stamps together.

"Can't you tack on the commission," Sharpe, suggested the Duke, "and make it round numbers?"

"And make it round numbers? Why, no, your Grace, I don't think I could do that, not altogether to-day; my banker's account is a leetle low. You grand people don't know what that is, your Grace, but the banks look very sharply after poor fellows like me." And Mr. Sharpe, appearing to consider that there lurked some exquisite fun in calling himself a poor fellow, sniggered merrily. He never laughed; he merely showed his teeth, and had spasms of the mouth and convulsions of the shoulders, when he was merry —if he was ever merry.

The Duke got his money, Mr. Sharpe sending one of his clerks with the cheque after his Grace had endorsed it. There was no need to take any extraordinary precautions with so old a customer; and the Duke was far too fast enclosed in the lawyer's clutches to quarrel with him under any conceivable circumstances now.

His Grace took the bank-notes after three months' interest at eighty per cent. had been deducted from them, for he was too old a hand to think it high or to wrangle with a money-lender, and he placed them in his pocket-book; then he buttoned up the large sum of money of which he had no need in his breast-pocket, and drew himself to his full height, putting on a dignified and melancholy aspect, though he had been in excellent spirits ten minutes before.

"I am quite destroyed, Sharpe," he observed, with a dejected air and extreme haughtiness, which was odd and laughable enough, though not without an absurd sort of pathos. "I am quite destroyed—I have not a guinea now. Lord George, that is Lord Punjaub, is in possession of my estates."

"Never mind, your Grace; it will all come right. Lord George! he ain't a very sharp creditor—he ain't. He has never drawn the Cornish rents, I happen to know; and there they are quite snug for your Grace."

"No! oh, no! I assure you," murmured the Duke, gravely, "they are all absorbed."

"The dooce they are, your Grace," replied Mr. Sharpe, quickly, for he had advanced his last loan on this security. "They weren't three days ago; and there was, let me see," added the lawyer, referring with trembling fingers to a memorandum-book—"there was 26,000*l*. doo, arrears most of it, because Lord Trecorne had obtained an injunction in Chancery, which Lord George settled for us last week."

"All gone! all gone!" repeated the Duke, mournfully.

Mr. Sharpe made a great gulp, but reflecting that the Duke had still some other assets, he merely grinned. "Ah! that *is* a riddle, your Grace. Now, I shouldn't have guessed that: I shouldn't indeed, your Grace, though I have known your Grace some time now," the lawyer added, reflectively.

"Very fine weather, Sharpe," said the Duke, to change the conversation.

"Very; so it is, your Grace. Going down to Richmond this afternoon, your Grace?"

"No," replied the Duke, drearily; "my misfortunes are too great. Besides, I have not the means, Sharpe, for any extravagance of that kind. I do not know when I have had five pounds in my purse. I am completely destroyed."

Mr. Sharpe smiled deferentially. He began to think again, as he had often thought before, that the Duke was a monomaniac about money; and probably he was right. No person who reasoned correctly could have said he had not a guinea, with thousands bulging out of the breast-pocket of his coat.

"By the way, Sharpe," said the Duke, after a pause, and quite recovering his good spirits, now all conversation about business was at an end, "you have not heard my riddle."

"Another riddle?" inquired Mr. Sharpe, in some alarm, for his Grace could whistle down even such an old bird as he sometimes; and had sometimes got a loan he should not have had on strict financial principles. "I'm afraid we must put it off till next week, your Grace. I can meet you then, if you will give me an order on the manager of your tin mine."

"Ah! then, we'll talk about that. When shall it be—on Monday morning? I shall be in town on Monday morning, Sharpe, if that will suit you," said the Duke, graciously. Then he put his head a little on one side with that innocent childlike smile of his, and asked, "Can you tell me who the deuce is a Captain Brown, Lord Punjaub's aide-de-camp?"

"He! he!" laughed Mr. Sharpe, slyly. "Well, perhaps I could if I tried, your Grace."

"I thought so," replied the Duke, drawing his chair closer to the money-lender, in an excited way he had when amused. "Damn it, Sharpe, you know everything. Who the deuce is he, now?"

"Captain Brown, of the 1st Lancers, your Grace means?" asked Mr. Sharpe, to make sure about the person inquired after.

"Ay! that's the man I mean," smiled the Duke.

"Captain Brown, of the 1st Lancers," replied the lawyer, demurely, "is your Grace's son. His mother was barmaid of the 'Chequers' inn at Wakefield-in-the-Marsh. She was your uncle's daughter by the Scotch marriage, and therefore Countess of Winguid in her own right. She was married to Thomas Brown, a Northumberlandshire man, before her son's birth, and he is therefore in law Earl of Winguid now, for she is dead. In that mottled tin box, on the fourth shelf, marked A. B. in white letters, your Grace, are the proofs of his mother's marriage, which I took for heriot, as agent to Sir Richard Porteous, under whom she was a copyholder, your Grace; or young Brown might now have been Earl of Winguid if he had employed a sharp solicitor; though we should have made a fight for it, your Grace—we should have made a fight for it."

"Ah!" said the Duke, grandly, without any trace of emotion, "I thought you might know. Going to Richmond, Sharpe, this afternoon? It's a monstrous fine day, and I hear my horses fretting outside there. Pleasant weather."

Five minutes afterwards the Duke of Courthope was driving with exquisite skill down Bond Street, and Mr. Stultz remarked to his foreman how well his Grace looked that day, though perhaps he was a little flushed. Towards eight o'clock he dined at White's, and played high stakes during the evening, winning largely, for the game was whist, which wants a cool head.

CHAPTER XVIII.

Conclusion.

THE Duke of Courthope did not, possibly, choose to make a parade of his feelings to Mr. Sharpe. It is not, however, fair to infer that the communication which he received from the money-lender made no impression upon them. He was, however, a slow and rather indistinct thinker, and he had not made up his mind as to what he should do, or whether he should do anything. It no longer signified much to him, personally, who should be heir to the Winguid estates. His life-interest in them, as in all the rest of his property which he had not inherited from his mother, Lady Pencarrow, had been recently assigned to Lord Punjaub. It did not matter, therefore, one straw to him whether Captain Brown became Earl of Winguid, or whether Amabel Wyldwyl became a Countess in her own right, after his decease. Any idea of dispossessing him now, during his lifetime, was, he well knew, utterly absurd. He would be dead long before such a case could be carried into Court by the most expert and diligent lawyèrs; and he thought of the term of human life with a sly satisfaction, because it would now enable him to get the better of any possible enemies. Meanwhile, all talk or gossip which might arise on the subject would be utterly indifferent to him. He had been early hardened to public praise and public censure, and cared just as much for one as for the other. When he had been a young man, and the bitter clergyman of *The Times* had written a leader upon him and the game laws, he had felt very sore about it; now, the bitter clergyman or anybody else might write what they pleased about him—it would not disturb his rest or diminish his appetite.

He had not a very good appetite, and could no longer eat a couple of lunches at the farm-houses on his own land when he went out shooting. He was obliged to be abstemious, and to content himself with a cutlet and a pint of claret after very moderate fatigue on his shooting pony. By the way, Captain Brown had broken that shooting pony for him, and taught the beast to amble and to stand fire like a rock. Captain Brown was always turning up. Well, "blood is thicker than water," thought his Grace, who was fond of old proverbs; and perhaps after all it was natural that Captain Brown should turn up.

The Duke, who had much experience of life, had long observed that the handsome young officer, who was so like what he had been once upon a time, had made considerable progress in the good graces of Miss Wyldwyl; and he had watched their intercourse and walks and rides together with the somewhat mischievous amusement of a man of the world, who does not mean to interfere with what does not concern him. He did not care how the matter ended then; and when their approaching marriage had been announced to him, it had not taken him by surprise. He had wished them joy as lord-lieutenant of his county, and shaken hands with Lord Punjaub, as is usual on such occasions, also with Captain Brown, whom he had asked to take wine with him. The Captain would be a rich man soon, and his Grace had noticed that young fellows who had just come into property could be often induced to invest it upon security tendered by their connections, though it was not strictly marketable.

What if he were to take up young Brown, and handsomely acknowledge the relationship between them? How would that work? The Duke rubbed his chin, and something seemed to answer, "Doubtfully." All the best cards were on the other side. Egad, he would have done better years ago if he had married that village girl at Wakefield; but how could he tell then that she was his first-cousin, and heiress to the Winguid property? The parsons would tell him that in any case he should have married her, and that a life passed under the law is always more prosperous than a life of licence; bearing many good seeds in it, which always blossom in due time; whereas the other life grows ever such bitter weeds. Perhaps the parsons were right; but it was over now. He had made his choice, and must abide by it. His eyes grew moist, and there was an oppression on his chest when he thought of this. Was his heart yearning towards the young soldier? Would he have really wished to have that stout arm to lean upon in his old age, and to be able to say in the face of the world, "This is my son; look at him—see how brave and good he is. I am not childless; I have a companion and a friend, as well as an heir, who shall transmit my name to unborn generations?"

The Duke was an unscrupulous man, and he knitted his brows till they met while he sought for a solution of this difficulty. Few obstacles had ever stood in the way of those resolute Wyldwyls. He might, it was quite possible—he might declare that he had been privately married to Madge over the border; and Sharpe, if it served his purpose, could produce witnesses in support of the statement. It might be easily done, and the sovereign might revive all his titles in the person of an undoubted Earl of Winguid. But how could the real marriage of Madge with Thomas Brown be got over? It was unfortunate that the English laws do not recognise the right of adoption. To be sure, the Duke was a Count of the Holy Roman Empire among other things, and by declaring his marriage in Italy, Young Brown would become a Count of the Holy Roman Empire too; but that was only giving him a fine historic title, which perhaps he would not appreciate, and means must be taken to make him Duke of Courthope. His Grace would think over them, and take advice. Mortmain was of no use in troubled waters, but Sharpe, who knew the whole story, would go any lengths. Lord Overlaw, the Premier, too, who had just succeeded Lord Hanaper, as usual, was his firmest friend now living, and could understand a gentleman's wishes in such a case. Much might be done in this way with time and management. There were at least two other dukedoms which had been manipulated. They might begin by making Young Brown a baron on his marriage with Lord Punjaub's heiress, or give him the remainder in the General's patent; then shortly afterwards he could be raised to an earldom, as had been done in a recent case. He might take the Wyldwyl name, too ostensibly in right of his wife. "Oh, yes," muttered the Duke, drawing down the corners of his mouth, "I think I can pull him through."

Having made up his mind to acknowledge his own son, the Duke determined to be quick about it; for he was eager to enter into possession of the only affection left to him; he thought with complacency how keen an interest he would begin to take again in politics, with the new objects which he had in view. Nevertheless, there was more than one hitch in the way of putting things upon the footing which he desired they should occupy. The Captain treated him with deference and respect; but his manners had grown somewhat cooler of late, because he had not been able to resist the conviction, which an intimate knowledge of the Duke's affairs had forced upon him, that his Grace had not behaved altogether honourably towards Lord Punjaub. The Duke could not go up to him all at once and say, "You are my son; I have left you to starve for nearly a quarter of a century, or to beg, or to steal, and now I want to make you a peer of the realm, because I am a lonely old nobleman with a heartache." Some more cautious way of breaking the business gently must be found, and the Duke, upon consideration, became convinced that no better mediator could be found between them than Dean Mowledy.

The priest came readily at the summons of the noble, and they conferred long together in that fine old library where the fortunes of the Courthopes had been so often decided. The Dean was much distressed, though his Grace spoke with infinite tact and delicacy; but the upshot of it all was that the only woman he had ever loved had been betrayed, that her heart had been broken, and that her destroyer stood before him, one of the princes of his people, and now sought a

CONCLUSION. 285

reward for his crime, instead of submitting meekly to the punishments which were due to it.

"I cannot—I dare not help your Grace," said the Dean, bowing his head upon his hands. "It is not for for me to judge what you have done; I beseech you to ask forgiveness where pardon may be found for all those who repent."

The Duke was not prepared for this view of the case. He had been satisfied with himself, and thought he was doing a becoming and generous act. He was annoyed to find that a new-fledged Dean presumed to consider him as a reprobate, beyond the benefit of clergy. His Grace changed the conversation in a dry way he had when displeased, without condescending to discuss the merits of the topic in dispute; and he left an invitation to stay at Beaumanoir, which he was prepared to give the Dean, unuttered, as well as the implied promise of a bishopric which he had also prepared; not without a fair chance of being some day able to fulfil it through Lord Overlaw, because Dean Mowledy was an unknown man, and there were no potent rivalries likely to be aroused by his promotion.

Then the Duke decided to act for himself; and one morning, after lunch, he took Captain Brown with winning familiarity by the arm, and walked about with him up and down the south terrace, where the monthly roses grew in gay profusion. The Duke was a wise and skilful gardener, and took great pains with them himself; having a natural taste for flowers, as he had for everything which was pretty, and bright, and fragrant. He often led his guests apart there when he had anything to say to them of a confidential character, and walked with them out of ear-shot up and down the terrace, while the roses nodded and tossed their fair heads to every light air that wantoned with them.

What passed between the two gentlemen on this occasion was never known. It is possible that the Duke spoke in his grand, kind, protecting way, and let the truth rather appear than told it. He had the art of raising those he spoke to up to himself, if he so willed it, and had considerable command of pathos.

Miss Wyldwyl, observing them from her balcony, thought they made a stately picture, as they walked slowly amidst the statues, fountains, and flowers which surrounded them, with here and there a peacock strutting and displaying his gorgeous colours in the noonday sun. The Duke was fond of peacocks.

Their talk grew very earnest after a while, and then Miss Wyldwyl saw the Duke shade his eyes with one hand, stretch out the other, and place it upon his companion's shoulder; but the younger man turned away, and Miss Wyldwyl knew, by that subtle sympathy which is part of a deep affection, that there was indignation or sudden anger in the movement which he made. Still they walked on again presently; though her lover's head was downcast, and his whole form drooped in a dejected manner, as though he were weary or humbled. By-and-by they ceased speaking; some embarrassment was visible between them, and they parted. The Duke returned to the library, where he was for ever writing letters now; but William Brown did not seek her as he was wont. He took his way alone towards the sombre beech-woods of the park, with his hand hanging down listlessly, and an air of brooding sadness which she had never seen before.

She thought they must have been talking of the dead Marquis, and never penetrated that mystery, if mystery it was; though in after-life she guessed at it. They were married soon afterwards, and lived very happily: being rich—very rich—for the fortune of Mr. Brown, the Indian merchant, was bequeathed to them; and they were also prosperous and honoured, which is better still than being rich.

Her husband's behaviour to the Duke of Courthope was henceforth subdued and respectful. He seemed to be always on the watch to render his Grace some service; and when he mounted the broad flight of steps on the terrace of Beaumanoir somewhat stiffly and feebly, her husband placed his hand beneath the Duke's arm and supported him. Captain Brown never addressed the Duke, but listened when he spoke as though under the influence of some spell which he dared not break; and once she saw him hold the Duke's stirrup when they rode out together. It was not usual for Captain Brown to show such deference to mere rank, and she observed it in her womanly way, then grew accustomed to it, and perhaps divined the cause.

His Grace died suddenly of an affection of the heart one day while dressing for dinner, and honest George Wyldwyl became the last Duke of Courthope and Revel. The titles were never revived, the late peer having been called away, before his schemes were ripe, to a place where dukedoms are of little worth. But in the fulness of years Amabel Wyldwyl became Countess of Winguid, as Madge should have been; so that, after all, William Brown and her descendants suffered little by the law of inheritance. For Time works wonders, and Wisdom is justified of her children.

THE END.

www.ingramcontent.com/pod-product-compliance
Lightning Source LLC
Chambersburg PA
CBHW031339230426
43670CB00006B/380